Familiar Poems,
Annotated

Annotations and Interpretations by Isaac Asimov

Asimov's Guide to the Bible (in 2 volumes)
Asimov's Guide to Shakespeare (in 2 volumes)
Asimov's Annotated Don Juan
Asimov's Annotated Paradise Lost
Familiar Poems, Annotated

ISAAC ASIMOV

Familiar Poems,
Annotated

DOUBLEDAY & COMPANY, INC.
GARDEN CITY, NEW YORK
1977

ISBN: 0-385-11686-1
Library of Congress Catalog Card Number 76-2747
Copyright © 1977 by Isaac Asimov
All Rights Reserved
Printed in the United States of America
First Edition

Library of Congress Cataloging in Publication Data
Main entry under title:

Familiar poems, annotated.

    1. English poetry. 2. American poetry.
I. Asimov, Isaac, 1920–
PR1175.F22   821'.008

To my sister, Marcia Repanes.
Her hair may be red, but her heart is gold.

Poems Included

Introduction

I think I had better explain the purpose of this book to avoid misunderstanding, and to begin with, I had better explain who I am.

I am Isaac Asimov and I have made my name chiefly in the writing of science fiction and science fact. I have, however, also written on a variety of other subjects including history, humor, and literature.

Am I presenting myself as a literary expert? Not at all. Few people have engaged in the *practice* of writing as copiously and as successfully as I myself, but I recognize the fact that this does not make me an expert in literary criticism—and certainly not in poetry, even though I have published some comic verse.

But then I am making no effort in this book to discuss the metric techniques, the uses of imagery and symbolism, the deeper and subtler values of poetry. I am merely talking about particular words and phrases used in constructing the poems.

Consider, for instance, the line:

Quinquireme of Nineveh from distant Ophir

which begins a poem named *Cargoes* by John Masefield, one of the thirty-seven included in this book. In this poem, Masefield apparently intends to juxtapose the glamorous and picturesque life imagined as characteristic of ancient times with the harsh and unpleasant reality of modern times.

Masefield makes the comparison of times plain, not only through the sense of the words he uses but also through the very sound of them. "Quinquireme of Nineveh from distant Ophir" is a slow and dreamy line, exotic in the strangeness of individual words that fall naturally into a softly drawn-out pronunciation.

Compare this with the first line of the third stanza which juxtaposes the reality of the present:

Dirty British coaster with a salt-caked smokestack

It is not only the words themselves that describe the unglamorous now; it is all those t's and k's that break up the words and force the line to be pronounced in a kind of jittery breathlessness that mimics the unsteady heaving of a small ship on rough water.

In this book I don't try to explain matters such as those I have taken up in the preceding paragraphs for the very good reason that I don't know how to do it. I will allow you to do that for yourself, therefore. I hope you will read each poem by itself without paying any attention to what I say about it; getting the sound of it and the pleasure of the images and symbols and emotional evocations for yourself.

Then, when you've done all you think you can do for yourself in this direction, you may go on, if you wish, to more prosaic matters. You can then afford to ask questions not about the poem as a poem, but about its component parts. The answers I give may not make the poem any more beautiful or significant, but they may satisfy your curiosity.

For instance, in connection with the first line of Masefield's *Cargoes*, it may occur to you to wonder what the devil a quinquireme might be. And who is Nineveh and why does she happen to have a quinquireme? And where, oh, where, is Ophir, since you won't find it in the atlas.

After all—once you have the answer to these questions, as I give them to you, you may then go back to the line and, having lost none of the beauty of the sound, find that you have gained an added appreciation of the sense.

Now that you see exactly what it is I want to do, you can decide whether you want to read the book or not.

—A few more words.

I've selected thirty-seven poems for this book. Some are good poems in my opinion, even great ones. Some are not so good poems, even wretched ones. However, I'll let you decide for yourself which are good and which are bad. (Not everyone may come to the same conclusions, and I certainly won't force mine on you, since I have no expertise in this matter.)

What the thirty-seven poems have in common is that they are familiar; they appear in numerous anthologies; they are quoted on numerous occasions; they are liable to have been forced down your throat at school, and so on. Therefore, each of you may well have read most (or even all) of the poems here included and may just possibly find new dimensions in the familiar lines, once you go through the annotations. That may please you; it would certainly please me.

I selected these particular poems, rather than other equally familiar ones, because they invited annotation. For instance, I might have chosen Kipling's *If* rather than his *Recessional* since *If* is undoubtedly the more familiar of the two poems. However, I can't think of much to say about *If* in the way of annotations, and there is a great deal I want to say about *Recessional*. Therefore, since it is every author's privilege to please himself before going on to please editors and readers, I chose *Recessional*.

The poems are placed in chronological order; not in order of publication, but in order of the time at which the key event described in the poem takes place. Thus, Shelley's *Ozymandias*, published in 1817, comes first in the list because the individual whose actions and statements are of central importance in the poem was at the height of his power in 1250 B.C.

ISAAC ASIMOV
July, 1976

Familiar Poems,

Annotated

Ozymandias[1]

PERCY BYSSHE SHELLEY[2]

(1250 B.C.)

I met a traveller from an antique land[3]
Who said: Two vast and trunkless legs of stone
Stand in the desert.[4] Near them, on the sand,
Half sunk, a shattered visage lies, whose frown
And wrinkled lip and sneer of cold command
Tell that its sculptor well those passions read
Which yet survive, stamped on these lifeless things,
The hand that mocked them and the heart that fed[5];
And on the pedestal these words appear:
My name is Ozymandias, king of kings[6]:
Look on my works, ye Mighty, and despair!"
Nothing beside remains. Round the decay
Of that colossal wreck, boundless and bare,
The lone and level sands stretch far away.[7]

---

1. The poem deals with a mighty monarch named Ozymandias,
but you will find no such monarch in the standard history books.
This doesn't mean that the poem is utterly fictional; it is, in fact,

based on a rather distorted version of reality. The distortion begins with the name itself.

A monarch, usually referred to as Rameses II, was, in his time, the most powerful person in the world, reigning for two-thirds of a century, from 1304 to 1237 B.C. One of his honorific names was "User-ma-Ra," and in the hands of the Greek historian, Diodorus Siculus, writing in the time of Julius Caesar, this became Ozymandias.

2. Percy Bysshe Shelley, was born on August 4, 1792, on his family estate in Sussex, England. Highly individual and eccentric, he was expelled from Oxford in 1811 for openly championing atheism. He married, then abandoned his wife to run off with another woman; he ran through his money and into debt, fled to the Continent, and in all ways was a most notorious person for his time.

From the age of eighteen he was publishing poetry, and although insufficiently appreciated in his own times, he is now recognized as one of the great poets in the English language. In 1817, while Shelley and his second wife (she later wrote the famous book *Frankenstein*) were in England again, he wrote a long poem which was eventually named *The Revolt of Islam. Ozymandias* is a portion of that poem.

Shelley was drowned on July 8, 1822, a month before his thirtieth birthday, when his small yacht was lost in a squall off Leghorn, Italy.

3. The antique (ancient) land referred to here is Egypt and, indeed, I have seen the poem entitled, *Ozymandias of Egypt.* This is fair enough, too, since Rameses II was ruler of that land.

Egypt was the antique land par excellence to the people of Shelley's day, and even to the people of ancient Greece, who stood in awe of its long history. Interest in Egypt had risen sharply in the early 1800s. In 1799, M. Boussard, an officer of engineers in Napoleon's army (which was then occupying Egypt) found a black stone near the town of Rosetta, which contained some sort of routine inscription dating back to 195 B.C. That inscription, however, was repeated in three different languages: Greek and two forms of ancient Egyptian.

The importance of this Rosetta Stone was that Greek was well-known to Europeans of the time and it might be used, therefore, as a key to the unlocking of the Egyptian language, which at that time could not be read. The English physician and physicist Thomas Young began work on transcribing the Rosetta Stone in 1814, and was producing results at just about the time that Shelley was writing this poem, so that at the time Egypt and things Egyptian were very much in the air.

4. The Egyptians were the first to perfect the art of building large structures in stone, and almost at once, in the pyramids, set a mark in sheer vastness that was never to be exceeded in any pre-industrial civilization, except by the Great Wall of China. The Great Pyramid, the largest and most magnificent of these early Egyptian constructions, was completed about 2680 B.C., over fourteen centuries before the time of Rameses II.

Obelisks, tall thin structures carved out of single rocks were built a thousand years after the pyramids, and the tallest of these that survives is some 32 meters (105 feet) high and was built about 1500 B.C.

The Egyptians also built large statues and colossal temples, and this aspect of their art reached its apex during the reign of Rameses II. That monarch filled his capital city of Thebes with huge temples, the largest of which had its stone roofs resting on a veritable forest of 134 giant pillars, some of which were 12 feet thick and 69 feet high. These temples contained enormous statues of Rameses himself.

None of these Theban temples remains intact; they exist today as colossal ruins. The reports of travelers concerning these ruins are undoubtedly what gave rise to Shelley's notion of "two vast and trunkless legs of stone."

5. One of the statues of Rameses II in the great temple at Thebes did indeed, in breaking (or being broken), lose its head of black granite. That head now lies in the sand near the ruins of the temple.

Shelley's notion, however, that the face was a realistic portrait, as though it were carved in Roman times, is quite wrong. The Egyptians, with very rare exceptions, made no attempt to carve naturalistically. Their statues and paintings conformed to arbitrary rulings,

3

and the heads of statues of their monarchs were always serene, unemotional, and god-like. There would be no "wrinkled lip and sneer of cold command."

6. Rameses II did, indeed, plaster his name all over the gigantic statuary of Egypt. His long, long reign not only gave him the opportunity to have innumerable statues raised to himself, but also made it possible for him to chip away the names of earlier monarchs, in some cases, and substitute his own name. The large broken statue in Thebes does, indeed, bear the name of Rameses II and, moreover, it seems really to have represented him.

The monarch of Egypt was called "per-o" from about 1570 B.C. onward. The word means "the big house," that is, the palace. This has come down to us as "Pharaoh." The title "King of Kings" is not, however, characteristically Egyptian. It is Asian, rather. The Persian monarch, who ruled over a number of nations that retained their cultural identity, and had had kings of their own, called himself "king of kings," and so this came to be thought of as the typical title for an eastern monarch. (It was also given, metaphorically, to Jesus and to God.)

7. As a thrilling picture of the evanescence of human accomplishments, nothing more chilling and concise exists than this poem. And yet, if the poem is considered as a literal description of what exists of the artifacts of Egyptian civilization, it is a gross underestimate. Much of the works of the artisans employed by Rameses II remain in pretty good condition—notably the temple and statues at Abu Simbel, which had to be rescued from the rising waters of an artificial lake established for irrigation purposes along the Nile at Aswan, Egypt. A surprising amount has survived the ravages of thirty-five to forty-five centuries.

Considering that ancient Egyptian artisans and laborers worked with the simplest tools plus human muscle, they did very well, and the picture of lone and level sands stretching far away does them an injustice. It is certain that none of the achievements of the modern industrial world will survive the civilization that built them as long as did the achievements of Egypt.

The Destruction of Sennacherib[1]

GEORGE GORDON BYRON[2]

(701 B.C.)

The Assyrian came down like the wolf on the fold,[3]
And his cohorts were gleaming in purple and gold[4];
And the sheen of their spears was like stars on the sea,
When the blue wave rolls nightly on deep Galilee.[5]

Like the leaves of the forest when Summer is green,
That host with their banners at sunset were seen:
Like the leaves of the forest when Autumn hath blown,
That host on the morrow lay withered and strown.

For the Angel of Death[6] spread his wings on the blast,[7]
And breathed in the face of the foe as he passed;
And the eyes of the sleepers waxed deadly and chill,
And their hearts but once heaved, and for ever grew still![8]

And there lay the steed with his nostril all wide,
But through it there rolled not the breath of his pride:
And the foam of his gasping lay white on the turf,
And cold as the spray of the rock-beating surf.

And there lay the rider distorted and pale,
With the dew on his brow, and the rust on his mail;
And the tents were all silent, the banners alone,
The lances unlifted, the trumpet unblown.[9]

And the widows of Ashur are loud in their wail,[10]
And the idols are broke in the temple of Baal[11];
And the might of the Gentile,[12] unsmote by the sword,
Hath melted like snow in the glance of the Lord![13]

---

1. Sennacherib was a king of ancient Assyria. His name is the English version of the Hebrew version of "Sin-akhe-eriba" (Sin has increased the brothers). Apparently, he was a younger son and his mother was grateful to the moon-god, Sin, for the number of boys she bore. Sennacherib succeeded to the throne of his kingdom in 705 B.C., and the poem is based on the biblical story of the siege of Jerusalem by his army in 701 B.C.

2. George Gordon Byron, 6th Baron Byron (and therefore usually known as Lord Byron) was born on January 22, 1788. By the time this poem appeared in 1815 (included in a volume called *Hebrew Melodies*) he had already made himself the most talked-about poet in Europe with his *Childe Harold's Pilgrimage*, published in 1812. Byron said, "I awoke one morning and found myself famous."

He had also made an atrociously bad marriage on January 2, 1815, and when *Hebrew Melodies* came out his wife was pregnant. Byron was to have a daughter on December 10, but his wife left him the next month and Byron fled to the Continent never to return.

In Italy, he wrote some of his greatest poems, including *Don Juan*. In 1823 he sailed to Greece to help the Greeks in their war for independence against Turkey, and there, on April 19, 1824, he died.

3. Egyptian power declined after the reign of Rameses II and

6

never recovered. Assyria, a nation in the upper Tigris-Euphrates valley, in what is now Iraq, gained importance in its place over the early civilizations of southwestern Asia and northeastern Africa. Assyria had its ups and downs but remained an important power during the six centuries prior to the time of the poem, and at times extended absolute empire over the region.

The Assyrian army was the first to be equipped entirely with iron weapons; it developed the art of siegecraft beyond that of other armies of the time; and under some of its kings, notably Ashurnasirpal II, who ruled from 883 to 859 B.C., it cultivated a deliberate policy of cruelty and frightfulness designed to terrorize opponents into submission. Under Sennacherib's father, Sargon II, Assyria rose to new heights of power, though Sargon initiated a more humane policy of warfare. In 722 B.C. he took Samaria, the capital of Israel, but did not slaughter its inhabitants. Instead, he took the leaders and deported them to other regions of his realm.

That left the smaller kingdom of Judah as the only remnant of the empire of David. It was huddled about its one sizable city, Jerusalem. Assyria was mighty and Judah was tiny, but when Sargon died and his son Sennacherib succeeded in 705 B.C., Judah felt she could count on the disorders that almost inevitably accompanied a change in monarch in those days. She therefore refused to pay tribute, which was a kind of "protection money" that served to keep an invading army away.

Sennacherib did have his troubles in the first four years of his reign and had to put down rebellions here and there, but by 701 B.C., he had straightened out his affairs to the point where he could trouble himself about such a tiny nuisance as Judah. His armies marched southwestward from Nineveh, his new capital on the upper Tigris River.

Considering the difference in strength between the two powers, the Assyrian advance was indeed rather like a wolf on a flock of sheep ("fold"). The Judeans could do nothing but cower behind the walls of Jerusalem and hope that after the Assyrian army had tired of ravaging the countryside and sitting before those walls, they would retire. Based on past performance, however, any dispassionate observer would judge that this would not happen; that Jerusalem would fall and the kingdom of Judah would be extinguished.

4. The cohort, strictly speaking, was a unit of the Roman army, a subdivision of the legion, consisting of from three hundred to six hundred men. It could be used, more generally, for any armed body of men. The association with Rome which, for over a thousand years after its fall remained for Europeans a vision of ultimate power, serves to accentuate the feeling of the strength of the Assyrians so the anachronism is worth it.

The "purple and gold" accentuate the wealth and the imperial trappings of the attacking host. The color of purple achieves its association with royalty through a dye called "Tyrian purple" which was obtained from certain Mediterranean shellfish. It was the best dye available to the ancients and was very expensive. A thousand years after the time of Sennacherib, the rulers of the East Roman, or Byzantine, Empire, reserved the right to use the dye to the Imperial family. Hence, "the Purple" came to be a synonym for the Emperor.

5. Galilee is probably the most overestimated body of water in the world. Because it is called a sea (Sea of Galilee) and because of its association with Jesus, there is a tendency to think of it as a large body of water. It isn't. It is a lake that is 21 kilometers (13 miles) long and 12 kilometers (7.5 miles) wide. It has an area of 166 square kilometers (64 square miles), which makes it about the size of Washington, D.C., and only $\frac{1}{16}$ as large as the state of Rhode Island. Its greatest depth is about 49 meters (157 feet.) The Sea of Galilee is rarely mentioned in the Old Testament and never by that name. Its use in this poem gives it the only New Testament touch in an otherwise completely Old Testament atmosphere.

6. "Angel" is from the Greek word for messenger, and the use of the term in the Bible would make it appear that God did most of His work among men through such messengers. It was an easy thought to suppose that there would be different emissaries, each specialized in a particular function. Thus, there might well be a particular angel who was skilled at destruction. When King David had offended God, for instance, "the Lord sent a pestilence upon

8

Israel from the morning even to the time appointed: and there died of the people from Dan even to Beersheba seventy thousand men. And when the angel stretched out his hand upon Jerusalem to destroy it, the Lord repented him of the evil, and said to the angel that destroyed the people, It is enough: stay now thine hand" (2 Samuel 24:15–16).

Again, when the Israelites were in Egypt, receiving instructions from Moses as to how to avoid suffering the fate of the Egyptians with respect to the loss of the first-born, they were told, "when he seeth the blood upon the lintel, and on the two side posts, the Lord will pass over the door, and will not suffer the destroyer to come in unto your houses to smite you" (Exodus 12:23). The "destroyer" is, presumably, the angel specializing in death and destruction.

From this to the notion of an "Angel of Death" is almost inevitable. The phrase does not actually occur in the Bible but is to be found frequently in post-Biblical Rabbinical literature. Since the Angel of Death plays no part in the Christian tradition, the use of the phrase emphasizes the Old Testament character of the poem. (The Moslems, by the way, personify the Angel of Death, by giving him a name—Azrael.)

7. There is a biblical echo here, too. The Psalmist, in the course of describing God as manifested in the storm, says: "And he rode a cherub and did fly: yea, he did fly upon the wings of the wind" (Psalms 18:10).

8. What the Bible says is that when all seemed lost for the Judeans, "—it came to pass that night, that the angel of the Lord went out, and smote in the camp of the Assyrians an hundred fourscore and five thousand: and when they arose early in the morning, behold, they were all dead corpses. So Sennacherib king of Assyria departed, and went and returned, and dwelt at Nineveh" (2 Kings 19:35–36).

As you see, it was not Sennacherib, in the literal sense of the word, who was destroyed, but merely his soldiers, who were, presumably, loyal patriots following the orders of their king.

Incidentally, people sometimes laugh at the fact that "they" (the Assyrians) "arose early in the morning" and "behold, they were all dead corpses." The biblical writers were not as careful in matching

9

pronouns and antecedents as we are. The "they" who arose early in the morning were not the dead Assyrians, but the very much alive Judeans within the city.

9. The Bible says nothing about the slaying of horses, but it makes a dramatic picture for those not troubled by the casual slaughter of innocent horses for the fault of human beings. The description in these two verses is much more closely what would be expected of a medieval army of knights rather than of an ancient Assyrian army of infantry.

10. Ashur is the name of the kingdom in its own Semitic tongue; Assyria being the Greek version of that name. Ashur is also the name of the national deity of the Assyrians and of the city that first served as their capital. To have god, city, and nation all of the same name is not unusual and is a testament of the national character of some early gods. Thus, the republic of Athenai (Athens, in English) had as its capital the city of Athenai, and for its patron goddess, Athene.

11. "Baal" is a Semitic word for lord and was used as a common title for various gods in Canaan and Mesopotamia. The Israelites used the word in that sense, too, but since it was used for the "false gods" of other nations, it came to seem wicked and was used no more. Baal came to be synonymous with idols in general.

The notion of a broken idol in this last verse was probably inspired by the biblical tale of Dagon, a god worshipped in the Philistine city of Ashdod. The Philistines had taken, in battle, the Israelitic Ark of the Covenant, the Holy of Holies, and had placed it in the temple of Dagon as a war trophy. The Bible says, "And they of Ashdod arose early on the morrow, behold, Dagon was fallen upon his face to the earth before the ark of the Lord. And they took Dagon, and set him in his place again. And when they arose early on the morrow morning, behold, Dagon was fallen upon his face to the ground before the ark of the Lord; and the head of Dagon and both the palms of his hands were cut off upon the threshold; only the stump of Dagon was left to him" (1 Samuel 5:3–4).

12. "Gentile" is from the Latin word *gens*, meaning a tribe. Members of the same clan or tribe were "gentiles" and, in Roman

times, the Jews began to use it for Romans and, in general, for non-Jews.

13. But what did happen at the siege of Jerusalem? The fact is that Jerusalem *was* under siege and was *not* taken. Even if we discount the tale of the miracle, *something* must have happened. Of course, in those days of innocence of hygiene, pestilence almost invariably struck, sooner or later, at a besieging army which was living in close quarters, eating irregularly, and drowning in their own excrement. It also struck the people being besieged within the city.

Herodotus, the Greek historian, doesn't mention Jerusalem or the Judeans, but he does tell of a disaster that overtook an Assyrian army—a plague of mice nibbled the Assyrian bowstrings, left the host insecurely armed, and forced a retreat.

What seems more likely and more prosaic is that Sennacherib was not entirely without other troubles. An Egyptian army was threatening to come to the relief of Jerusalem (for fear that Egypt would be next on the Assyrian menu—and it was, for Egypt was taken thirty years later by Sennacherib's son.) Sennacherib defeated the Egyptians but weakened his own forces in the process. When news reached him that the Babylonians were on the verge of another of their periodic rebellions, Sennacherib raised the siege. Jerusalem wasn't important enough to risk Babylon.

On the whole, Judah could have had very little cause to celebrate. It retained its king and its national identity, but its land was devastated and it had to pay an enormous tribute. Judah learned its lesson, too. Never as long as Assyria existed, did Judah revolt again.

So the event, despite the one-sided account in the Bible, was far more nearly the destruction of Judah than the destruction of Sennacherib.

The Vision of Belshazzar[1]

GEORGE GORDON BYRON

(539 B.C.)

The King was on his throne,[2]
   The Satraps thronged the hall[3];
A thousand bright lamps shone
   O'er that high festival.[4]
A thousand cups of gold
   In Judah deemed divine,—[5]
Jehovah's vessels hold
   The godless Heathen's wine![6]

In that same hour and hall,
   The fingers of a hand
Came forth against the wall,
   And wrote as if on sand:
The fingers of a man;—
   A solitary hand
Along the letters ran,
   And traced them like a wand.[7]

The monarch saw, and shook,
   And bade no more rejoice;

All bloodless waxed his look,
And tremulous his voice.[8]
"Let the men of lore appear,
The wisest of the earth,
And expound the words of fear,
Which mar our royal mirth."[9]

Chaldea's seers are good,
But here they have no skill;
And the unknown letters stood,
Untold and awful still.[10]
And Babel's men of age[11]
Are wise and deep in lore;
But now they were not sage,
They saw,—but knew no more.

A captive in the land,
A stranger and a youth,[12]
He heard the King's command,
He saw that writing's truth.
The lamps around were bright,
The prophecy in view:
He read it on that night,—
The morrow proved it true.[13]

"Belshazzar's grave is made,
His kingdom passed away,
He, in the balance weighed,
Is light and worthless clay[14];
The shroud, his robe of state,
His canopy, the stone;
The Mede is at his gate!
The Persian on his throne!"[15]

1. This poem follows the biblical version of the last days of Babylon under native rule. By that version, Belshazzar (the biblical way of saying "Bel-shar-ushur") is described as the last king of the land. This is not quite so. Nabonidus was the last king, and Belshazzar was his son.

Nabonidus, however, was a quiet, unwarlike king, interested chiefly in antiquarian pursuits and engaged in studying the relics of a Babylonia that was already ancient in his time. The defense of the land was therefore in the hands of Belshazzar, who thus seemed to the biblical writers (who wrote their account centuries later) to have been the king in fact.

2. The King is Belshazzar and the time is 539 B.C. Babylon was, at this time, the capital of what is known in the history books as the "Chaldean Empire."

The Chaldeans were a group of tribes who had entered Babylonia from the Arabian lands to the southwest some three hundred years before the incident described in this poem. Under their leadership, Babylonia revolted against Assyrian overlordship repeatedly. Finally, in 612 B.C., the Chaldeans, in alliance with the Median tribes northeast of Assyria, took Nineveh and destroyed Assyria (less than a century after Sennacherib's siege of Jerusalem).

In 586 B.C. the greatest monarch of the Chaldean Empire, Nabukudurri-usur, or Nebuchadrezzar, as the name is given in the Book of Jeremiah in the Bible, did what Sennacherib could not do. Nebuchadrezzar took Jerusalem, destroyed its temple, and carried off the upper classes of the nation into exile.

After Nebuchadrezzar's death in 561 B.C., however, the Chaldean Empire declined rapidly. Nabonidus was a usurper who came to power in 555 B.C. and neither he nor his son was related to Nebuchadrezzar in any way, though in the Bible, Belshazzar is described as Nebuchadrezzar's son.

3. "Satrap" is from Persian words meaning "protector of the king" and was used for the governor of provinces of the Persian Empire, which had, in fact, just been founded and was now threatening the Chaldeans. Its use for Chaldean noblemen is, strictly speaking, wrong, but the word can be used, in the more general sense, as any great subsidiaries of a monarch.

14

4. The biblical story that this poem relates is to be found in the Book of Daniel. This was written in the second century B.C., nearly four centuries after the events described by the writer. At the time of the writing, the Jews were being threatened with extinction by a Greek monarch, and the Book of Daniel is probably a piece of historical fiction, a wonder tale to inspire enthusiasm among the beleaguered Jews by telling them of the bad end of an earlier persecutor.

The biblical tale begins, "Belshazzar the king made a great feast to a thousand of his lords, and drank wine before the thousand" (Daniel 5:1).

5. The writer of the Book of Daniel is so unfamiliar with the actual facts of history with which he is dealing that he even misspells Nebuchadrezzar (and so popular is the book that the misspelled name is the more familiar to the general public). The biblical story goes on to say:

"Belshazzar, while he tasted the wine, commanded to bring the golden and silver vessels which his father Nebuchadnezzar had taken out of the temple which was in Jerusalem; that the king, and his princes, his wives, and his concubines, might drink therein. Then they brought the golden vessels that were taken out of the temple of the house of God which was at Jerusalem; and the king, and his princes, his wives, and his concubines, drank in them" (Daniel 5:2–3).

Because these were vessels that had been in the temple, and had been devoted to the service of God, they were vessels that were "in Judah deemed divine."

6. That they were now being used by "godless Heathen" is emphasized in Daniel, which says, "They drank wine, and praised the gods of gold, and of silver, of brass, of iron, of wood, and of stone." (Daniel 5:4.) They used the captured vessels of Jehovah to honor their own gods, in other words. This called for punishment and it came at once.

7. The Bible says: "In the same hour came forth fingers of a man's hand, and wrote over against the candlestick upon the plaister of the wall of the king's palace: and the king saw the part of the hand that wrote" (Daniel 5:5).

8. The Bible says: "Then the king's countenance was changed, and his thoughts troubled him, so that the joints of his loins were loosed, and his knees smote one against another" (Daniel 5:6).

9. The Bible says: "The king cried aloud to bring in the astrologers, the Chaldeans, and the soothsayers. And the king spake, and said to the wise men of Babylon, Whosoever shall read this writing, and show me the interpretation thereof, shall be clothed with scarlet and have a chain of gold about his neck, and shall be the third ruler in the kingdom" (Daniel 5:7).

10. The Bible says: "Then came in all the king's wise men: but they could not read the writing, nor make known to the king the interpretation thereof."

11. "Babel" is the Hebrew version of "Bab-ilu" ("the gate of the god") which was the actual name to the city as known to its inhabitants. The Greeks distorted this to Babylon, and it is by that name that it is known to us, too.

12. The "captive in the land" is Daniel, who apparently had come to Babylonia with those Judeans who had been taken by Nebuchadrezzar at the time of the fall of Jerusalem and the destruction of the Temple in 586 B.C. The first four books of Daniel detail occasions when Daniel advised Nebuchadrezzar and interpreted dreams for him. The first occasion of dream interpretation took place early for ". . . in the second year of the reign of Nebuchadnezzar, Nebuchadnezzar dreamed dreams, wherewith his spirit was troubled, and his sleep brake from him" (Daniel 2:1).

Assuming that the second year of the reign of Nebuchadnezzar means the second year of the captivity or 584 B.C., we might allow Daniel to have been a youth then—say eighteen years old. He could scarcely have been a youth at the time of Belshazzar's feast in 539 B.C. He must then have been sixty-three years old at least. To be sure, the Bible does not speak of Daniel as young on this occasion. The word is Byron's addition.

13. According to the Book of Daniel, Belshazzar's queen remembered the dream-interpreting power of Daniel in Nebuchadrezzar's time and urged Belshazzar to send for him. Daniel came, lectured Belshazzar on his wickedness and said, "And this is the writing that was written, Mene, Mene, Tekel, Upharsin" (Daniel 5:25).

14. In the Bible, Daniel is described as saying, "This is the interpretation of the thing: Mene; God hath numbered thy kingdom, and finished it. Tekel; Thou art weighed in the balances, and art found wanting" (Daniel 5:26-27).

Actually, the meaning of the words Mene, Tekel, and Upharsin are unknown. Since they appear in the Bible, a great deal of effort is put into translating them in the light of what Daniel says, but it seems very likely that the writer of Daniel simply made up gibberish. After all, it needed heavenly inspiration to translate it. If the words were in some known language, surely the Babylonian experts would have read and interpreted it.

15. Daniel continues his interpretation: "Peres; Thy kingdom is divided, and given to the Medes and Persians . . . In that night was Belshazzar the king of the Chaldeans slain. And Darius the Median took the kingdom . . ." (Daniel 5:28, 30-31).

The Book of Daniel (which Byron follows) is no more accurate in this case than in any other where history is concerned. Belshazzar did not die when Babylon fell to its conquerors. He died outside the city some uncertain time later, falling bravely in battle.

Moreover, it was not "Darius the Median" who took the kingdom; but Cyrus the Persian.

Cyrus, before he conquered Babylon, had, in 550 B.C., conquered the Medes and ruled over both Medes and Persians. The two groups of people spoke much the same language and had much the same culture. They were therefore almost interchangeable to foreigners. The Greeks came in contact with the Medes before the latter were conquered; they therefore tended to use the term "Medes" to refer to the Persians as well. At the time the Book of Daniel was written, the Jews were under the strong influence of Greek culture, and they might refer to Persians as Medes, too.

Furthermore, the Greeks had no great direct contact with Cyrus. A half century later, however, they came into contact with Darius I of Persia, a distant cousin of Cyrus, who succeeded to the throne when Cyrus's son had died. Darius's armies conquered Thrace and Macedon to the north of Greece and finally threatened Greece itself, but were defeated by the Athenians at the Battle of Marathon in 490 B.C.

The Greeks, therefore, were very aware of "Darius the Median," and the writer of the Book of Daniel, very weak in history, made the mistake of thinking Darius had conquered Babylon. In other books of the Bible, such as the latter part of Isaiah, written at a time closer to the period in question, it is clear that it is Cyrus the Persian who was the conqueror.

Alexander's Feast[1]

Or, The Power of Music: An Ode[2] in Honor of St. Cecilia's Day, 1697[3]

JOHN DRYDEN[4]

(331 B.C.)

I

   'Twas at the royal feast for Persia won
By Philip's warlike son—[5]
Aloft in awful state
The godlike hero sate[6]
On his imperial throne;
His valiant peers were placed around,[7]
Their brows with roses and with myrtles bound,
   (So should desert in arms be crowned)[8];
The lovely Thais by his side[9]
Sat like a blooming Eastern bride

In flower of youth and beauty's pride:—
Happy, happy, happy pair!
None but the brave
None but the brave
None but the brave deserves the fair![10]

CHORUS—*Happy, happy, happy pair!*
None but the brave
None but the brave
None but the brave deserves the fair!

II

Timotheus, placed on high[11]
Amid the tuneful choir,
With flying fingers touched the lyre:
The trembling notes ascend the sky
And heavenly joys inspire.
The song began from Jove[12]
Who left his blissful seats above—
Such is the power of mighty love!
A dragon's fiery form belied the god[13];
Sublime on radiant spires he rode
When he to fair Olympia pressed,[14]
And while he sought her snowy breast,
Then round her slender waist he curled,
And stamped an image of himself, a sovereign of the world.[15]
—The listening crowd admire the lofty sound!
A present deity! they shout around[16]:
A present deity! the vaulted roofs rebound:
With ravished ears
The monarch hears,
Assumes the god,
Affects to nod[17]
And seems to shake the spheres.[18]

Alexander's Feast

CHORUS—*With ravished ears*
   The monarch hears,
   Assumes the god,
   Affects to nod
   And seems to shake the spheres.

III

The praise of Bacchus then the sweet musician sung,[19]
Of Bacchus ever fair and ever young:
The jolly god in triumph comes!
Sound the trumpets, beat the drums!
Flushed with a purple grace[20]
He shows his honest face:
Now give the hautboys breath[21]; he comes, he comes!
Bacchus, ever fair and young,
Drinking joys did first ordain;
Bacchus' blessings are a treasure,
Drinking is the soldier's pleasure:
Rich the treasure,
Sweet the pleasure,
Sweet is pleasure after pain.[22]

CHORUS—*Bacchus' blessings are a treasure,*
   Drinking is the soldiers pleasure:
   Rich the treasure,
   Sweet the pleasure,
   Sweet is pleasure after pain.

IV

Soothed with the sound, the king grew vain;
Fought all his battles o'er again,
And thrice he routed all his foes, and thrice he slew the slain!

The master[23] saw the madness rise,[24]
His glowing cheeks, his ardent eyes;
And, while he Heaven and Earth defied,
Changed his hand and checked his pride.
He chose a mournful Muse[25]
Soft pity to infuse:
He sung Darius great and good,[26]
By too severe a fate
Fallen, fallen, fallen, fallen,
Fallen from his high estate,
And weltering in his blood[27];
Deserted at his utmost need
By those his former bounty fed;
On the bare earth exposed he lies
With not a friend to close his eyes.
—With downcast looks the joyless victor sate,[28]
Revolving, in his altered soul,
The various turns of Chance below[29];
And, now and then, a sigh he stole,
And tears began to flow.

CHORUS—*Revolving, in his altered soul,*
The various turns of Chance below;
And, now and then, a sigh he stole,
And tears began to flow.

V

The mighty master smiled to see
That love was in the next degree;
'Twas but a kindred-sound to move,
For pity melts the mind to love.
Softly sweet, in Lydian measures[30]
Soon he soothed his soul to pleasures.

War, he sung, is toil and trouble,
Honor but an empty bubble;
Never ending, still beginning,
Fighting still, and still destroying;
If the world be worth thy winning,
Think, O think it worth enjoying:
Lovely Thais sits beside thee,
Take the good the gods provide thee!
—The many rend the skies with loud applause;
So Love was crowned, but Music won the cause.
The prince, unable to conceal his pain,
Gazed on the fair
Who caused his care,
And sighed and looked, sighed and looked,
Sighed and looked, and sighed again:
At length with love and wine at once oppressed
The vanquished victor sunk upon her breast.

CHORUS—*The prince, unable to conceal his pain,*
Gazed on the fair
Who caused his care,
And sighed and looked, sighed and looked,
Sighed and looked, and sighed again:
At length with love and wine at once oppressed
The vanquished victor sunk upon her breast.

VI

Now strike the golden lyre again:
A louder yet, and yet a louder strain!
Break his bands of sleep asunder
And rouse him, like a rattling peal of thunder.
Hark, hark! the horrid sound
Has raised up his head:

As awaked from the dead,
And amazed he stares around.
Revenge, revenge, Timotheus cries,[31]
See the Furies arise![32]
See the snakes that they rear
How they hiss in their hair,[33]
And the sparkles that flash from their eyes!
Behold a ghastly band,
Each a torch in his hand!
These are Grecian ghosts, that in battle were slain
And unburied remain
Inglorious on the plain[34]:
Give the vengeance due
To the valiant crew!
Behold how they toss their torches on high,
How they point to the Persian abodes
And glittering temples of their hostile gods.
—The princes applaud with a furious joy:
And the King seized a flambeau with zeal to destroy;
Thais led the way
To light him to his prey,
And, like another Helen, fired another Troy![35]

CHORUS—*And the king seized a flambeau with zeal to destroy;*
Thais led the way
To light him to his prey,
And, like another Helen, fired another Troy!

VII

—Thus, long ago,
Ere heaving bellows learned to blow,
While organs yet were mute,[36]
Timotheus, to his breathing flute

And sounding lyre,
Could swell the soul to rage, or kindle soft desire.
At last divine Cecilia came,
Inventress of the vocal frame[37];
The sweet enthusiast from her sacred store
Enlarged the former narrow bounds,
And added length to solemn sounds,[38]
With Nature's mother-wit, and arts unknown before.
—Let old Timotheus yield the prize
Or both divide the crown;
He raised a mortal to the skies;
She drew an angel down![39]

GRAND CHORUS—*At last divine Cecilia came,*
Inventress of the vocal frame;
The sweet enthusiast from her sacred store
Enlarged the former narrow bounds,
And added length to solemn sounds,
With Nature's mother-wit, and arts unknown
before.
—Let old Timotheus yield the prize
Or both divide the crown;
He raised a mortal to the skies;
She drew an angel down!

---

1. "Alexander" is Alexander the Great, the most renowned and successful conqueror in western history. He was born in 356 B.C., in Macedonia, a kingdom which, until then, had been a minor power north of Greece. It had, for a time, been under the control of the Persian Empire, which, two centuries before, had established itself as ruler of western Asia after the conquest of Media and Babylonia by Cyrus.

Alexander's father, Philip II, had raised Macedonia to the rank of the dominant power in the Greek world. When Philip was assassinated in 336 B.C., Alexander, twenty years old, succeeded to the throne. He rapidly put down revolts by the tribes to the north and west of Macedon, and by the Greek cities to the south—all of which thought they could take advantage of an inexperienced youth. Then, in 334 B.C., he took an army into Asia with the intention of conquering the vast Persian Empire.

2. An ode (from a Greek word for song) was originally a poem intended to be set to music, with choral responses. And, indeed, each of the seven stanzas of this poem ends with a choral repetition of the last section.

3. Saint Cecilia, according to a popular legend, was a Christian maiden of second century Rome. She had vowed herself to a life of celibacy but was forced to marry a nobleman. She managed to convert him without losing her virginity, and both were eventually martyred. The day of her reputed martyrdom is November 22 (which is therefore "Saint Cecilia's Day"). On Saint Cecilia's day it was the custom for the organized musicians of London to join in procession and to go to divine service at St. Paul's, since the ancient martyr was the patron saint of music and musicians. This poem was written for the occasion of the procession in 1697.

4. John Dryden, born in Aldwinkle, England, on August 19, 1631, was the greatest English poet of the last half of the seventeenth century. He was rather a trimmer who saw to it that his political views matched those that were predominant in the nation. In 1668, he received his reward when he was appointed Poet Laureate. He supported Charles II steadily, and when Charles's brother, a Catholic, succeeded to the throne as James II, Dryden turned Catholic, too. When James II was driven out of the land, and the Protestant monarchs, William III and Mary II were in power, Dryden lost his Laureateship. *Alexander's Feast* was a product of his old age, and he died in London, on May 1, 1700.

5. The feast described here takes place in 331 B.C. at the time of Alexander's climactic victory, here being celebrated. In the three years since Alexander had invaded the Persian Empire, he had taken Asia Minor in two great victories, beaten down Tyre after a long siege, occupied Egypt bloodlessly, and then, finally, in July,

331 B.C., beat the full Persian army in the great Battle of Gaugamela.

The Persian Empire had thus been "won by Philip's warlike son." Nothing was left but to pursue the fleeing army contingents that had not yet surrendered.

After the Battle of Gaugamela, Alexander moved eastward to Persepolis (in what is now south-central Iran), which was the ceremonial capital of the Persian kings. It was in Persepolis that they were crowned and, eventually, buried. It was in the king's palace at Persepolis that Alexander feasted and celebrated his victory.

6. It was customary for Homer to refer to the heroes of the Trojan war as "god-like" and, indeed, many of them were supposed to be the sons of one god or another. The adjective is appropriate here for Alexander consciously modeled himself on Achilles, the greatest of Homer's heroes, and the son of a goddess.

7. Philip had gathered around himself a remarkable group of generals whom he himself trained. They went on to help Alexander win his victories and (after his death) to tear apart his empire. Now they, "his valiant peers," are with him to help him celebrate his triumph.

8. The ancient Greeks rewarded winners in certain games with crowns of laurel leaves because the laurel tree was sacred to Apollo, the god of music and athletic contests. The association of triumphs of any kind with wreaths of leaves thus arose.

9. Thais (THAY-is) was an Athenian courtesan, who was supposed to have been Alexander's mistress and to have traveled with his army. That this could have been so is doubtful because it would appear that Alexander was not terribly interested in women. The great love of his life was Hephaestion, a man, on whose premature death Alexander went into dramatic transports of grief (perhaps in conscious imitation of Achilles' grief at the death of Patroclus).

The presence of Thais at this feast, and the story of what happens in the course of it is drawn by Dryden from a history of Alexander written by Clitarchus, who wrote about thirty years after the death of the conqueror. Clitarchus wrote in a very high-flown manner, with great stress upon the dramatic. That made him the most popular in later times of all the writers on Alexander—but also the least trustworthy. Only fragments of his history now survive.

10. The notion is older in its negative form: "Faint heart never won fair lady." The positive form of the saying is stronger and tends to remind one of the connection of soldiers and women, something symbolized by the love-making of Ares and Aphrodite (Mars and Venus) in the Greek myths. Less poetically, but more realistically, the connection of brave and fair may have arisen from the frequency with which victorious soldiers commit mass rape on the women of the conquered cities, though this, of course, is not what Dryden has in mind here.

11. Timotheus was a musician of the Greek city of Miletus on the Asia Minor shore who, because of his daring innovations, at first could not get a hearing in Athens, the cultural center of the Greek world. Eventually, however, the Athenians grew used to his strange sounds, and he became enormously popular. He could scarcely have been at Alexander's feast, just the same, since he died in 357 B.C., the year before Alexander was born—and he was supposed to have been ninety years old by then.

12. Jove is from the genitive form of the Roman name, Jupiter, and is often used as an alternate name for the chief god of the Romans. The Romans equated their dull and uninteresting gods with the fascinating deities of the Greeks. Since the west Europeans obtained their knowledge of ancient literature by way of Latin, it is only comparatively recently that the Greek gods have been given their Greek names once more. The god here referred to should be called Zeus, and would certainly be known by that name to Timotheus.

13. Zeus, in the Greek myths, fathered a horde of human heroes by way of a variety of maidens who attracted his fancy. In order to accomplish his purpose, Zeus (according to the myths) often took the guise of various animals. It was in the shape of an eagle that he carried off Ganymede, in the shape of a bull that he abducted Europa, in the shape of a shower of gold that he came to Danae, and in the shape of Alcmene's husband, he enjoyed Alcmene.

A similar myth was created in Alexander's lifetime in order to make a demi-god of him. Again Zeus was described as taking up an animal form to accomplish his purpose, becoming a serpent. The word "dragon," used by Dryden, originally applied to large serpents. Even the wonder-additions of wings and fiery breath, designed to make dragons more dangerous, are, in a way, poetic exaggerations of the snake. The wings represent the hidden way in which serpents can progress, crawling unobserved through the underbrush, and the act of breathing fire is an obvious metaphor for the poisoned bite of the venomous varieties.

14. Olympia, more properly Olympias, was the mother of Alexander, a ferocious shrew of a woman (apparently) of whom Philip eventually tired. It was when Philip was marrying another and younger woman that he was assassinated, very possibly at Olympia's instigation. She was not averse to making it appear that Alexander (whom she outlived by seven years, by the way) was not the son of Philip, but of a serpent-Zeus.

15. To the Greeks of Alexander's time, the well-known world consisted of the Greek cities spread over the shores of the Mediterranean and Black seas, plus the Persian Empire. The only region, well-known to the Greeks, that was neither Greek nor Persian was the city of Carthage on the north-central African coast.

Most of the Greeks owed allegiance to Alexander, and when he conquered Persia there was little of the world within the Greek horizon that was left. There was more beyond, for Alexander eventually penetrated as far as the land we now call Pakistan and wished to go further still, but his troops knew only very vaguely of such distant lands and refused to budge into the unknown.

To the ancient view, then, Alexander had conquered "the world" and on his soldiers rebelling is supposed to have wept at the fact that there were no more worlds left to conquer. To be sure, Carthage remained independent, but some feel that Alexander was preparing an expedition westward against Carthage at the time of his death. (Actually, by modern knowledge, he had conquered only a twentieth of the land area of the world.)

16. Alexander faced difficulties in ruling a large, heterogeneous empire and tried to adapt himself to the various customs of the people he ruled. He assumed the modes and dress of an Oriental monarch, for instance, and forced his soldiers to take Persian wives.

Then, too, since the Egyptians had for thousands of years considered their rulers to be gods, Alexander decided to accept divine honors as well.

His own generals, and the Greeks generally, were not as pleased to promote Alexander to godhood as this passage makes it sound.

17. In the first book of the *Iliad*, Thetis, the goddess-mother of Achilles, pleads with Zeus to honor her wronged son. Reluctantly, Zeus grants the pleas and says,

" 'I will manage to do what you want. Look here. I will bow my head to you that you may believe me. That is my sure and certain sign here among us; when I bow my head, my word can never be recalled, and never deceive, and never fail.'

"As he spoke, Zeus bowed his black brows; the Lord's ambrosial locks swung forward from his immortal head, and high Olympus quaked."

When Phidias, the greatest of the Greek sculptors, formed his masterpiece, a statue of Zeus that was regarded by the ancients as one of the seven wonders of the world, he attempted to illustrate this passage of the *Iliad*.

18. Alexander, pictured here as attempting to duplicate Zeus's ability to rule the universe by a nod, goes beyond Homer's description of the feat. Zeus only shook a mountain. The "spheres" refer to the concentric enclosures that held the various planets and the outer fixed stars according to the Greek view of the universe.

19. Timotheus, as he does throughout the poem, shifts his music from one kind to another, forcing Alexander through the emotional hoops. From exalted images of godhood, he changes to a drinking son. Bacchus (or Dionysus) was the god of the vine and to praise him is to praise the delights of drinking and conviviality.

Alexander's fault was that he drank too much. In the end, eight years after this banquet, he held another in Babylon, and, after a prolonged drinking bout, sickened and died on June 13, 323 B.C., at the age of thirty-three.

20. Bacchus was supposed to have introduced the culture of the vine to mankind. He wandered through the world, for the purpose, along with a large accompaniment of woodland deities, all flushed

with wine, hence with a "purple grace." Those who received Bacchus were treated kindly and granted the gift of wine; those who rejected him were terribly punished.

21. A "hautboy" (*haut-bois,* French for "high-wood") is what we now call an oboe.

22. Alexander had marched his army through a thousand miles and more into a vast land and against an empire no one could reasonably imagine he could take. He had sent them against huge armies no one could reasonably imagine he could defeat. After the pain of labor and suspense for his soldiers came the pleasure of rest and triumph in the enemy capital.

23. The "master" is Timotheus. The title is a common one to give an accomplished musician, though we are more familiar with the Italian version, "maestro."

24. Alexander responds to Timotheus' second song by drinking and becomes drunk, and when he was in his cups, he was apt to become dangerous. He was an absolute monarch as it was, and was feared by everyone since the extent of his victories showed him, if not a god, somehow more than a man. When drink loosened what inhibitions existed in him, his arbitrary actions might seem those of a madman.

The most celebrated case of this came three years after the feast described here. This later feast took place in Maracanda (the modern Samarkand) in the northeastern corner of what had been the Persian Empire. Those who wished to flatter Alexander praised his victories and described how much greater he was than was Philip, his father. At this, one of the Macedonian generals, Cleitus, who had fought under Philip, and who had saved Alexander's life in the course of the first battle on Asian soil, rose to praise Philip for having trained the army and having devised the tactics that alone made it possible for Alexander to be a conqueror.

Alexander, far gone in drink and infuriated, hurled a spear at Cleitus and killed him.

25. To keep Alexander from going out of control, Timotheus shifts to a sad song. The Muses, in the Greek myths, were the daughters of Zeus and Mnemosyne (memory). Eventually, nine

Muses were named and identified as each presiding over individual arts. The term could be used, more generally, as here, to signify creative inspiration.

26. Darius III was the last king of the Persian Empire, coming to the throne in 356 B.C., just as Alexander was succeeding to his kingdom. He was a gentle, kindly monarch, but was great only by virtue of his position, which he was incompetent to serve as an adversary of Alexander. He faced Alexander in two battles, and fled in defeat each time. After the second battle, that of Gaugamela, he was a fugitive, no longer a king. He fled madly into the eastern recesses of the Empire, seeking only personal safety.

27. Actually, this describes an event that took place about a year after Alexander's occupation of Persepolis and of the feast that is the subject of the poem. In midsummer 330 B.C., Alexander took off in pursuit of Darius in order to prevent a rallying of Persian forces in the east. By that time, though, Darius was a virtual prisoner of Bessus, the governor of Bactria, one of the easternmost Persian provinces.

Since Alexander's forces seemed relentlessly intent on getting Darius, Bessus decided that it was not worthwhile keeping him. If Darius were handed over to the pursuing forces, Alexander might have enough and turn westward again.

Bessus therefore ordered Darius stabbed and left behind, dying, for Alexander to find. The Persian forces then hastened on eastward.

28. Alexander, intent on ruling a pacified Persia, knew the value of the grand gesture that would win hearts. He had earlier returned to Darius the king's harem and treasures which Alexander had taken in battle. Now when he found Darius' body, he mourned the king rather ostentatiously, and saw to it that Darius received a stately funeral with full honors. When Bessus was finally caught, Alexander had him first mutilated, then executed.

29. It might be reasonable for Alexander to feel sadness at the thought of Darius' fate. If he could look into the future (as Dryden could on his behalf), he would see that "the various turns of Chance below" were indeed such as to darken his present triumph

and happiness. After his own premature death, all those of his family; his wife, son, mother, half-brother, would die ignominiously, while his Empire was torn to shreds by his generals.

30. The Greeks arranged the eight notes of the octave in different combinations of half-intervals and full-intervals. Each arrangement was a different mode. One of them, the "Lydian mode" was thought to be particularly adapted to soft, erotic, and enervating music, and it is this to which Timotheus now shifts.

It is called Lydian because, in the sixth century, B.C., western Asia Minor made up the kingdom of Lydia which, to the inhabitants of the poor and rocky Greek mainland, seemed incredibly rich and luxurious. A form of music that seemed made to celebrate pleasure and luxury would naturally be the Lydian mode.

31. Timotheus, having used his music to induce, in turn, religious feelings, joy, sadness, and love, now uses it to incite to war. In 480 B.C., Persian armies had invaded Greece and, though they had been repelled at last, had created much havoc. In particular, they had driven the Athenians out of their city and burned the Athenian temples. According to Clitarchus, it was Thais, Alexander's Athenian mistress, who remembered this now and who egged him on to a symbolic revenge.

32. The Furies (or the Erinyes) were monsters who pursued criminals and drove them to madness. They were, perhaps, the personification of the guilty conscience.

33. The ancient authors vied with each other in inventing horrible physical characteristics for the Furies. Aeschylus described them as having hair formed of living snakes.

34. Actually, in the Persian wars of a century and a half before, the Greeks had won almost all the key battles. Their dead were buried with due honor, and if any corpses were dishonored and inglorious, it was those of the defeated Persians.

35. The Trojan war, which ended with the besieging Greeks putting the torch to Troy and burning it down, was occasioned by the kidnapping of the Spartan queen, Helen, by the Trojan prince, Paris. In that indirect fashion, Helen can be said to have burned Troy as Thais now burned Persepolis. Actually, historians don't be-

lieve Alexander fired Persepolis out of revenge. Either there was re-
sistance at Persepolis, and it was burned in the course of battle, or
Alexander burned it for political advantage.

36. The organ was not invented until some five centuries after the
burning of Persepolis.

37. Saint Cecilia is supposed to have invented the organ, and it is
for that reason that she is considered the patron saint of musicians.
She is usually presented in art as playing the organ.

38. Before the invention of the organ, musical sounds were made
by percussion, by plucking the strings (Timotheus' method) or by
blowing the breath through pipes. The individual notes in percus-
sion and plucking were short, and in wind instruments they could
be prolonged only while the human breath lasted without renewal.
Since organs made use of a bellows arrangement, a kind of
artificially prolonged breath, notes could be sustained for indefinite
periods. The organ music exceeded in majesty anything that had
preceded and became (and remains) the typical music-producer in
Christian churches.

39. The legend of Cecilia explains that after she was forcibly
married and persuaded her husband to accept Christianity, he went
off to be baptized. On his return from the ceremony, he saw an
angel talking to Cecilia.

Another version of the story, and the one that Dryden refers to, is
that an angel fell in love with Cecilia when he heard the beautiful
music she produced on the organ. He descended to give her and
her newly baptized husband a crown of martyrdom.

Antony to Cleopatra[1]

WILLIAM HAINES LYTLE[2]

(30 B.C.)

I am dying, Egypt, dying![3]
  Ebbs the crimson life-tide fast,
And the dark Plutonian shadows[4]
  Gather on the evening blast;
Let thine arms, O Queen, enfold me,
  Hush thy sobs and bow thine ear,
Listen to the great heart-secrets
  Thou, and thou alone, must hear.

Though my scarred and veteran legions[5]
  Bear their eagles high no more,[6]
And my wrecked and scattered galleys
  Strew dark Actium's fatal shore[7];
Though no glittering guards surround me,
  Prompt to do their master's will,
I must perish like a Roman,[8]
  Die the great Triumvir still.[9]

Let not Caesar's servile minions[10]
  Mock the lion thus laid low;

'Twas no foeman's arm that felled him,
   'Twas his own that struck the blow[11]:
His, who pillowed on thy bosom,
   Turned aside from glory's ray—
His who, drunk with thy caresses,
   Madly threw a world away.[12]

Should the base plebeian rabble
   Dare assail my name at Rome,
Where the noble spouse, Octavia,[13]
   Weeps within her widowed home,
Seek her; say the gods bear witness,—
   Altars, augurs, circling wings,—[14]
That her blood, with mine commingled,
   Yet shall mount the throne of Kings.[15]

As for thee, star-eyed Egyptian—[16]
   Glorious sorceress of the Nile!—
Light the path to Stygian horrors,[17]
   With the splendor of thy smile;
Give the Caesar crowns and arches,
   Let his brow the laurel twine:
I can scorn the Senate's triumphs,[18]
   Triumphing in love like thine.

I am dying, Egypt, dying!
   Hark! the insulting foeman's cry;
They are coming—quick, my falchion![19]
   Let me front them ere I die.
Ah, no more amid the battle
   Shall my heart exulting swell;
Isis and Osiris guard thee—[20]
   Cleopatra—Rome—farewell![21]

1. After the death of Alexander, his Empire was torn apart by his generals and Egypt fell to the share of Ptolemy. Ptolemy's descendants ruled over Egypt for two and a half centuries, and the last ruler of his line was a woman, Cleopatra VII, whose rule (at first in conjunction with a brother) began in 51 B.C.

Meanwhile, Rome, which had ruled only over central Italy in Alexander's time had expanded its power until it controlled almost all the Mediterranean area. Egypt remained independent in theory, but Julius Caesar brought an army there in 48 B.C. and made a puppet state of it.

After the assassination of Julius Caesar in 44 B.C., his erstwhile lieutenant, Marcus Antonius (usually known in the English-speaking world as Mark Antony), was one of the two most powerful men in Rome. The other was the young Octavian, great-nephew of Caesar, and only nineteen years old at the time of the assassination. There was rivalry between them, and then a division of the realm, with Octavian taking the west, including Rome itself, and Antony taking the wealthy east.

In the east Antony met Cleopatra and the two fell in love. The clever Octavian was able to use that love to convince the Romans that Antony was planning to bestow half or all the Roman realm upon the foreign queen.

For years there was rivalry and, sometimes, open war between the two Romans. In the end Antony was defeated and this poem is the poet's impression of what the defeated Antony's last speech to Cleopatra might have been like.

2. William Haines Lytle was born in Cincinnati, Ohio, on November 2, 1826. He fought in the Civil War, attaining the rank of brigadier-general, and died in action at the Battle of Chickamauga on September 20, 1863. Of the poetry he wrote, *Antony to Cleopatra* is the only well-known example.

3. This is a quotation from William Shakespeare. At the end of the fourth act of Shakespeare's *Antony and Cleopatra*, Antony, while dying, so addresses Cleopatra, and Lytle can find no better way of introducing Antony's speech.

Antony is not, of course, addressing Egypt in general, but Queen Cleopatra specifically. It was customary in medieval times to address a nobleman by his estate, so that the Duke of Lancaster, for instance, can be addressed as "Lancaster." And so Lytle (and Shakespeare) has Cleopatra addressed as "Egypt" in accord with a medieval custom that did not prevail in Antony's time.

4. Pluto was the ancient god of the underworld so that "the dark Plutonian shadows" is a reference to death.

5. The legions were the tactical unit of the Roman army. They consisted of from four to six thousand heavily armed infantrymen supported by cavalry units and by more lightly armed infantrymen who used missiles rather than swords. It was rather equivalent to our modern army divisions.

6. Each of the legions had its own standards about which its men could rally. In several cases, eagles were represented on those standards. The fierceness, speed, and strength of eagles seems to make them a fitting emblem for martial valor from Babylonian times to the present. (The bald eagle is, today, a symbol of the United States.)

7. The final war between Octavian and Antony reached its climax off the shores of northwestern Greece near a promontory called Actium. There a naval battle was fought on September 2, 31 B.C. Antony's ships, to which Cleopatra added a fleet of sixty Egyptian vessels, were larger and more powerful than those brought against them by Agrippa, Octavian's general.

Agrippa's ships were more maneuverable, however, and he was the better tactician. Agrippa nudged Antony into stretching his line so that Agrippa's ships could dart through the openings that resulted, making straight for the Egyptian fleet that lay in reserve.

Cleopatra, in a panic, ordered her ships to sail off and Antony, abandoning his men and his vessels, got into a small ship and sailed after the queen. Without their commander, Antony's fighters lost heart—and the battle.

After Actium, Antony and Cleopatra retreated to Alexandria, capital of Egypt. There was nothing for them to do but wait for Octavian to find the time to go to Egypt after them. They spent a last year of fleeting happiness together and then, in July, 30 B.C., Octavian led his army from Judea into Egypt.

8. It was considered an act of Roman honor, in Antony's time to kill one's self rather than to allow one's self to fall into the hands of an enemy to be imprisoned and humiliated. Thus, Cato the Younger in 46 B.C., sixteen years before the events described in the poem, killed himself rather than fall prisoner to Julius Caesar, and later generations admired the act. Ordinarily, a military commander might order some aide to run him through with a sword, but Antony was alone and must see to it himself that he would "perish like a Roman."

9. After the initial bout of rivalry following Caesar's assassination, Antony and Octavian reached a compromise through the good offices of a general named Marcus Aemilius Lepidus. All three agreed to rule the Roman realm together. Such a union of three men was referred to as a triumvirate (from the Latin words for "three men") and each individual was a triumvir. This was, in fact, the Second Triumvirate, for the first had been that of Julius Caesar, Gnaeus Pompeius, and Marcus Crassus in 60 B.C.

10. "Caesar" refers, here, to Octavian, who had adopted his great-uncle's name and called himself now, Gaius Julius Caesar Octavianus. Because of the great fame of Julius Caesar, all the Roman Emperors who followed could be referred to as Caesar even when those who ruled were in no way related to the great Julius. The name became equivalent to Emperor even in modern times. "Kaiser" and "Tsar" are both versions of Caesar.

11. Once Octavian was in Egypt there was no hope of resistance. Antony's army melted away and capture and disgrace was all the erstwhile triumvir could expect. He fell on his sword on August 1, 30 B.C., and he is pictured as making this speech to Cleopatra while bleeding to death.

12. It has pleased the romancers of the world to think that Mark Antony was a great man and a great soldier who would have won undisputed rule over Rome if he had not been besotted by Cleopatra. This is probably not so. He seems to have been an incapable man and by no means a great soldier. He was often defeated, both in Italy and in Parthia, under conditions that had nothing to do with Cleopatra. The thought of "losing all for love," however (as in the

case of the thoroughly undistinguished Edward VIII of Great Britain) catches the fancy of the world, and defeat is attributed romantically to love instead of being blamed prosaically on incompetence.

13. Mark Antony was married several times. When his wife, Fulvia, died in 40 B.C., there seemed an opportunity for another try at making peace between Octavian and Antony. Antony consented to marry Octavia, the pretty and virtuous sister of Octavian. He spent a couple of years with her in Athens and had two daughters by her, but friction with Octavian continued, and eventually Antony returned to Egypt—and Cleopatra.

14. The Romans routinely sought for hints of the future in meaningless appearances they felt were sent by the gods to guide them. The entrails of slaughtered animals were studied at the altar by specialists in such matters, who were called "augurs." It was also thought significant to follow the flight of birds—how many and in what direction. In fact, the word "augur" may be related to the Latin word for "bird."

15. Well yes. One of the daughters of Mark Antony by Octavia, married Lucius Domitius Ahenobarbus and had a son Gnaeus Domitius Ahenobarbus, who married Agrippina, who was a great-granddaughter of Octavian. They had a son who was, therefore, the great-grandson of Mark Antony and Octavia, and also the great-great-grandson of Octavian. This son *did* "mount the throne of kings" and become Roman emperor in A.D. 54, eighty-four years after the death of Antony.

However, that Emperor-descendant was none other than Nero, whose reputation, in still later times, was blackened as a monster of cruelty and depravity. He ended his reign in disgrace, committing suicide, as his ancestor Antony had done, in order to avoid capture and execution. He was the last of the line of Julius Caesar and Octavian to rule in Rome. (Cleopatra never had a chance to see Octavia, however, and give her the news of this royal future—assuming she would have wanted to.)

16. Cleopatra was an Egyptian in the sense that she was born and lived in Egypt. She was, however, Greek in descent. There were no native Egyptians among her ancestors.

17. The Styx was one of the rivers of the underworld in the

Greek legends. Indeed, the Styx forms the boundary of Hades, separating it from the world of mortal man. The "Stygian horrors," then, are the horrors of death and Hell.

18. The "triumph" was a Roman method of honoring a victorious general, and was awarded by the vote of the Senate, which was the ruling body of the state up to Julius Caesar's time. The general, decorated in a laurel crown denoting victory and followed by his army and by notable prisoners, moved in his chariot along decorated streets between cheering onlookers, to the Capitol where religious services were held. The day then ended in a great feast. (It was rather like our modern ticker-tape parade.)

19. A falchion is a variety of sword—a medieval variety, so the use here is rather anachronistic. Actually, by the time Octavian entered Alexandria, Antony was already dead.

20. Isis and Osiris were the heads of the Egyptian pantheon, and both were eventually worshipped in Roman dominions. There were temples to the Egyptian goddess, Isis, as far away as in Britain.

21. Cleopatra was left behind in considerable danger. She would surely be taken by Octavian and then brought to Rome to follow behind his chariot wheels in his triumph.

She sought an interview with Octavian after he entered Alexandria and found him friendly, but knew that the friendliness was only intended to soothe her till she could be carried off captive. There was only one way out. She pretended complete submission, but when, later on, Octavian's messengers arrived to order her to accompany them, they found her dead.

Octavian had foreseen the possibility of suicide and had had all cutting utensils and other instruments of death removed, but Cleopatra had somehow managed to commit suicide and trick the Roman of the final capstone to his victory.

The tradition arose that she had made use of a poisonous snake which she had had smuggled to her in a basket of figs, but no one knows if that is really true. It is very likely that no one will ever know.

The Angels' Song[1]

EDMUND HAMILTON SEARS[2]

(4 B.C.)

It came upon the midnight clear,[3]
   That glorious song of old,
From angels bending near the earth
   To touch their harps of gold[4]:
"Peace on the earth, good will to men
   From heaven's all-gracious King"—[5]
The world in solemn stillness lay
   To hear the angels sing.[6]

Still through the cloven skies they come
   With peaceful wings unfurled,
And still their heavenly music floats
   O'er all the weary world;
Above its sad and lowly plains
   They bend on hovering wing,
And ever o'er its Babel-sounds[7]
   The blessed angels sing.

But with the woes of sin and strife
   The world has suffered long;
Beneath the angel-strain have rolled
   Two thousand years of wrong[8];
And man, at war with man, hears not
   The love-song which they bring;—
Oh, hush the noise, ye men of strife,
   And hear the angels sing![9]

And ye, beneath life's crushing load,
   Whose forms are bending low,
Who toil along the climbing way
   With painful steps and slow,
Look now! for glad and golden hours
   Come swiftly on the wing;—[10]
Oh, rest beside the weary road
   And hear the angels sing!

For lo! the days are hastening on
   By prophet bards foretold,
When with the ever circling years
   Comes round the age of gold[11];
When Peace shall over all the earth
   Its ancient splendors fling,
And the whole world give back the song
   Which now the angels sing.[12]

---

1. Octavian, after the death of Mark Antony, reorganized the Roman government, creating what came to be called the Roman Empire with himself, under the name of Augustus, as the first Emperor. During his reign, Jesus was born in Galilee. The exact year is not known. In the sixth century, a Christian monk decided it was in the year we now call A.D. 1, but this has turned out to be at least

four years too late. Therefore, the birth of Jesus is usually placed in 4 B.C.

The birth is annually celebrated at Christmas, in connection with which hymns of praise and religious joy (carols) are sung. Individual Christmas carols have originated at different times and in different places. This one, one of the most popular in this country, was written in the United States in 1850.

2. Edmund Hamilton Sears was born in Sandisfield, Massachusetts, in 1810. He was a Unitarian minister whose most notable work was a scholarly treatment of the Gospel of St. John. What he is remembered for, however, is this Christmas carol. He died in Weston, Massachusetts, on January 14, 1876.

3. Christmas carols are so often sung and so rarely read that one scarcely ever thinks of them as having titles or even authors. Generally, a carol is known by its first line (all the more since that is very often the only line that casual singers know with assurance). This carol is usually referred to, therefore, as "It Came Upon the Midnight Clear," although the proper title, "The Angels' Song" is much more appropriate. The "midnight clear" is, of course, the one immediately following the birth of Jesus.

4. This comes from the description of the nativity in Luke. After an angel appeared to shepherds in the field, announcing the birth of a Messiah, then, "suddenly there was with the angel a multitude of the heavenly host praising God, and saying—" (Luke 2:13).

There is no specific reference to songs or singing, but it is a fair inference that the angels were chanting their praise. The use of harps in heaven is a common belief that has no direct biblical basis. However, David played on a stringed instrument of some sort before Saul. The stringed instrument, kinnor, is translated as "harp" in the King James Version, although it was probably more like a lyre. If David, always associated with the Psalms, accompanied himself on a harp while praising God, surely so would the angels— and just as surely, a harp of anything less worthy than gold would be unworthy of heaven.

5. The corresponding verse in the Bible is "Glory to God in the highest, and on earth, peace, good will toward men" (Luke 2:14).

6. At the time of the Nativity, the Roman world, after many dec-

ades of civil war, was at peace internally and had been for the quarter of a century since Antony's death. It is sometimes suggested that the earth had been plunged into peace in order to prepare itself for the birth of Jesus—that no sign of war and violence mar the day and year of his birth.

Unfortunately, the vision of world-wide peace holds true only if we consider that small portion of the world that lay within the boundaries of the Roman realm. Not only must there have been fighting in many places outside the Roman Empire, but between 16 B.C. and A.D. 9 the Empire itself was attempting to extend its sway over Germany, and there was continual fighting east of the Rhine.

The fighting in Germany culminated in a great Roman defeat in A.D. 9, a defeat that marked a major turning point in Roman history. After three and a half centuries of continued expansion, Rome fell on the defensive and remained so to the end of its history, with a few brief and rare exceptions. This turning point also marks the Nativity.

7. The reference is to the Tower of Babel in Genesis 11. The people of the earth, after the Flood, all spoke a single language, and a group of them endeavored to build a tower high enough to reach heaven. God, in disapproval, said, "Go to, let us go down, and there confound their language, that they may not understand one another's speech." (Genesis 11:7).

In this way, the builders, in mutual incomprehension, were foiled. They scattered into smaller groups, each, presumably, with a different language. This was the biblical way of accounting for differences in language among people, and "Babel-sounds" would therefore represent the wildly incoherent aimless activities of men who had lost sight of God. The picture is helped on by the purely accidental similarity between the word "Babel" (see page 16) and "babble."

8. This is a slight exaggeration at the time the carol was written since only 1,854 years had then passed since the birth of Jesus. At the time of the present writing, the time elapsed is 1,980 years, so the verse has become considerably nearer the literal truth. In another quarter of a century, it will undoubtedly be converted into an underestimate.

45

9. Actually, the carol was written at a time of comparative peace in the world. What wars were being fought were brief and comparatively unbloody. The Austrians won victories in Italy in 1849, and the British were fighting blacks in Africa. There had been no major wars since the Battle of Waterloo in 1815.

Yet if anyone believed that the history of human warfare was tapering to a close, he was mistaken. Sears lived to see the first of the modern wars, long-enduring, bloody, and fought to a finish, and saw it in his own country, too. In 1861, the United States was convulsed in the bloodiest Civil War the Western World had ever seen.

10. Narrowly interpreted, this might refer to the Christmas respite that is supposed to come each year when much is made of the spirit of love and brotherhood, as though there is some special time when such a spirit ought to be expected to exist more than another. (The satirist, Tom Lehrer, in his *Christmas Song* puts it this way: "On Christmas Day, you can't be sore/Your fellow-men you must adore/There's time to cheat him all the more/The other three hundred and sixty-four.") Sears, however, goes on to make the thought a more general one—

11. Many cultures, notably the Greek, described humanity as having experienced an idyllic period at the beginning of its existence, an "Age of Gold," in which human beings did not labor nor age, and when all was joy and merriment. This is not surprising in view of the fact that human beings tend to idealize the past and that each individual, when aged, recalls for himself the golden age of his youth.

The Jews, after the destruction of their kingdom and Temple, and the end of their line of kings of the Davidic dynasty at the hands of Nebuchadrezzar, began to dream of a time in the future when somehow a king (an "anointed one" or Messiah) of that old line would arise and be reinstated and there would be a *return* of the Age of Gold.

Jesus was, and is, held by Christians to be the Messiah foretold in the Old Testament, but when Jesus' birth and death was not followed by a return to the Age of Gold, a modification was forced upon the believers. There would have to be a *Second* Coming, and the results of that were told in great (and confusing) detail in Revelation, the last book of the New Testament.

12. In the Old Testament, the vision of a world finally at peace is given its best-known expression thus—"And he [God] shall judge among the nations, and shall rebuke many people: and they shall beat their swords into plowshares, and their spears into pruninghooks: nation shall not lift up sword against nation, neither shall they learn war any more" (Isaiah 2:4).

Boadicea[1]

WILLIAM COWPER[2]

(60)

When the British warrior queen,
   Bleeding from the Roman rods,[3]
Sought, with an indignant mien,
   Counsel of her country's gods,

Sage beneath a spreading oak
   Sat the Druid,[4] hoary chief,
Every burning word he spoke
   Full of rage and full of grief:

"Princess! if our aged eyes
   Weep upon thy matchless wrongs,
'Tis because resentment ties
   All the terrors of our tongues.

"Rome shall perish[5]:—write that word
   In the blood that she has spilt;
Perish, hopeless and abhorred,
   Deep in ruin as in guilt.

"Rome, for empire far renowned,
    Tramples on a thousand states;
Soon her pride shall kiss the ground,—
    Hark! the Gaul is at her gates.[6]

"Other Romans shall arise
    Heedless of a soldier's name[7];
Sounds, not arms, shall win the prize,
    Harmony the path to fame.[8]

"Then the progeny that springs
    From the forests of our land,
Armed with thunder, clad with wings,
    Shall a wider world command.[9]

"Regions Caesar never knew[10]
    Thy posterity shall sway[11]
Where his eagles[12] never flew,
    None invincible as they."

Such the bard's prophetic words,
    Pregnant with celestial fire,[13]
Bending as he swept the chords
    Of his sweet but awful lyre.

She, with all a monarch's pride,
    Felt them in her bosom glow,
Rushed to battle,[14] fought and died[15];
    Dying, hurled them at the foe.

"Ruffians! pitiless as proud,
    Heaven awards the vengeance due;
Empire is on us bestowed,[16]
    Shame and ruin wait for you!"

1. The island of Britain was first invaded by Romans under Julius Caesar in 54 B.C., but the permanent occupation took place a century later in A.D. 43, and for decades the British tribes remained restless under the Roman yoke. The Iceni, a British tribe living in what is now Norfolkshire, were, however, quiet under their local ruler who maintained a careful loyalty to the Romans.

About 60, the ruler of the Iceni died, leaving his widow, Boudicca (that name being frequently written as Boadicea, a Romanized version) and two daughters. The dead father had taken the precaution of leaving part of his wealth to the emperor Nero in the hope that this would win the family favored treatment and that his daughters would be allowed to rule over the land. What followed that is the subject of the poem.

2. William Cowper was born in Great Berkhamsted, Hertfordshire, England on November 26, 1731. He was subject to depressions, attempted suicide in his twenties, was confined to an asylum for a year and a half, and found consolation in religion. He began to publish poetry in middle life, religious poetry at first, and several of his hymns have remained famous. His most popular poem, however, has always been the comic ballad, *The Journey of John Gilpin,* which was published in 1783. The year before that, he published *Boadicea,* which has also remained popular. He died in East Dereham, Norfolk, on April 25, 1800.

3. The care taken by the ruler of the Iceni to placate the Romans went for nothing. He had died without a male heir, so it seemed to the Roman governor on the spot, his lands had become directly Imperial and belonged to the Emperor. The claims of the young daughters to the succession were disallowed and, the story goes, they were raped by the Roman soldiery. When the queen mother, Boadicea, objected with very natural indignation, she was ordered whipped.

4. The Druids were the priestly caste of the ancient Celtic tribes in Gaul and Britain. The Celts were not yet literate, and it was the Druids who retained the oral traditions of their people, putting them into swinging poetry for easier memorization.

The Romans suppressed Druidism, and by no gentle means, since the Druids remained the center of anti-Roman sentiment. To excuse their actions, the Romans described Druidism as extraordinarily evil, involving black magic and human sacrifice. It is quite likely, however, that Druidism was no worse than other primitive religions.

The Druid referred to in this poem would naturally keep his post "beneath a spreading oak." Trees are a common object of worship in primitive religions, and in Britain, the oak tree, for its size, majesty, and longevity, is a natural candidate as the greatest of trees. Druidism seems to have centered about oak-worship, and the very word, Druid, is from Celtic words meaning "knowing the oak tree" (that is, being able to use it to foretell the future.)

5. Druids were deemed learned enough in the ways of oaks and stars to be able to predict the future. This tradition continued, underground, among the Britons despite all the Romans could do to suppress it. It was only after the Romans left, in fact, that the last and greatest of the Druids of tradition arose—Merlin. Under a thin guise of Christianity, Merlin, the great Druid, was made a part of the King Arthur cycle of legends.

6. When Rome was still an inconsiderable city-state, all but unknown to the civilized centers of the Mediterranean world, she was taken and pillaged by Gallic invaders. This was in 390 B.C., four and a half centuries before the time of Boadicea.

The Romans never forgot the terror and disgrace of the event, and this no doubt contributed to the brutality with which Caesar conquered Gaul a century before Boadicea's time, and the heavy hand with which they suppressed the Druids.

As a result, the phrase, "the Gaul is at her gates" can be used to serve as a general reference for the destruction of the Empire. Actually, though, when the time came for Rome to fall, it was not the Gauls or any Celtic tribe that did the pushing. By that time the Celts were thoroughly Romanized, and the fall of Rome was their fall as well.

It was the Germanic barbarians from east of the Rhine and north of the Danube that precipitated the fall—the Goths and the Franks. And behind them, were the central-Asian tribes known as the Huns.

The use of the word "soon" in predicting the fall, however, is a kind of prophetic license. There was no "soon" about it, in human terms. It was to be four centuries yet before an Emperor ceased to reign in Rome—and even then, the eastern provinces remained Roman in tradition for another thousand years.

7. As a matter of fact, the Romans were losing their martial traditions already in Boadicea's time. The Empire was still expanding, somewhat, despite the Druid's prediction of its imminent fall, and would not reach its maximum territorial extent till another half-century had passed. Nevertheless, the army was beginning, more and more, to consist of paid mercenaries from the provinces who felt little loyalty to the Empire or Emperor, but only to their general. In the later centuries of the Empire, the army grew barbarized, with many of the soldiers Germans from beyond the borders, who learned Roman ways and were excellent warriors, but who felt virtually no loyalty to the Empire.

After the fall of the Roman Empire, Italy never regained a martial tradition. It was never again the home of a conquering people and, in Cowper's time (and for three centuries before that) much of the peninsula remained under foreign domination.

8. In early modern times Italy was taking the leadership in the development of new musical trends. It was in Italy, for instance, that modern opera developed in the 1600s, and Italians were the most accomplished musicians in Cowper's time. It was in this sense that "sounds, not arms" would become the mark of Italy—and would remain so, for the trend has continued unabated since Cowper's time.

9. The British Empire in Cowper's time was already impressively large. In the New World, Canada was British, and in the Old World, large sections of India were. Furthermore, Great Britain commanded the sea, and there were many islands and coastal points that were used as bases for British ships. This British sway represented a far wider world, indeed, than that known to the Romans.

The British who had conquered his Empire were "armed with thunder" in the sense that they possessed gunpowder, which the Romans did not. They were "clad with wings" in reference to the sails of their ocean-controlling ships, as compared to the Mediterranean galleys of the Romans which were propelled by oars.

10. Caesar is not merely Julius Caesar. It is the generic term for the Roman Emperor (see page 39).

11. Not really so! When the declining Romans finally left Britain in 410, that was an utter catastrophe for the Britons who might well, in years to come, have longed to see Boadicea's oppressors return. Beginning in 456, Germanic invaders, Jutes, Angles, and Saxons, arrived and treated the Britons far more ruthlessly than ever the Romans did, pushing them bodily into the corners of the island—into Cornwall and Wales, with some Britons fleeing to the Gallic peninsula that came to be called Brittany in consequence. Add to this, the invasions of Danes and Normans that were to follow, and it is doubtful how much of the ancestry of the modern Englishman can be traced back to the Britons of Boadicea's time.

12. (See page 37.)

13. Could Cowper have been writing the poem out of a certain dejection? The time was 1782 and the Americans who were rebelling against Great Britain, as once the Britons had rebelled against Rome, had clearly won. The next year, in fact, Great Britain was to recognize the independence of the United States. Was Cowper writing this paean to the British Empire because he feared it was falling apart?

It wasn't. Great Britain survived the American rebellion and, in a way, learned its lesson, ruling other colonies with a lighter hand so that the Empire continued to grow, reaching a peak a century and a third after this poem was written. At its maximum, a quarter of the land area of the globe, and a quarter of its population, were ruled from London.

14. Actually, Boadicea did not rush to battle as wildly as all that. She waited, grimly, till a good part of the Roman army was off in the western hills, subduing the tribesmen there. She then seized the opportunity to raise a rebellion of her own, leading her tribesmen southward, burning the local Roman camp at Colchester and utterly destroying London. Her army slaughtered every Roman it could find and many of the pro-Roman Britons as well. Roman reports (possibly exaggerated) placed the number of those killed at seventy thousand, a heavy payment for the callousness of their brutal officials to a widow and her two orphaned daughters.

15. The Roman army returned from the west eventually and Boadicea was defeated, whereupon she killed herself. The entire Roman structure in Britain had broken down, however, and the work of the conquest had to be done all over again.

16. Yet no empire is eternal. It was three and a half centuries after the Roman Empire had reached its territorial peak before the western provinces fell, and the city of Rome itself was in a barbarian grip. It took less than half a century after the British Empire had reached its territorial peak for that empire to disappear, although Great Britain itself remains free and is still recognizably the Great Britain of Cowper's day.

The Pied Piper of Hamelin[1]

ROBERT BROWNING[2]

(1284)

I

Hamelin Town's in Brunswick,[3]
  By famous Hanover city[4];
  The river Weser, deep and wide,[5]
  Washes its wall on the southern side;
  A pleasanter spot you never spied;
But, when begins my ditty,
  Almost five hundred years ago,[6]
  To see the townsfolk suffer so
From vermin was a pity.

II

  Rats!
They fought the dogs and killed the cats,
  And bit the babies in the cradles,
And ate the cheeses out of the vats,
  And licked the soup from the cooks' own ladles,

Split open the kegs of salted sprats,
Made nests inside men's Sunday hats,
And even spoiled the women's chats
By drowning their speaking
With shrieking and squeaking
In fifty different sharps and flats.[7]

III

At last the people in a body
To the Town Hall came flocking:
"'Tis clear," cried they, "our Mayor's a noddy;
And as for our Corporation,[8]—shocking
To think we buy gowns lined with ermine[9]
For dolts that can't or won't determine
What's best to rid us of our vermin!
You hope, because you're old and obese,
To find in the furry civic robe ease?
Rouse up, sirs! Give your brains a racking,
To find the remedy we're lacking,
Or, sure as fate, we'll send you packing!"
At this the Mayor and Corporation
Quaked with a mighty consternation.

IV

An hour they sat in council,—
At length the Mayor broke silence:
"For a guilder[10] I'd my ermine gown sell;
I wish I were a mile hence!
It's easy bid one rack one's brain,—
I'm sure my poor head aches again,
I've scratched it so, and all in vain.
Oh for a trap, a trap, a trap!"

Just as he said this, what should hap
At the chamber-door but a gentle tap?
"Bless us," cried the Mayor, "what's that?"
(With the Corporation as he sat,
Looking little though wondrous fat;
Nor brighter was his eye, nor moister
Than a too-long-opened oyster,
Save when at noon his paunch grew mutinous
For a plate of turtle[11] green and glutinous)
"Only a scraping of shoes on the mat?
Anything like the sound of a rat
Makes my heart go pit-a-pat!"

V

"Come in!" the Mayor cried, looking bigger:
And in did come the strangest figure!
His queer long coat from heel to head
Was half of yellow and half of red,
And he himself was tall and thin,
With sharp blue eyes, each like a pin,
And light loose hair, yet swarthy skin,
No tuft on cheek nor beard on chin,
But lips where smiles went out and in;
There was no guessing his kith and kin:
And nobody could enough admire
The tall man and his quaint attire.
Quoth one: "It's as my great-grandsire,
Starting up at the Trump of Doom's tone,[12]
Had walked this way from the painted tombstone!"

VI

He advanced to the council-table:
And, "Please your honors," said he, "I'm able,

ROBERT BROWNING

By means of a secret charm, to draw
All creatures living beneath the sun,
That creep or swim or fly or run,
After me so as you never saw!
And I chiefly[13] use my charm
On creatures that do people harm,
The mole and toad and newt and viper;
And people call me the Pied Piper."[14]
(And here they noticed round his neck
A scarf of red and yellow stripe,
To match with his coat of the self-same check,
And at the scarf's end hung a pipe;
And his fingers, they noticed, were ever straying
As if impatient to be playing
Upon his pipe, as low it dangled
Over his vesture so old-fangled.)
"Yet," said he, "poor piper as I am,
In Tartary I freed the Cham,[15]
Last June, from his huge swarms of gnats;
I eased in Asia the Nizam[16]
Of a monstrous brood of vampire-bats;
And as for what your brain bewilders,—
If I can rid your town of rats,
Will you give me a thousand guilders?"
"One? fifty thousand!" was the exclamation
Of the astonished Mayor and Corporation.

VII

Into the street the Piper stepped,
    Smiling first a little smile,
As if he knew what magic slept
    In his quiet pipe the while;
Then, like a musical adept,
    To blow the pipe his lips he wrinkled,

58

And green and blue his sharp eyes twinkled,
Like a candle-flame where salt is sprinkled[17];
And ere three shrill notes the pipe uttered,
You heard as if an army muttered;
And the muttering grew to a grumbling;
And the grumbling grew to a mighty rumbling;
And out of the houses the rats came tumbling.
Great rats, small rats, lean rats, brawny rats,
Brown rats, black rats, gray rats, tawny rats,
Grave old plodders, gay young friskers,
    Fathers, mothers, uncles, cousins,
Cocking tails and pricking whiskers;
    Families by tens and dozens,
Brothers, sisters, husbands, wives,—
Followed the Piper for their lives.
From street to street he piped advancing,
And step for step they followed dancing,
Until they came to the river Weser,
Wherein all plunged and perished!
—Save one who, stout as Julius Caesar,
Swam across[18] and lived to carry
(As he, the manuscript he cherished)
To Rat-land home his commentary,[19]
Which was: "At the first shrill notes of the pipe,
I heard a sound as of scraping tripe,
And putting apples, wondrous ripe,
Into a cider-press's gripe,—
And a moving away of pickle-tub-boards,
And a leaving ajar of conserve-cupboards,
And a drawing the corks of train-oil-flasks,
And a breaking the hoops of butter-casks;
And it seemed as if a voice
(Sweeter far than by harp or by psaltery
Is breathed) called out, 'Oh rats, rejoice!
The world is grown to one vast drysaltery!

59

So munch on, crunch on, take your nuncheon,
Breakfast, supper, dinner, luncheon!'
And just as a bulky sugar-puncheon,
Already staved, like a great sun shone
Glorious scarce an inch before me,
Just as methought it said, 'Come, bore me!'—
I found the Weser rolling o'er me."

VIII

You should have heard the Hamelin people
Ringing the bells till they rocked the steeple;
"Go," cried the Mayor, "and get long poles!
Poke out the nests and block up the holes!
Consult with the carpenters and builders,
And leave in our town not even a trace
Of the rats!"—when suddenly, up the face
Of the Piper perked in the market-place,
With a "First, if you please, my thousand guilders!"

IX

A thousand guilders! the Mayor looked blue;
So did the Corporation too.
For council-diners made rare havoc
With Claret, Moselle, Vin-de-grave, Hock[20];
And half the money would replenish
Their cellar's biggest butt with Rhenish.[21]
To pay this sum to a wandering fellow
With a gypsy coat of red and yellow!
"Beside," quoth the Mayor, with a knowing wink,
"Our business was done at the river's brink;
We saw with our eyes the vermin sink,
And what's dead can't come to life, I think.

So, friend, we're not the folks to shrink
From the duty of giving you something to drink,
And a matter of money to put in your poke;
But as for the guilders, what we spoke
Of them, as you very well know, was in joke.
Beside, our losses have made us thrifty;
A thousand guilders! Come, take fifty!"

X

The Piper's face fell, and he cried,
"No trifling! I can't wait! beside,
I've promised to visit by dinner time
Bagdat,[22] and accept the prime
Of the Head Cook's pottage, all he's rich in,
For having left, in the Caliph's[23] kitchen,
Of a nest of scorpions no survivor:
With him I proved no bargain-driver;
With you, don't think I'll bate a stiver![24]
And folks who put me in a passion
May find me pipe after another fashion."

XI

"How?" cried the Mayor, "d'ye think I brook
Being worse treated than a Cook?
Insulted by a lazy ribald
With idle pipe and vesture piebald?
You threaten us, fellow? Do your worst,
Blow your pipe there till you burst!"

XII

Once more he stepped into the street;
    And to his lips again

Laid his long pipe of smooth straight cane;
    And ere he blew three notes (such sweet
Soft notes as yet musician's cunning
Never gave the enraptured air)
There was a rustling that seemed like a bustling
Of merry crowds justling at pitching and hustling;
Small feet were pattering, wooden shoes clattering,
Little hands clapping, and little tongues chattering;
And, like fowls in a farm-yard when barley is scattering,
Out came the children running:
All the little boys and girls,
With rosy cheeks and flaxen curls,
And sparkling eyes and teeth like pearls,
Tripping and skipping, ran merrily after
The wonderful music with shouting and laughter.[25]

XIII

The Mayor was dumb, and the Council stood
As if they were changed into blocks of wood,
Unable to move a step, or cry
To the children merrily skipping by,—
And could only follow with the eye
That joyous crowd[26] at the Piper's back.
But how the Mayor was on the rack,
And the wretched Council's bosoms beat,
As the Piper turned from the High Street
To where the Weser rolled its waters
Right in the way of their sons and daughters!
However, he turned from south to west,
And to Koppelberg Hill[27] his steps addressed,
And after him the children pressed;
Great was the joy in every breast.

"He never can cross that mighty top!
He's forced to let the piping drop,
And we shall see our children stop!"
When, lo, as they reached the mountain-side,
A wondrous portal opened wide,
As if a cavern was suddenly hollowed;
And the Piper advanced and the children followed;
And when all were in, to the very last,
The door in the mountain-side shut fast.
Did I say, all? No! One was lame,
And could not dance the whole of the way;
And in after years, if you would blame
His sadness, he was used to say,—
"It's dull in our town since my playmates left!
I can't forget that I'm bereft
Of all the pleasant sights they see,
Which the Piper also promised me;
For he led us, he said, to a joyous land,
Joining the town and just at hand,
Where waters gushed, and fruit-trees grew,
And flowers put forth a fairer hue,
And everything was strange and new;
The sparrows were brighter than peacocks here,
And there dogs outran our fallow deer,
And honey-bees had lost their stings,
And horses were born with eagles' wings;
And just as I became assured
My lame foot would be speedily cured,
The music stopped and I stood still,
And found myself outside the hill,
Left alone against my will,
To go now limping as before,
And never hear of that country more!"

XIV

Alas, alas for Hamelin!
   There came into many a burgher's pate
   A text which says that heaven's gate
   Opes to the rich at as easy rate
As the needle's eye takes a camel in![28]
The Mayor sent East, West, North and South,
To offer the Piper, by word of mouth,
   Wherever it was men's lot to find him,
Silver and gold to his heart's content,
If he'd only return the way he went,
   And bring the children behind him.
But when they saw 'twas a lost endeavor,
And piper and dancers were gone forever,
They made a decree that lawyers never
   Should think their records dated duly
If, after the day of the month and year,
These words did not as well appear,
"And so long after what happened here
   On the Twenty-second of July,
Thirteen hundred and seventy-six"[29]:
And the better in memory to fix
The place of the children's last retreat,
They called it, the Pied Piper's Street—[30]
Where any one playing on pipe or tabor
Was sure for the future to lose his labor.
Nor suffered they hostlery or tavern
   To shock with mirth a street so solemn;
But opposite the place of the cavern
   They wrote the story on a column,
And on the great church-window painted
The same, to make the world acquainted

How their children were stolen away,
And there it stands to this very day.
And I must not omit to say
That in Transylvania[31] there's a tribe
Of alien people[32] who ascribe
The outlandish ways and dress
On which their neighbors lay such stress,
To their fathers and mothers having risen
Out of some subterraneous prison
Into which they were trepanned
Long time ago in a mighty band
Out of Hamelin town in Brunswick land,[33]
But how or why, they don't understand.

XV

So, Willy, let me and you be wipers
Of scores out with all men—especially pipers!
And, whether they pipe us free from rats or from mice,
If we've promised them aught, let us keep our promise![34]

---

1. After the fall of Rome in the fifth century, western Europe remained depressed and backward for centuries. It was not until the eleventh century that western Europe began the climb back to prosperity, and by the thirteenth century, prosperous commercial towns dotted France and Germany.

This poem is based on a legendary event supposed to have taken place in 1284 in one of these towns. The tale was first brought to the English-reading public about 1650 in the writings of James Howell. The poem presented here, however, written in 1845, placed the legend in its best-known form.

2. Robert Browning was born in London on May 7, 1812, the son of a bank clerk. He is best known to the non-poetry-reading public for his courtship of the invalided Elizabeth Barrett. It was just

about the time this courtship was beginning that he wrote this poem. The next year, in 1846, they married (secretly, to avoid trouble with Mrs. Browning's harsh and despotic father). They then left for Italy and spent fifteen happy years together till Mrs. Browning died in 1861. Robert Browning then returned to London. He died in Venice, Italy, on December 12, 1889.

3. Hamelin is now known as Hameln. It is located in West Germany in the province of Niedersachsen (Lower Saxony). Prior to 1870, however, Germany was a crazy quilt of more or less independent regions of various sizes, with boundaries varying widely from decade to decade.

In the medieval times in which the poem is set, there was a Duchy of Brunswick ("Braunschweig" in the German spelling) located in north-central Germany, and Hamelin was located in that Duchy.

4. Hanover ("Hannover" in German) is a much larger city than Hamelin, and is about 45 kilometers (28 miles) to the northeast. It was the capital of the Duchy of Brunswick, and in 1692 the Duke of Brunswick was raised to the higher honor of Elector of Hanover.

What made Hanover particularly famous to the British of Browning's time was that in 1714, the Elector of Hanover succeeded to the British throne as George I. From that time on, for a century and a quarter, the same man was King of Great Britain and Elector of Hanover, although there was no other connection between the two lands. The connection with Hanover brought nothing but trouble to Great Britain, for the latter nation was entangled in wars on the continent of Europe on some occasions over Hanoverian interests that meant little to the British.

In 1837, eight years before this poem was written, Queen Victoria came to the British throne and then the connection was broken. Women might succeed in Great Britain, but they could not in Hanover. Nevertheless, because of the long connection, Hanover remained more "famous" in British eyes than other German cities were.

5. The Weser River is about 440 kilometers (275 miles) long and flows generally northward and northwestward. After passing to the

west of Hamelin, it flows on to the city of Bremen and there enters the North Sea.

6. Browning places the events in the late fourteenth century. In Hamelin itself the events of the legend are placed in the late thirteenth century. And, in actual fact, the historical event that may have given rise to the legend came in the early thirteenth century.

7. Sharps and flats are musical terms. A sharped note is higher by half a tone than the note itself, and a flatted one is lower by half a tone. The noise of the rats was not only interfering, it was discordant as well.

8. The "Corporation" is the body of municipal authorities taken as a whole. There is a Corporation of the City of London, for instance, and that is what the English readers of the poem would be used to. We in the United States would say "city officials" instead. (Apparently, the attitude of the citizens of Hamelin toward natural disaster is exactly that of modern city dwellers. Attack the mayor!)

9. Ermine is the fine white winter fur of the stoat or weasel and is traditionally used for royal robes, so it has become the mark of high governmental position.

10. A guilder is the name given to a variety of gold coins in use in Germany at various times. (The word itself is derived from "gold.") A coin by that name is the unit of currency in the Netherlands today and is worth about an American quarter. The coins of the past had much more buying power than modern coins (of what there was in the past to buy, that is).

11. A plate of turtle *soup* is what is meant. It is a typical luxury food demonstrating the ease of life of the officials; something also shown by the references to their fatness.

12. The "Trump of Doom" is the sound of trumpet that is supposed to herald the Day of Judgment ("doom" means "judgment"). At the sound of the trumpet, the dead would be no longer dead but would rise from their graves according to a legend based on a biblical quote: ". . . the trumpet shall sound, and the dead shall be raised incorruptible . . ." (1 Corinthians 15:52). The implication is that the newcomer has a costume so old-fashioned as to resemble those worn a century and more earlier.

13. *"Chiefly,"* not invariably. It is a quiet warning that the officials do not note, or disregard.

14. The pie is a black-and-white bird, and its most common variety is the magpie. (This name comes from the addition of the common name Mag, short for Margaret, to the name of the bird, as in Jenny Wren, and Cock Robin.) Because of the coloring of the pie, any other animal that is colored in large swatches of black and white is "pied" and so is any human dressed up in such a particolored costume. By extension, the word came to be applied to costumes made up of large swatches of any two contrasting colors— yellow and red, as described here.

15. Tartary is the region of the Tartars (more properly, Tatars) or Mongols. At the time of the legend, 1284, the Mongols had established a huge land Empire over most of Asia and eastern Europe —roughly the equivalent of the modern Soviet Union and China combined. They were at the peak of their prosperity then under the enlightened rule of Kublai Khan. "Cham" is a distorted version of "Khan," a Turkish word that is roughly the equivalent of our king.

16. "Nizam" is a Hindu word meaning ruler. The only region ruled by someone officially known by that title was Hyderabad, a large land-locked region in southern India. The line of Nizams only began in 1713, so in this case, the reference is anachronistic.

17. There are indeed salt-like chemicals which when sprinkled into a candle flame will cause it to turn green or blue, and which are used in fireworks for that purpose. Ordinary salt, the kind we use to salt our food, does not do this. It turns the flame a yellow-orange.

18. Browning seems to have things twisted here. The most famous literary expression of the tale is in William Shakespeare's *Julius Caesar*. There, the conspirator, Caius Cassius, tells that one time Caesar dared him to swim across the Tiber, fully armed, on a raw, gusty day. Both plunged in, but Caesar *couldn't* make it and Cassius had to help him across.

19. This carries on the reference to Caesar, who described his wars in Gaul in a book he named *Commentaries*.

20. These are various expensive wines of which the Corporation would have to run short if they paid out the thousand guilders.

Claret is a clear, red wine (from the Latin word for "clear") from the region of Bordeaux. Moselle is a white wine produced in the valley of the Moselle River, which runs through northeast France and then through western Germany into the Rhine. Hock is short for Hochheimer, a wine from Hochheim, a city in the German Rhineland.

21. "Rhenish" is a general term for any of the several wines produced in the Rhine valley.

22. The city referred to here is usually spelled Baghdad. It was founded in 762 to serve as the capital of the Moslem Empire of the Abbasids, which, during the ninth century, was the most powerful in the world. Even though the Abbasid Empire quickly went into a decline after the ninth century, Baghdad remained a great city and stayed, in European consciousness, as an abode of distant exotic glory.

In the early eighteenth century a collection of Arabic wonder stories was translated into French, and then into other European languages. This collection, *The Thousand Nights and a Night,* more popularly known as *The Arabian Nights,* contained many stories set in Baghdad at its height, thus reinforcing the European notion of its glamour.

And yet at the time the Pied Piper is supposed to have done his work in Hamelin, 1284, Baghdad had already suffered a catastrophe from which it did not recover for centuries. In 1258, Mongol invaders took the city and virtually destroyed it. Thereafter it remained a shadowy remnant of what it had been till the modern nation of Iraq came into being in the twentieth century. Now the modern city, Baghdad, capital of Iraq, has a population of over two million—more than it ever had in the great days of *The Arabian Nights.*

23. "Caliph" is from the Arabic word meaning successor. For centuries after the death of Mohammed, founder of Islam, those who ruled the expanding Moslem realm, considered themselves his successors. Their realm was therefore the "Caliphate."

Only briefly did the Moslem Empire remain united, first under a line of Caliphs called the Ommayads, and then (with Spain subtracted) under the Abbasids mentioned in the previous note. When the Abbasid Empire fell apart and the Caliphs possessed very little political and military power, they retained a kind of religious primacy.

The most famous of all the Caliphs to Westerners, is Harun ar-Rashid (Aaron the Just), who ruled over the Caliphate at its height, from 786 to 809. This fame derives largely from the fact that he was a hero of a number of tales in *The Arabian Nights* where he is sometimes pictured as moving among his subjects in disguise in order that he might reward virtue and punish villainy.

But though the Caliph was a glamorous figure in the memories of Europeans of Browning's time, it so happens there was no Caliph in Baghdad in the time of the Pied Piper. The last Caliph was killed by the invading Mongols in 1258. (One story is that he was kicked to death by the Mongol soldiery.) In Egypt, supposed descendants of the Abbasid line were called Caliphs, and in the sixteenth century, the Turkish Sultan took over the title. Thus, in the Pied Piper's time, there was a Caliph of sorts, not in Baghdad, but in Cairo, and in Browning's time, there was one not in Baghdad, but in Constantinople. Since 1924, there has been no Caliph anywhere.

24. A "stiver" was a coin worth about $\frac{1}{20}$ of a guilder. In modern terms, if the piper were asking a thousand dollars, he would be swearing he would not take a nickel less.

25. The piper is drawing the children after him, as earlier he had drawn the rats. This is the picture of the Pied Piper frozen in our minds. It has become a metaphor. Anyone who leads people happily to their doom through the charisma of his words and personality is called a "pied piper" by those who happen to be immune to his charm.

Sadly enough there was, apparently, a basis for the legend. No piper drew the children of one small town away from home by magic piping; much worse took place on a much larger scale.

Western Europe had by then so far recovered from the fall of Rome that it moved into the offensive against the Moslem powers which were in the slow process of destroying the last vestiges of the Roman heritage in the east. This was the period of the Crusades.

The warriors of the First Crusade, which set out eastward in

1096, had wrested Jerusalem and the Holy Land from the Moslems. The Moslems counterattacked repeatedly and in 1187 retook Jerusalem, after having crushed an ineffective Second Crusade some decades before. The Third Crusade, the most dramatic of all, failed to turn the Moslem tide, and a Fourth Crusade was diverted in 1204 and took the Christian city of Constantinople.

Then, in 1212, some boys claimed to have seen a vision of Jesus and their tale led, somehow, to the widespread belief that children would be the key to final victory for the Christians in the Holy Land. Young men, like one called Nicholas of Cologne, recruited children in the towns of France and Germany, and drew them from their homes Pied-Piper fashion.

Some fifty thousand children left to follow some sort of vision of a heavenly conquest. They straggled southward, dying in droves of hunger and exposure, and those who reached the Mediterranean were taken on board by ship masters (who, presumably, considered themselves to be Christians) and were sold into Moslem slavery in Africa.

Hamelin must have lost children in this sad episode of human folly and cruelty, and perhaps they romanticized and misplaced the time of the event into the tale of the Pied Piper.

26. The legend has it that 130 children followed the Piper.

27. "Koppelberg" means, in itself, Koppel Hill in German. To add a second "Hill" is superfluous.

28. The reference is to Matthew 19:23–24: "Then said Jesus unto his disciples, Verily I say unto you, That a rich man shall hardly enter into the kingdom of heaven. And again I say unto you, It is easier for a camel to go through the eye of a needle, than for a rich man to enter into the kingdom of God." (This was said in the early days when the followers of the new Messiah were a group of poor men who resented the wealthy of the religious Establishment of the day. In later years, when there was a new and wealthy Christian Establishment, there were many interpretations produced to take away the plain meaning of these verses.)

The significance of the reference is that the Mayor and Council in keeping their wealth by refusing to keep their bargain, now found they could no more enter the hole in the mountain that had taken their children than a camel could pass through the eye of a needle.

29. This is ninety-two years later than the date fixed for the event by the people of Hamelin.

30. Modern Hamelin (Hameln) does make much of rat catching in line with the legend. The town has a rat-catcher collection in the local museum and a "Rattenfängerhaus" (Rat-catcher's House).

31. Transylvania (the name means "beyond the forest" in Latin) is a region in what is now northwestern Rumania. It is chiefly famous these days as the homeland of the legendary vampire, Count Dracula. Since he entered our consciousness only with the publication of Bram Stoker's horror novel, *Dracula,* in 1897, the region at the time the poem was written had no uneasy vampirish connotation.

32. Although the population of Transylvania is mostly Romanian in speech, the area was dominated by Hungary for five centuries beginning in 1003. One of the methods by which the Hungarians retained control was to introduce settlers from outside who could develop the land and who were sure to be faithful to the Hungarian rulers since they had to count on the Hungarians to protect them from the hostile native population. Among those settlers were Germans (usually referred to as Saxons) who lived in a coherent group in southeastern Transylvania and were clearly an "alien people" to the surrounding peasantry.

33. Transylvania is some 1,400 kilometers (850 miles) from Hamelin, but presumably, the Pied Piper had magic powers that made the long trip through the mountain a quick one. There are still about half a million Germans in Romania, bearing witness to the medieval *"drang nach osten"* (push to the east) that sent medieval Germans as far east as the Volga River. Some think that the loss of young people to the lure of the east gave rise to the legend of the Pied Piper.

34. This call to fiscal responsibility in this particular poem may be thought of as having originated the phrase "to pay the piper," which is often used as a reference to suffering the unpleasant consequences of some pleasant interlude.

The phrase, however, dates much farther back than this poem. It

The Pied Piper of Hamelin

was used as long ago as 1681 by the English poet, Thomas Flatman, who said of a politician, "After all this dance he has led the Nation, he must at last come to pay the piper himself." This however, was after England had been introduced to the legend of the Pied Piper, and that may have influenced the saying.

Bruce to His Men at Bannockburn[1]

ROBERT BURNS[2]

(1314)

Scots, wha hae wi' Wallace bled,[3]
Scots, wham Bruce has aften led[4];
Welcome to your gory bed,
   Or to victory!

Now's the day, and now's the hour[5]:
See the front o' battle lour:
See approach proud Edward's[6] power,—
   Chains and slavery!

Wha will be a traitor knave?
Wha can fill a coward's grave?
Wha sae base as be a slave?
   Let him turn and flee!

Wha for Scotland's king and law
Freedom's sword will strongly draw,

Freeman stand, or freeman fa',
    Let him follow me!

By oppressions' woes and pains!
By your sons in servile chains,
We will drain our dearest veins,
    But they shall be free!

Lay the proud usurpers low!
Tyrants fall in every foe!
Liberty's in every blow!—
    Let us do or die![7]

---

1. The turmoil in Britain following the departure of the Romans led, after six and a half centuries, to the formation of a strong monarchy under a line of kings from Normandy in France. The Norman monarchs, ruling over what was now known as England, had an expansive foreign policy. They took Wales, the last remnant of the Celtic Britons, and secured a foothold in eastern Ireland.

The main thrust of English expansion, however, was northward against that part of the island that had never been under Roman rule and that now made up the kingdom of Scotland.

The hostility between the two nations was endemic, and each side raided across the border at will. The English won almost every large battle so that Scotland seemed forever in danger of falling prey to the larger and wealthier nation to the south. That danger was the greatest toward the end of the thirteenth century when Scotland seemed, for a while, to be finally conquered.

Margaret, Queen of Scotland, had died in 1290, and at that time Edward I ruled England in strong and capable fashion. There were several Scottish noblemen who claimed the throne by virtue of descent from a younger branch of the royal line. Edward I put his influence behind the candidate he thought most likely to be subservient to himself, and when that candidate was not sufficiently subservient, Edward led an army into Scotland and, in a five months' campaign in 1296–97, conquered the country.

The conquest, however, was not permanent, and the struggle reached its climax two decades later at a battle near the small town of Bannockburn some 32 kilometers (20 miles) northeast of Glasgow. The poem purports to give the words of the leader of the Scottish army to his men on the eve of the battle.

2. Robert Burns was born at Alloway, Ayrshire, on January 25, 1759. His father was a farmer who died defeated by his farm, and Burns, in his turn, took up the task and could do no better. However, Burns had the gift of poetry, writing often in the Scottish dialect. In 1785, he published a book of verse that brought him instant fame (enhanced by his own deliberate pose as more of an uneducated ploughman than he really was). *Bruce to His Men at Bannockburn* was published in 1794, and Burns died, still young, in Dumfries, Scotland, on July 21, 1796.

3. This, by slight spelling changes becomes the formal English: "Scots, who have with Wallace bled." The first three words, as written, and pronounced "Scots wah hay," is sometimes used as the title of the poem.

The Wallace referred to is Sir William Wallace, who led a band of Scottish patriots against the occupying English forces in 1297, soon after Edward I had made himself king of Scotland. In true Robin Hood fashion, he defeated the surprisingly inept English garrisons and virtually cleared the land. In October 1297 he was even able to raid northern England.

Edward I, however, was in France at the time, so that the hand was not yet truly played out. In 1298 Edward returned to England, and in July of that year he led an army into Scotland. On July 22 there was a pitched battle at Falkirk, just about halfway between Glasgow and Edinburgh, and the result was (as almost always) an overwhelming English victory. The Scottish army was composed almost entirely of spear-carrying infantry, while the English had skillful archers using the longbow, who could gall the Scots from a distance, plus cavalry who could then ride down the demoralized battalions and scatter them.

The battle of Falkirk put an end to Wallace's rebellion, and de-

spite scattered resistance, Edward finally completed a second con-
quest of Scotland by 1304. Wallace was captured on August 5,
1305, condemned for treason, and hanged in the cruel way of the
times—which involved being taken down and disembowelled while
still alive.

4. Robert Bruce, born July 11, 1274, who is here pictured as
speaking to his men, was the great-great-great-grandson of David I,
who had ruled Scotland two centuries before, and he claimed the
throne on that basis. In 1306 he picked up the fight against Eng-
land (he appears to have been only a cautious and lukewarm sup-
porter of Wallace) and on March 25 of that year had himself
crowned as the Scottish king—which put him in direct rebellion
against the redoubtable Edward I.

Bruce had a rough road ahead of him. He was defeated on six
different occasions and, for a while, was forced to flee and hide.
(The legend arose that, when about to despair and give up, he
watched a spider trying to fix its thread to a beam six times and
fail, then succeed on the seventh—and this heartened him to try
again.)

The turning point came when Edward I, leading an army into
Scotland for a third campaign of conquest (which he probably
would have carried off successfully once again), died en route on
July 7, 1307, at the age of sixty-eight.

In the confusion that inevitably followed, Bruce and his followers
could finally make headway. One by one they took the English-held
castles until only Stirling Castle was left to the English. Bruce laid
that last castle under siege in 1314, and now the new English king
was stirred to a major effort. He took a large army northward to
break and destroy the Scottish army, and the two forces neared
each other on June 23, 1314, just west of Bannockburn. The battle
took place the next day.

5. It is hard to judge the ifs of history. Was this really the crucial
moment, the day, the hour and the battle that would decide every-
thing? In hindsight, it was.

The English had conquered Scotland. After one rebellion, they
conquered it again. Now, if after a second rebellion, they conquered
it a third time; if they defeated Bruce at Bannockburn, as they had

defeated Wallace at Falkirk (10 kilometers, or 6 miles, to the south-east) sixteen years before, they would go on to conquer Scotland a third time in less than twenty years—and this time it might have stuck.

6. This was not, of course, Edward I, who had conquered Scotland twice, but his unworthy son, Edward II. Edward II, whose abilities were limited, was under the sway of his favorites (he was homosexual) and made enemies of the English barons. He spent the first years of his reign in quarrels and intrigues, and it wasn't till Scotland was nearly lost that he could find the time and the means to lead an army northward.

7. Actually, Bruce's plea might have seemed useless. The English army consisted of 20,000 men against Bruce's 6,000. And, as usual, the English had archers and horsemen, while Bruce had none of the first and few of the second. The Scottish cause seemed hopeless.

Bruce, however, knew that the English were coming to relieve Stirling Castle and that the battle would be fought near the castle. He therefore picked an appropriate spot to station his army. He chose a spot between woods and stream, behind a marshy area where the English would, on attacking, be penned into a narrow front where their superior numbers would do them no good, and where they would have to cross the marsh to reach the Scots. Furthermore, Bruce had holes dug with pointed stakes at the bottom and brush covering them.

The English might have ravaged the countryside to try to draw the Scots out of their position and force them to fight a battle on English terms—but Edward II was not a shrewd general. In addition, repeated victories had made the English overconfident, and they scorned such devious tactics.

The English launched the battle with a bombardment of arrows, and Bruce sent what cavalry he had against the bowmen to break them up, at least for a while. The English then charged; and the horses stumbled in the pits and impaled themselves on the stakes, while the men and horses both were mired in the marsh. The English line was thrown into confusion and the soldiers could scarcely use their weapons, and at the proper moment, Bruce sent his spearmen forward. It was a slaughter. Edward II withdrew with the remnant of his forces into England and spent the rest of his reign fighting his own barons (eventually, he was made to abdicate and was then cruelly murdered). His successors were more interested in conquering France, and Scotland was left to itself so that the battle of Bannockburn assured its independence.

Robert Bruce reigned as Robert I of Scotland till 1329, and his descendants reigned after him. His daughter married one Walter Stuart, and her descendants formed the line of the Stuarts, who still ruled Scotland in 1603. In that year, James VI of Scotland, a tenth-generation descendant of Robert Bruce (and also the great-great-grandson of Henry VII of England) ascended the English throne as James I.

Lepanto[1]

GILBERT KEITH CHESTERTON[2]

(1571)

White founts falling in the Courts of the sun,
And the Soldan of Byzantium[3] is smiling as they run;
There is laughter like the fountains in that face of all men
    feared,[4]
It stirs the forest darkness, the darkness of his beard,
It curls the blood-red crescent, the crescent of his lips,[5]
For the inmost sea of all the earth[6] is shaken with his ships.
They have dared the white republics up the capes of Italy,[7]
They have dashed the Adriatic round the Lion of the Sea,[8]
And the Pope[9] has cast his arms abroad for agony and loss,
And called the kings of Christendom for swords about the
    Cross.[10]
The cold Queen of England[11] is looking in the glass;
The shadow of the Valois[12] is yawning at the Mass;
From evening isles fantastical[13] rings faint the Spanish gun,
And the Lord upon the Golden Horn[14] is laughing in the sun.

Dim drums throbbing, in the hills half heard,
Where only on a nameless throne a crownless prince has stirred,

Where, risen from a doubtful seat and half attainted stall,[15]
The last knight of Europe[16] takes weapons from the wall,
The last and lingering troubadour[17] to whom the bird has sung,
That once went singing southward when all the world was
    young.[18]
In that enormous silence, tiny and unafraid,
Comes up along a winding road the noise of the Crusade.[19]
Strong gongs groaning as the guns boom far,
Don John of Austria is going to the war,
Stiff flags straining in the night-blasts cold,
In the gloom black-purple, in the glint old-gold,
Torchlight crimson on the copper kettle-drums,
Then the tuckets, then the trumpets, then the cannon, and he
    comes.
Don John laughing in the brave beard curled,
Spurning of his stirrups like the thrones of all the world,
Holding his head up for a flag of all the free.
Love-light of Spain—hurrah!
Death-light of Africa![20]
Don John of Austria
Is riding to the sea.[21]

Mahound[22] is in his paradise above the evening star,
(*Don John of Austria is going to the war.*)
He moves a mighty turban on the timeless houri's knees,[23]
His turban that is woven of the sunsets and the seas.
He shakes the peacock gardens as he rises from his ease,
And he strides among the tree-tops and is taller than the trees,
And his voice through all the garden is a thunder sent to bring
Black Azrael[24] and Ariel[25] and Ammon[26] on the wing.
Giants and the Genii,[27]
Multiplex of wing and eye,
Whose strong obedience broke the sky
When Solomon was king.[28]

They rush in red and purple from the red clouds of the morn,
From temples where the yellow gods shut up their eyes in
    scorn[29];
They rise in green robes roaring from the green hells of the
    sea,[30]
Where fallen skies and evil hues and eyeless creatures be.
On them the sea-valves cluster and the grey sea-forests curl,
Splashed wth a splendid sickness, the sickness of the pearl[31];
They swell in sapphire smoke out of the blue cracks of the
    ground,—
They gather, and they wonder and give worship to Mahound.[32]
And he saith, "Break up the mountains where the hermit-folk can
    hide,
And sift the red and silver sands lest bone of saint abide,[33]
And chase the Giaours[34] flying night and day, not giving rest,
For that which was our trouble[35] comes again out of the west.

"We have set the seal of Solomon[36] on all things under sun,
Of knowledge and of sorrow and endurance of things done,
But a noise is in the mountains, in the mountains, and I know
The voice that shook our palaces—four hundred years ago[37]:
It is he that saith not 'Kismet'[38]; it is he that knows not Fate;
It is Richard,[39] it is Raymond,[40] it is Godfrey at the gate![41]
It is he whose loss is laughter when he counts the wager worth,
Put down your feet upon him, that our peace be on the earth."
For he heard drums groaning and he heard guns jar,
(*Don John of Austria is going to the war.*)
Sudden and still—hurrah!
Bolt from Iberia![42]
Don John of Austria
Is gone by Alcala.[43]

St. Michael's on his Mountain in the sea-roads of the north,[44]
(*Don John of Austria is girt and going forth.*)

Where the grey seas glitter and the sharp tides shift
And the sea-folk labour and the red sails lift.
He shakes his lance of iron and he claps his wings of stone[45];
The noise is gone through Normandy; the noise is gone alone;
The North is full of tangled things and texts and aching eyes[46]
And dead is all the innocence of anger and surprise,
And Christian killeth Christian[47] in a narrow dusty room,
And Christian dreadeth Christ that hath a newer face of doom,[48]
And Christian hateth Mary that God kissed in Galilee,[49]
But Don John of Austria is riding to the sea.
Don John calling through the blast and the eclipse,
Crying with the trumpet, with the trumpet of his lips,
Trumpet that sayeth ha!
Domino Gloria![50]
Don John of Austria
Is shouting to the ships.[51]

King Philip's in his closet[52] with the Fleece about his neck,[53]
(*Don John of Austria is armed upon the deck.*)[54]
The walls are hung with velvet that is black and soft as sin,
And little dwarfs creep out of it and little dwarfs creep in.
He holds a crystal phial that has colours like the moon,
He touches, and it tingles, and he trembles very soon,
And his face is as a fungus of a leprous white and grey
Like plants in the high houses that are shuttered from the day,
And death is in the phial and the end of noble work,[55]
But Don John of Austria has fired upon the Turk.
Don John's hunting, and his hounds have bayed—
Booms away past Italy the rumour of his raid.
Gun upon gun, ha! ha!
Gun upon gun, hurrah!
Don John of Austria
Has loosed the cannonade.[56]

The Pope was in his chapel before day or battle broke,
(*Don John of Austria is hidden in the smoke.*)
The hidden room in man's house where God sits all the year,[57]
The secret window whence the world looks small and very dear.
He sees as in a mirror on the monstrous twilight sea
The crescent of the cruel ships whose name is mystery[58];
They fling great shadows foe-wards, making Cross and Castle
   dark,
They veil the plumèd lions on the galleys of St. Mark[59];
And above the ships are palaces of brown, black-bearded chiefs,
And below the ships are prisons, where with multitudinous griefs,
Christian captives sick and sunless, all a labouring race repines[60]
Like a race in sunken cities, like a nation in the mines.
They are lost like slaves that swat, and in the skies of morning
   hung
The stairways of the tallest gods when tyranny was young.

They are countless, voiceless, hopeless as those fallen or fleeing on
Before the high Kings' horses in the granite of Babylon.[61]
And many a one grows witless in his quiet room in hell
Where a yellow face looks inward through the lattice of his cell,
And he finds his God forgotten, and he seeks no more a sign—[62]
(*But Don John of Austria has burst the battle-line!*)
Don John pounding from the slaughter-painted poop,
Purpling all the ocean like a bloody pirate's sloop,
Scarlet running over on the silvers and the golds,[63]
Breaking of the hatches up and bursting of the holds,
Thronging of the thousands up that labour under sea,
White for bliss and blind for sun and stunned for liberty.[64]
Vivat Hispania![65]
Domino Gloria!
Don John of Austria
Has set his people free!

Cervantes[66] on his galley sets the sword back in the sheath,
(Don John of Austria rides homeward with a wreath.)[67]
And he sees across a weary land a straggling road in Spain,
Up which a lean and foolish knight for ever rides in vain,[68]
And he smiles, but not as Sultans smile,[69] and settles back the
blade. . . .
(*But Don John of Austria rides home from the Crusade.*)[70]

---

1. From the time of Alexander the Great (see page 25) to the fall of the Roman Empire, European-based powers had remained supreme in the Mediterranean center of western civilization. In A.D. 622, however, a man named Mohammed began to form the nucleus of a new religion, loosely based on Judeo-Christian tenets, which became known as Islam (or Mohammedanism), while its practitioners were Moslems (or Mohammedans).

By 632 Islam had made itself supreme in the Arabian peninsula and had begun to spread beyond. By 732 all of southwestern Asia, northern Africa, and even Spain had become part of the Moslem Empire. The only great defeats suffered by the Moslems were failures to take the city of Constantinople, capital of what remained of the Roman Empire, first in 678, then in 718. The Roman remnant, confined now to the Balkans and Asia Minor, is usually called the Byzantine Empire from then on.

The Moslems were also stopped in the west in 732 by the Franks under Charles Martel at the Battle of Tours. The Moslems remained on the offensive nevertheless, took Sicily and Crete in the following century, and even invaded Italy.

The next big surge of Moslem advance came after 1037, when the Seljuk Turks began to dominate western Asia. Most of Asia Minor became Turkish before the end of that century, and they took over Palestine as well from other Moslems. In response, western Christians marched eastward in a series of wars (the "Crusades") designed to take Palestine (the "Holy Land") and make it Christian. Parts of it were indeed taken, but after two centuries, the Moslems had it all back.

About 1300, a new tribe of Turks, the Osmanlis or Ottomans, gained power in Asia Minor and a new period of expansion began. In 1354 the Ottoman Turks moved into southeastern Europe, which was now subjected to Moslem conquest for the first time, and began to spread throughout the Balkans. In 1453 they took Constantinople, and the last remnant of the Roman Empire came to an end.

Under Suleiman the Magnificent, who came to the throne in 1520, the Ottoman Turks reached the height of their power, taking Hungary, and even laying unsuccessful siege to Vienna in 1529. When Suleiman died in 1566, he was succeeded by Selim II (called "the Sot" because he was an alcoholic). Though Selim was not as capable as his predecessor, the realm was still the most powerful military force in Europe, and it set about clearing out what was left of Christian strongholds in the eastern Mediterranean.

This poem deals with the Christian reaction to this new Ottoman offensive.

2. Gilbert Keith Chesterton was born in London, on May 29, 1874. He is best known for his detective stories, featuring the short, plump, deliberately-made-ordinary Catholic priest, Father Brown. In these, as well as in his essays, he cultivated the habit of speaking in apparent paradoxes to puncture what he felt to be wrong and uphold what he felt to be right. He tended to a social and religious archaism (he was converted from Anglicanism to Catholicism in 1922) and to a resolute denunciation of any view that could be dated later than the sixteenth century. Given the choice between saying something reasonable and dull, and saying something nonsensical and witty, one could be pretty sure he would knowingly choose the nonsense every time. Even his poetry was old-fashioned, and in 1911, when he wrote *Lepanto,* he used a style that was at its peak in 1811 (but of which, I must admit, I happen to be very fond, just the same). He died in Beaconsfield, Buckinghamshire, on June 14, 1936.

3. Byzantium was the name of the Greek city on the Bosporus— the narrow strait at the southwestern end of the Black Sea that separates Europe from Asia.

In A.D. 330 the Roman Emperor, Constantine I, rebuilt the city and made it the new capital of the Roman Empire. It was named, in Greek, "Konstantinou polis" (Constantine's City) or Constantinopolis in Latin, or Constantinople in English. It remained the capital of the slowly shrinking Roman Empire until 1453, when the Turks took it. It then became the capital of the conquering Ottoman Empire under the new name of Istanbul. Chesterton chooses to use the old name, however, as a symbol of the Ottoman Empire.

The Ottoman ruler bore the title of "Sultan" from an Arabic word meaning "dominion." In medieval times, this was usually distorted, by way of French, to "Soldan" and Chesterton, out of deliberate archaism, chooses to use the distortion.

The "Soldan of Byzantium" in this poem is Selim the Sot, and the time is 1571, when Selim had been on the throne for five years.

4. The Ottoman Empire and its ruler were rightly feared by Christian Europe ("all men" in the Chestertonian view) since no Christian nation could withstand it singlehanded. The only hope for resistance rested in a coalition, and the Christian nations of Europe in those days (as in these days) were never very good at making coalitions.

5. Ancient Byzantium, in 340 B.C., had withstood a siege by Philip of Macedon (see pages 25–26). Philip's last attempted surprise assault had been given away when moonlight broke through the clouds. The Byzantines thereafter struck commemorative coins bearing the crescent moon and a star as their thanks to the moon-goddess, Hecate, whom they worshipped. The crescent moon remained the symbol of the city forever after, even when the Ottoman Turks took it over. During the Ottoman heyday, the Crescent became the symbol of Islam, as the Cross was that of Christianity.

6. To the Greeks and Romans the Mediterranean Sea was the center of civilization, with great cities on its northern, southern, and eastern shores. It was open to the ocean only at the narrow strait of Gibraltar in the west; everywhere else it was surrounded by land. The name "Mediterranean" is Latin for "in the middle of the land," and "the inmost sea of all the earth" is the Mediterranean.

7. After the first flood of Moslem conquest, Moslem ships became a power in the Mediterranean. They were held off at first by the Byzantine navy, but by A.D. 1000, it was the various commercial

cities of Italy, Venice, Genoa, Pisa, and so on, that became the chief naval opponents of the Moslems.

These Italian republics, however, reached their peak in the fifteenth century. In 1494 the French, under Charles VIII, invaded Italy, and the peninsula became a battleground for French, Spanish, and German armies. The coasts of battered and helpless Italy were open to the raids of Moslem corsairs.

8. The "Lion of the Sea" is Venice, at the northwestern end of the Adriatic Sea. It alone of the Italian republics retained its independence and its naval power through the sixteenth century. To be sure, she was past her greatest days, but she still held important bases in the eastern Mediterranean, bases she had picked up during the Crusades, over three centuries before, and that she continued to hold even against the overwhelming force of the Ottoman Empire. She held various islands off the shores of Greece and Asia Minor, for instance, the two most significant being Crete and Cyprus.

It was these islands against which the new Ottoman offensive was being chiefly waged. In 1570 the Ottoman Empire was at war with Venice and had landed forces in Cyprus. (It was the memory of this war, by the way, that influenced Shakespeare in his writing of *Othello* a generation later.)

9. The Pope is Pius V, who had gained the office in 1566. He was an ascetic and a firm supporter of orthodoxy. Under him any vestige of Protestantism (which had come into being in 1517) in Italy was wiped out, the Inquisition was strengthened, and Philip II of Spain (the arch-Catholic of Europe) was supported in his war against the Dutch Protestants who were rebelling against his rule.

10. Pius's relentless war against those Christians he considered heretics did not blind him to the Moslem danger. Aware that only in a coalition could the Christian nations find the strength required to oppose the Turks, he labored to organize a "Holy League."

11. Forming a Holy League wasn't easy, for if the Pope was the enemy of many of the Christian powers, they returned his enmity with interest. The "cold Queen of England" is Elizabeth I, who is "cold" because she publicized herself as a virgin (though we may suppose she was not entirely as cold as all that). She had been reigning since 1558.

There was no chance of her joining the League because, for one thing, she was a Protestant, who had been excommunicated by the Pope on February 24, 1570. Even while the Pope was trying to form the League, he was declaring the English throne forfeit, and Elizabeth was scarcely going to express her gratitude for this by offering to fight under his banner.

12. The French monarch at this time was Charles IX of the House of Valois. Twenty years old, he had been king for ten years now. He was a "shadow" because he had little ability and was completely dominated by his advisers, and particularly by his mother, Catherine de Medici. France was not likely to join the League because she considered Spain and the Holy Roman Empire (ruled by the same royal family) to be her prime enemies. Indeed, a half-century before, at a time when France had suffered a great defeat at the hands of Charles V, who then ruled both Spain and the Empire, the French king, Francis I, had actually come to an understanding with Suleiman the Magnificent. He had virtually allied himself with the Turks against his Christian enemies.

13. In 1492 Christopher Columbus, an Italian navigator sailing under Spanish auspices, had discovered the lands of the western hemisphere that were eventually to be known as North and South America. For decades the Spaniards had been settling and exploiting the islands of the Caribbean ("evening isles" because they were far to the west of Europe, and "fantastical" because Europeans had fantasized islands in the Atlantic long before they discovered the real ones).

After the abdication of Charles V in 1556, his son, Philip II, reigned over Spain, the Netherlands, and much of Italy. Philip II was heart and soul with any effort to halt the Ottoman Turks, but the need to control his empire in the "evening isles fantastical," and the beginnings of his struggle against the rebellious Netherlanders in 1567, weakened him and limited his ability to participate.

14. Just to the north of Constantinople is an inlet of the Bosporus which provides a wide, large, and beautiful harbor. This can hold any number of ships and can be easily defended. Because it broadens out like a horn, and because its existence made first Byzantium, then Constantinople, and finally Istanbul rich and powerful,

thanks to its usefulness in peaceful trade and warlike action, it was called the "Golden Horn."

15. By May 20, 1571, Pope Pius had managed to form his Holy League. It consisted of Venice and Spain, as the two chief naval powers, plus the Pope himself and various other Italian cities which, militarily, were negligible. Philip II, as the most powerful ruler involved, chose the leader of the actual military enterprise and his choice fell upon his half-brother, John, then twenty-four years old.

John was the illegitimate son of Charles V by the daughter of a German middle-class citizen. The stigma of illegitimacy gave him a "doubtful seat and half attainted stall," and made him a "crownless prince" with a "nameless throne."

It wasn't as bad as all that, however. After Philip became king, he recognized John as his half-brother, gave him the name "Don John of Austria," assigned him a considerable retinue, and had him treated with the honors due a relative of the king.

Though John was young he had already had experience in fighting the Moslems. He had fought Moslem pirates in the Mediterranean in 1568, and in 1569 he had led armies against the rebellious Moriscos in Spain. (These were descendants of the Moors who had ruled southern Spain up to 1492.) Don John of Austria had done well in these earlier assignments, and Philip felt he could entrust him now with the larger task.

16. To Chesterton and to others who worshipped an ideal past that had never existed, there seemed something glorious about knights who fought for glory or honor or the sheer love of it, as opposed to fighting merely for material gain. The wars in the Mediterranean were certainly fought for trading footholds and commercial advantage (the Venetians, at least, being a remarkably sane people, never fought for anything else) with religious differences serving merely to rouse enthusiasm among the common fighting men, who got none of the advantage, win or lose, and all of the sweat, scars, and death.

The young Don John, however, perhaps because he was middle class on his mother's side, was enamored of war, and Chesterton chooses to call him "the last knight of Europe."

17. The troubadours were the poets of the Middle Ages and from

about 1050 to 1300 they sang of romantic love—an idea that may have been picked up from Moslem literature, actually. Since an exaggerated respect for women was imposed on knights in the troubadour tales (though never, as far as anyone can notice, in reality) it is easy to equate knights and troubadours if one is romantic enough.

18. The troubadours flourished on the rim of Christendom, facing the Moslem world from which it drew its inspiration. It was strong in the Provençal land of southern France, northern Spain, and northern Italy. Its time was the High Middle Ages which, to medievalists like Chesterton, was the best of times—"when all the world was young."

The Albigensian heresy was concentrated in the highly civilized regions where the troubadours sang, and in the thirteenth century all of it—the civilization, the heresy, and the troubadours—was ruthlessly destroyed by the chill forces of orthodoxy from northern France—with the blessing of the powerful Pope Innocent III.

19. The word "crusade" dates back to 1095 when Pope Urban II called for a holy war against the earlier tribe of Seljuk Turks. Those who rallied to the cause wore crosses as the distinguishing mark of the fight on behalf of Christ against the Infidel. The nobility of southern France were prominent among them and their word for cross was *cruzada*. Hence, the war became a "crusade" in English and the soldiers were "crusaders."

Strictly speaking, the crusades are limited to the expeditions sent by west Europeans against the Moslems between 1095 and 1291, but in a larger sense, any war of Christian against Moslem can be called a crusade, and this war of 1571 of Spaniards and Venetians against the Turks could fairly come under the heading.

20. All of the north African coast was Moslem in 1571 and had been so for nine centuries. Although the core of Ottoman power was at the northeastern end of the Mediterranean coast, it was from the African shore that the Moslem pirates raided the south European coast, and it was African pirates that Don Juan had fought and defeated three years before.

21. Don John is heading for the coast where he will take ship to join the fleet gathering in Messina at the northeast corner of Sicily.

22. "Mahound" is a distortion of "Mohammed" and was

adopted in English in medieval times with the deliberate intention of sullying the name by using the syllable "hound." Chesterton here, too, makes use of an archaism to enhance the atmosphere of the poem.

23. Sex was a feature of the Islamic heaven, as harps seem to be a feature of the Christian heaven. Houris were black-eyed, white-skinned, ideally beautiful women, compounded of musk and spices, who existed in the Islamic afterworld for the delectation of the faithful. They were forever young (hence "timeless") and had the unusual faculty of remaining ever virginal despite the extent to which the faithful made use of them.

24. "Azrael" is the name given by Moslems to the Angel of Death.

25. "Ariel," which means "lion of God" in Hebrew, is used in the Book of Isaiah to represent Jerusalem. In Milton's *Paradise Lost*, however, it is the name given to one of the fallen angels, and Chesterton follows that. Chesterton here takes up the natural medieval notion that Mohammed, as a false prophet in league with the Devil, has at his command all the fallen angels, demons, and idolatrous gods.

26. The kingdom of Ammon was one of the idolatrous neighbors of Israel in Old Testament times. One of the Egyptian gods was Amen, or, in Latin, "Ammon." Thus, the name doubly suggests a false, idolatrous god.

27. The Jinni (singular, Jinn) were demons in the Islamic mythology, possibly fallen angels. Sometimes they were pictured as giants, often monstrous, but sometimes beautiful and all the more evil for that. The Latins used the word "genii" (singular, "genius") to represent a divine spirit assigned to a particular person. Jinni and Genii were confused, and the latter is the more common spelling for the Islamic demons with "Genie" the singular in this case.

28. Solomon, who ruled Israel in the tenth century B.C., is described in the Bible as being the wisest of men. In Islamic legend this was taken to mean that Solomon had astonishing magical powers, including the ability to talk to animals and to control the Jinni. He used a Jinn, for instance, as a means of transporting himself to the celestial spheres (breaking the sky, in a way) so that he might study the mechanics of the universe.

29. Chesterton lumps all non-Christian beliefs together. There is no use in trying to distinguish nicely between falseness and falseness. The far-eastern "yellow" deities (from the direction of "the morn"), the Buddhas, Brahmas, and so on are also minions of Mahound.

30. Solomon could punish Jinni who attempted recalcitrance. He forced them into bottles, sealed with divine force, and sank them in the sea. Mahound now calls them all forth.

31. Pearls are produced by oysters as a way of surrounding and neutralizing some foreign material that has found its way inside the oyster shell. The invasion is, in a sense, a sickness, and the pearl is the resulting scar—but because the pearl is beautiful in human eyes, it is the mark of a "splendid sickness."

32. The fallen angels in Christian mythology were imprisoned under the ground in hell, and Mahound calls these up as well. The poem here expresses the Christian Medieval view that the Islamic prophet was a false god worshipped by the forces of evil. Actually, Islamic thought makes it quite clear that Mohammed was entirely human. It was, in fact, an Islamic jeer against Christianity that it was the Christian prophet, Jesus, who had been made into a god and that it was the Christians who fell into the error of polytheism.

33. It was commonly felt in medieval days that the physical relics left behind by saintly individuals had power over evil spirits. Bones were the commonest relics, and presumably they had to be dug out or disposed of or Mahound and all his demons would not be able to defeat the gathering Christian force.

34. "Giaour" was the common Turkish word for a non-Mohammedan, particularly a Christian. It was the analog of the word "Saracen," used by Christians for their Islamic enemies.

35. The reference is to the Crusades, which had been at their height four centuries before Don John's time. Once again, western fighters were flooding eastward as in those old days.

Since the Christian forces in those earlier centuries of the Crusades had won few victories, had never succeeded in holding more than a narrow coastal strip, and had eventually been thoroughly defeated, it might seem that Mahound need not fear a renewal of such an attempt, but, of course, the poem is presented from a Christian viewpoint.

36. When Solomon imprisoned the Jinni in bottles, he marked the seals with the interlocking triangles commonly called "the Star of David." This mystic sign neutralized the power of evil within the bottle and kept the Jinni irrevocably imprisoned. It is therefore also called the "seal of Solomon," and it here represents the Moslem dominion over the forces opposing them.

37. The Crusades again.

38. "Kismet" is a Turkish word meaning lot; that is, whatever is assigned to a man. Islamic fatalism holds that all is decided by the far-seeing wisdom of God, and that whatever is, must be, for the greater design.

Therefore, when things go ill, the faithful Moslem says "Kismet" —that is, "So must matters be, so would Fate have it, and there is nothing to do but accept the will of God with humility." Infidels, in the Turkish view, rebelling against God, would not say "Kismet."

39. Richard I ("the Lionheart") of England was the most renowned of the Crusaders, in the English view. He was one of the leaders of the Third Crusade, from 1189 to 1192, and though he was fought off by the Turkish leader, Salah-al-Din ("Saladin"), a far more capable and civilized man, the Christian version of the war makes Richard the hero, of course.

40. Raymond IV of Toulouse was one of the leaders of the First Crusade (1096–99).

41. Godfrey of Bouillon was another leader of the First Crusade and was usually considered the most high-minded of them. He was one of the leaders of the assault that actually took Jerusalem itself in 1099, so that he can be described as "in the gate."

42. Iberia is the old Greek name for the peninsula occupied by Spain and Portugal. The name is taken from the Iberus (the Ebro River). The region is still the "Iberian peninsula" today.

43. Don John has reached the Spanish coast and heads east by sea.

44. Mont-Saint-Michel (St. Michael's Mountain) is a renowned religious center set on a rock just off the coast of the northern French province of Normandy.

45. The statue is naturally winged, for Michael was the great archangel described in Daniel 12:1 as the specially assigned guard-

ian of Israel, and in Revelation 12:7, as the leader of the loyal angels who expelled the rebel angels under Satan from heaven.

46. In the poem, the forces of evil are pictured as united behind Mahound, but the Christian world is not united. In 1517 Martin Luther began the questioning that led to the Protestant Reformation, and ever since northern Europe has been full of religious disputation (tangled things and texts and aching eyes"). In particular, there has been a Protestant movement in France, relatively small in numbers but large in dedication and resolve. In 1562 the first of a series of religious civil wars broke out in the nation and kept it from taking its share of the fight against the Turk.

47. For over a century after the beginning of the Reformation, religious wars wracked Europe, with Christian killing Christian in holy enthusiasm. This was done in warfare when forces were relatively equal, but by massacre when one side had the other at sufficient disadvantage.

Thus, in 1572, the year after the events narrated in this poem, French Catholics caught French Protestants by surprise on August 23 (St. Bartholomew's Day), because it was a time of truce, and massacred three thousand of them in Paris alone, plus many thousands more in the rest of France.

48. The French religious reformer, John Calvin, developed in 1536 a gloomy system of thought in which, rather Islamically, all was predestined. God knew in advance who would go to hell and who to heaven, but the individual human being did not know. Each man had to be as God-fearing as possible, then, in the hope that this meant he was predestined to heaven since otherwise he couldn't be that good. Naturally, the knowledge of the possible inescapable jaws of Hell waiting made life more fearful and gave Christ "a newer face of doom."

49. The Calvinists disapproved of the intricate ceremonies of the Catholic Church, considering them devices of paganism and idolatry. They disapproved, in particular, of the important role of the Virgin Mary, the mother of Jesus, in Catholic dogma and, even more, in the affections and superstitions of the common folk. It seemed to them a hangover from the goddesses (Athena, Isis) of pagan days. Where the Calvinists seized control, therefore, they

broke the religious statues, with particular attention to those of Mary.

50. "Glory to the Lord!"

51. By August 24, 1571, Don John was trying to make something of the allied fleet at Messina. There was considerable confusion and cross-purposes between the Spaniards and Italians, but Don John's enthusiasm and eagerness managed to override that, and for a while at least, he welded them into an effective fighting unit. As seems always to be the case with coalitions, however, the Holy League was moving slowly. While they were getting ready, the Turks had been driving the Venetians steadily back on Cyprus and had taken most of the island.

52. Though Philip II of Spain was the moving force behind the new crusade, he was an enemy of Protestant England, and he has gone down in English history books as one of the villains against whom the English gloriously fought. Even Chesterton cannot bring himself to picture Philip heroically, but must reserve the hero place for Don John.

Philip was almost a recluse, remaining in the large and gloomy palace, whose construction he had ordered begun in 1562. There, immured in his workroom ("closet") he attempted to keep track of, and direct, all the events in his vast dominions. No one can dispute the king's vast capacity for work and his intense devotion to his cause, but since one man can only do so much, his insistence on overseeing everything and giving all the orders, contributed to Spain's failure during his reign.

53. The Order of the Golden Fleece was instituted in 1430 by Philip the Good, Duke of Burgundy, the great-great-great-great-grandfather of Philip II of Spain. The Order was the most exclusive organization of its type. Its membership was drawn from only the highest noble houses, chiefly those of Spain and the Holy Roman Empire (both ruled by descendants of Philip the Good), and was restricted to Catholics.

54. The Turks, who were well aware of the fleet being gathered at Messina took up their post at the city of Navpaktos, 550 kilometers (350 miles) to the east. Navpaktos is half-way into the Gulf of Corinth, which nearly splits southern Greece from northern Greece.

It is only 110 kilometers (70 miles) southeast of Actium, the site of the greatest naval battle of ancient times (see page 38).

Many of the Greek cities at this time were known by Italian names since the Venetians had controlled much of the Greek coastline and islands for three centuries. The Italian name of Navpaktos was Lepanto. The advancing fleet of the Holy League met the Turks here and the resulting action is known as the Battle of Lepanto and, of course, the city also gives its name to the poem.

Don John of Austria, now "armed upon the deck" is maneuvering for the attack. He had 220 ships and 26,000 soldiers (the greatest Christian fleet the world had yet seen) against the 250 Turkish ships under their commander Ali Pasha. Each side underestimated the strength of the other and moved forward confidently. When each discovered the truth, it was too late to draw back, and the scene was set for the greatest naval battle since Actium, just sixteen centuries before.

55. To Protestant Europe, and to England in particular, Philip II was viewed as a sly and deadly schemer, hidden always in his palace, holding the strings of a hundred secret intrigues in his hand, and fighting to destroy Protestantism by all means. In particular, he was thought to be not above arranging assassinations of his enemies and thus putting an end to what those enemies might have considered to have been "noble work."

Philip approved of the St. Bartholomew Day's massacres and is said to have laughed at the news—the only time anyone had ever heard him laugh. William the Silent of the Netherlands, who led the revolt against Spain was assassinated in 1584; Henry III of France (Catholic, but not Catholic enough, apparently) was assassinated in 1589; and there were constant rumors of plots against Elizabeth's life in England. All such matters were thought to be the work of Philip II.

56. The battle of Lepanto was fought on October 7, 1571.

57. This is reminiscent of the Holy of Holies of the Temple in Jerusalem, which only the High Priest might enter, and which he could do on only one day—the Day of Atonement. In it was the ark of the covenant, and it was in this ark, more than anywhere else, that the presence of God was thought to be concentrated.

58. "The crescent of the cruel ships" is, of course, the Turkish fleet, and it is here compared to the great Whore of Babylon, described in the seventeenth chapter of the Book of Revelation, and interpreted as a type of the Antichrist. The Bible says, "And upon her forehead was a name written, MYSTERY . . ." (Revelation 17:5).

59. The chief allies of the Christian fleet are here indicated symbolically. The Cross is the Pope and the Castle is Spain. (The chief portion of Spain is "Castile," originally named from the castles established as strongholds of the Christian chieftains fighting the Moors during the long centuries of Moslem domination of Spain.) St. Mark is the patron saint of Venice, and when he is painted it is usually with a lion at his feet.

60. The Mediterranean Sea is not a particularly windy area of the ocean, and sails cannot be depended on for maneuvering in battle. Consequently, in ancient and medieval times, warships of the Mediterranean used oarsmen. The oarsmen could be freemen, as in the Athenian fleet of ancient times. They might also be "galley slaves," condemned to a life of back-breaking work on the poorest food and negligible care—to say nothing of certain death if the ship were smashed by the victorious prow of another.

The Battle of Lepanto was the last major sea fight fought by oarsmen. The Moslem ships had Christian slaves chained to the oars below, while the Moslem fighters ("brown, black-bearded chiefs") were ranked on the decks above.

61. In ancient times, the great battles fought by the Asian monarchs ("high kings") were generally commemorated in stone, and the tale was never spoiled through mistaken modesty. Generally, the enemy was shown fleeing helplessly before the all-powerful, large-hewn figure of the conquering king in his chariot.

62. In the Bible, a sign is sometimes asked of God, some indication of an event out of the course of Nature, to show that He is in charge and that things for His chosen will work out well. Then, when things look ill for the Kingdom of Judah, the prophet Isaiah urges King Ahaz to "Ask thee a sign of the Lord thy God" (Isaiah 7:11). Ahaz, however, in complete despair, refuses to ask for a

sign, feeling the case to be hopeless and too far gone even for God to help.

63. The Battle of Lepanto was, indeed, a great Turkish defeat. In the melee of ship against ship, the Allies were triumphant and the result was one-sided. After a ferocious fight of three hours, 80 Turkish ships were sunk and 130 captured. Only 40 ships of the Turkish fleet escaped. About 25,000 Turks, Spanish historians estimated, were killed (Ali Pasha among them) and 50,000 were captured.

On the Christian side, 8,000 were killed, two-thirds of them Venetians (who bore more than their share of the battle and of the credit for the victory). Only 15 ships of the Allied fleet were lost. It was a tremendous and unexpected victory. The news sent Christian Europe wild with joy—a joy that is still reflected in this poem.

64. No less than 12,000 of the enslaved Christian oarsmen were rescued from the captured Turkish ships and given their liberty.

65. "Long live Spain!"

66. Miguel de Cervantes, born in Alcala de Henares about September 29, 1547, is the supreme genius of Spanish literature. He was a contemporary of Shakespeare and, in some ways, is comparable to him. He did not achieve his literary glory till late in life, however. In his youth, he missed out on a university education, got into trouble with the law, and prudently left for Italy. When the Holy Alliance was striving to gather fighters to man the ships intended to fight the Turks, Cervantes volunteered and fought on the *Marquesa*. He conducted himself with great bravery, was wounded three times, one shot permanently maiming his left hand.

67. A wreath of leaves is the traditional reward of victory (see page 27).

68. The "lean and foolish knight" is Don Quixote, the hero of Cervantes' book of that name. It was published in 1605, nearly a quarter century after the Battle of Lepanto. It was the first work of literature that could be called a novel and is still the best of its class in the minds of many—including that of this author.

69. Although Cervantes led a life of what we would now call "quixotic" adventure and glory, his great book satirized the empty

worship of such a life as glamorized by the literary descendants of the troubadours, including—heaven help us—Chesterton himself, as expressed in this poem. Cervantes (as seen through his book) smiled not with the blood lust of a Sultan—or of a Don John—or even of a Chesterton who talks of a "slaughter-painted poop" and of "scarlet running over on the silvers and the golds." Rather, Cervantes smiles with gentle sadness at the folly of mankind.

70. The poem makes it all sound as though it ended happily, but it did not. The victory at Lepanto was great, but it fizzled in the aftermath. The Spaniards and Venetians quarreled at once, since the Spaniards wanted to follow the victory with an attack on North Africa while the Venetians wanted to take back Cyprus. When the Spaniards remained adamant, the Venetians dropped out of the alliance, made peace with the Turks, abandoned Cyprus, and handed over an indemnity of 300,000 ducats.

Don Juan, in 1573, carried on the projected North African offensive and took Tunis. He was, however, driven out again in 1574, and by that time the Turks had rebuilt their fleet and were again in control of the Mediterranean. It was almost as though the battle had never been fought.

Even the participants soon disappeared. Pope Pius V died in 1572, just too soon to see the failure of the Holy Alliance after Lepanto. Selim the Sot died in 1574, his capture of Cyprus overshadowed by the naval defeat. Don John of Austria died in the Netherlands in 1578, at the age of thirty-one, his failure in his assigned task of pacifying that rebellious land added to his failure in Tunis in dimming that one glorious day at Lepanto.

And yet Lepanto had two important results that helped change history—

Psychologically, if not actually, the defeat was disastrous for the Turks. Their aura of invincibility was forever gone. Christian Europe had learned that the Turks could be smashed. When, therefore, in a decade or so, internal decay, inefficiency and intrigue began to weaken the Ottoman Empire, Christian Europe, always remembering Lepanto, began to increase pressure against it steadily and to drive its boundaries back and back.

Psychologically, the victory was just as disastrous for the Span-

iards. Made overconfident by Lepanto, Philip II (the one principal
to survive for decades) was ready, sixteen years later, to send an-
other fleet against England. This time he was defeated. The decline
of the Ottoman Turkish Empire and of the Spanish Empire, loser
and winner of the Battle of Lepanto, began, thus, at about the same
time and continued in the same slow but remorseless manner for
each, ending in the complete or almost complete loss of that empire
by the early decades of the twentieth century.

And the heir of both was England.

The "Revenge"[1]

ALFRED TENNYSON[2]

(1591)

At Florés in the Azores[3] Sir Richard Grenville lay,[4]
And a pinnace,[5] like a fluttered bird, came flying from far
    away:
"Spanish ships of war at sea! we have sighted fifty-three!"[6]
Then sware Lord Thomas Howard[7]: "'Fore God I am no
    coward;
But I cannot meet them here, for my ships are out of gear,
And the half my men are sick.[8] I must fly, but follow quick.
We are six ships of the line[9]; can we fight with fifty-three?"

Then spake Sir Richard Grenville: "I know you are no coward;
You fly them for a moment to fight with them again.
But I've ninety men and more that are lying sick ashore.
I should count myself the coward if I left them, my Lord
    Howard,
To these Inquisition[10] dogs and the devildoms of Spain."

So Lord Howard passed away with five ships of war that day,
Till he melted like a cloud in the silent summer heaven[11];

But Sir Richard bore in hand all his sick men from the land
Very carefully and slow,
Men of Bideford in Devon,[12]
And we[13] laid them on the ballast down below;
For we brought them all aboard,
And they bless him in their pain, that they were not left to Spain,
To the thumbscrew and the stake, for the glory of the Lord.[14]

He had only a hundred seamen to work the ship and to fight,
And he sailed away from Florés till the Spaniard came in sight,[15]
With his huge sea-castles[16] heaving upon the weather bow[17]
"Shall we fight or shall we fly?
Good Sir Richard, tell us now,
For to fight is but to die!
There'll be little of us left by the time this sun be set."
And Sir Richard said again: "We be all good English men.
Let us bang these dogs of Seville,[18] the children of the devil,
For I never turned my back upon Don[19] or devil yet."

Sir Richard spoke and he laughed, and we roared a hurrah, and
    so
The little *Revenge*[20] ran on sheer into the heart of the foe,
With her hundred fighters on deck, and her ninety sick below;
For half of their fleet to the right and half to the left were seen,
And the little *Revenge* ran on through the long sea-lane
    between.[21]

Thousands of their soldiers looked down from their decks and
    laughed,
Thousands of their seamen made mock at the mad little craft
Running on and on, till delayed
By their mountain-like *San Philip*[22] that, of fifteen hundred
    tons,

And up-shadowing high above us with her yawning tiers of guns,
Took the breath from our sails, and we stayed.[23]

And while now the great *San Philip* hung above us like a cloud
Whence the thunderbolt will fall
Long and loud,
Four galleons[24] drew away
From the Spanish fleet that day,
And two upon the larboard and two upon the starboard lay,[25]
And the battle-thunder broke from them all.

But anon the great *San Philip*, she bethought herself and went,
Having that within her womb that had left her ill content;
And the rest they came aboard us,[26] and they fought us hand to
    hand,
For a dozen times they came with their pikes and musqueteers,
And a dozen times we shook 'em off as a dog that shakes his ears
When he leaps from the water to the land.

And the sun went down, and the stars came out far over the
    summer sea,
But never a moment ceased the fight of the one and the
    fifty-three,[27]
Ship after ship, the whole night long, their high-built galleons
    came,
Ship after ship, the whole night long, drew back with her dead
    and her shame.
For some were sunk and many were shattered, and so could
    fight us no more—
God of battles,[28] was ever a battle like this in the world before?

For he said, "Fight on! fight on!"
Though his vessel was all but a wreck;
And it chanced that, when half of the short summer night was
    gone,

With a grisly wound to be dressed he had left the deck,
But a bullet struck him that was dressing it suddenly dead,
And himself he was wounded again in the side and the head,
And he said, "Fight on! fight on!"

And the night went down, and the sun smiled out far over the
    summer sea,
And the Spanish fleet with broken sides lay round us all in a ring;
But they dared not touch us again, for they feared that we still
    could sting,
So they watched what the end would be.
And we had not fought them in vain,
But in perilous plight were we,
Seeing forty of our poor hundred were slain,
And half of the rest of us maimed for life
In the crash of the cannonades and the desperate strife;
And the sick men down in the hold were most of them stark and
    cold,
And the pikes were all broken or bent, and the powder was all of
    it spent;
And the masts and the rigging were lying over the side;
But Sir Richard cried in his English pride,
"We have fought such a fight for a day and a night
As may never be fought again!
We have won great glory, my men!
And a day less or more
At sea or shore,
We die—does it matter when?
Sink me the ship, Master Gunner—sink her, split her in twain!
Fall into the hands of God, not into the hands of Spain!"

And the gunner said, "Ay, ay," but the seamen made reply:
"We have children, we have wives,
And the Lord hath spared our lives.
We will make the Spaniard promise, if we yield, to let us go;

We shall live to fight again and to strike another blow."
And the lion there lay dying, and they yielded to the foe.

And the stately Spanish men to their flagship bore him then,
Where they laid him by the mast, old Sir Richard[29] caught at
   last,
And they praised him to his face with their courtly foreign grace:
But he rose upon their decks, and he cried:
"I have fought for Queen and Faith like a valiant man and
   true;
I have only done my duty as a man is bound to do.
With a joyful spirit I Sir Richard Grenville die!"

And he fell upon their decks, and he died.
And they stared at the dead that had been so valiant and true,
And had holden the power and glory of Spain so cheap
That he dared her with one little ship and his English few;
Was he devil or man? He was devil for aught they knew,
But they sank his body with honor down into the deep,
And they manned the *Revenge* with a swarthier alien crew,
And away she sailed with her loss and longed for her own;
When a wind from the lands they had ruined[30] awoke from sleep,
And the water began to heave and the weather to moan,
And or ever that evening ended a great gale blew,
And a wave like the wave that is raised by an earthquake grew,
Till it smote on their hulls and their sails and their masts and
   their flags,
And the whole sea plunged and fell on the shot-shattered navy
   of Spain,
And the little *Revenge* herself went down by the island crags
To be lost evermore in the main.

---

1. The successors of Edward I and Edward II of England failed
in the long run to conquer France, and England, despite certain
great victories over the French forces, remained a second-rate power

till the reign of Elizabeth I. She came to the throne in 1558 and thanks to her shrewdness, her charisma, and her mastery of the art of the politician, she established herself as the greatest of England's monarchs.

During her reign, Spain was the strongest power in Europe and had a world-wide empire. England was merely a part of one island, with no overseas possessions. She was David to the Spanish Goliath.

England did have good ships and able seamen, however, while Spain, having undertaken too much in the way of military adventurism, and suffering from a decaying economy at home, was about to enter into a decline from which she would never recover.

All that managed to keep Spain going as long as she did, despite the continuous drain of endless, unnecessary wars intended to make Europe safe for Catholicism, was the wealth that Spanish ships managed to bring in from Spain's colonies in the Americas. Protestant England, for which Spanish defeat was necessary, was in no position to dare Spain to a land war. England could only try to break Spain's lifeline to the Americas and to do it unofficially, so as to avoid actual war as long as possible.

For that reason, English sea rovers sailed the seas, plundering Spanish possessions in the Americas and lying in wait for the treasure ships en route to Europe. To Spain, these sea rovers were pirates, and so they were. Elizabeth always disowned them, and swore they did their deeds without her permission, but she made no effort to stop them, she shared in the loot, and she knighted Francis Drake, the most successful of the looters.

In the end, Spain brought together a huge fleet or "armada" with which to break England. The armada was to reach the English Channel, carry a Spanish army waiting in the Netherlands to England, and with that army to conquer the land, restore Catholicism and end its piratical forays. The armada sailed in 1588, but unfortunately for Spain, everything that could go wrong with it did go wrong, both before it sailed and after. Bad weather and English seamen virtually destroyed the fleet, and the Spanish army in the Netherlands remained there. From that moment on, Spain entered its slow decline, and England its slow rise to world power greater than Spain had ever had.

The defeat of the armada didn't reverse matters on the instant, however. Even with the armada destroyed, Spain still controlled the New World, still had the strongest armies in Europe, and still had plenty of ships. The English had to continue to fight by way of piracy.

This poem deals with a bit of intended piracy gone wrong in 1591, three years after the defeat of the armada.

2. Alfred Tennyson was born at Somersby rectory, in Lincolnshire, on August 6, 1809. He was writing poetry at an early age, and by the time he was in his twenties had already written some of the poetry for which he is now famous. The critics thought little of him at first, however, and it was not till 1850, that he became famous with his poem *In Memoriam* written after the death of his good friend, Arthur Hallam.

He was appointed Poet Laureate in that year, and in that post he was expected to turn out verse on the occasion of incidents important to the nation. He composed an ode on the death of the Duke of Wellington in 1852, for instance, and in 1855, he published *The Charge of the Light Brigade,* which appears later in this book. He wrote *The "Revenge,"* a jingoistic paean to a British feat at sea in 1878, at a time when war was threatening with Russia. He died in Aldworth, Surrey, on October 6, 1892, at the age of eighty-three.

3. In the Atlantic, about a thousand miles west of Spain, are a group of islands called the Azores. The name is from a Portuguese word meaning "hawks," for the Portuguese discoverers who sighted it in 1431 spied hawks in the air over it. The islands have been a Portuguese possession ever since, except for an eighty-year-long period—from 1580 to 1640—when Portugal and its possessions were taken over by Spain (whose Empire thus reached its maximum territorial extent). At the time the events in this poem were taking place, the Azores were Spanish territory.

In its vicinity, British ships were lying in wait for the Spanish treasure fleet. The Azores were the logical place to wait since they were in mid-Atlantic on the sea route from the chief Spanish ports in the New World. Of the nine islands of the group, Florés was the farthest west, the nearest to the Americas, and the first the Spanish fleet would have to pass.

4. Sir Richard Grenville, born about 1541, played a tangential

role in American history. His cousin, Sir Walter Raleigh, was interested in colonizing the coast of what is now the United States. In 1585 a fleet of ships carried about 100 colonists to what is now Roanoke Island off the shore of North Carolina. That fleet was under the command of Sir Richard Grenville. He returned the next year with provisions but found that the colonists had left. They had grown homesick and had been picked up by Francis Drake. (It was not till a quarter-century more had passed that a permanent English settlement was placed in America.)

In 1591 Grenville was sent out with a fleet of ships to the Azores, there to lie in wait for the Spanish treasure fleet. He was second in command.

5. A pinnace is a small sailing vessel that can be set out to scout the surrounding waters.

6. The ambushers were in danger of being themselves ambushed. Actually, only about twenty of the fifty-three Spanish ships were men-of-war, but even so it was a formidable array.

7. Lord Thomas Howard was the Earl of Sussex. He had distinguished himself in the fight against the Spanish armada, and he was first in command of the ships waiting off the Azores. He was Grenville's superior officer.

His greatest feat was yet to come. In 1596, five years after the events recounted in this poem, he was to lead an invading force against Spain and would succeed in taking and sacking the sea port of Cadiz on Spain's southwestern shore.

8. In those days, the diets on ships were inadequate. They might stave off hunger, but without refrigeration the only food that would keep during long voyages out of sight of land were such things as hardtack and salt pork. Better than nothing, but they were seriously deficient in Vitamin C. On such a diet, seamen would get scurvy after a time and were sufficiently weakened to fall prey to other ailments, too.

9. Actually, the British fleet consisted of fifteen ships, and the fight would have been between fifteen and twenty, not between six and fifty-three. Tennyson shades the odds in the time-honored fashion of favoring your own side. Still, Howard judged a defeat to be too likely and chose to retreat. It was a logical move. He wasn't

there to fight Spanish warships; he was there to loot treasure ships. If the latter wasn't possible, then the former was to be avoided.

10. One of the horrors of the religious wars that half-destroyed Europe in the century between 1550 and 1650 was that prisoners were apt to be looked upon as less than human because they happened to be Christians of another variety. Spain was particularly notorious for the cruelty with which it punished any deviation from accepted opinion and the harshness with which it treated prisoners of war (though other nations weren't very much better).

From 1478 on, the tool that defended Spanish orthodoxy against dissenters was the Inquisition (the "asking of questions") which used torture and terror as its chief weapons. The Spanish Inquisition became a byword of unjust cruelty that was not to be exceeded until the deeds of the German Nazis came to light. The Spanish Inquisition worked in the sense that it kept Spain completely Catholic, but in the long run it failed since it placed a blanket of terror and conformity over the land that completely choked off intellectual advance and reduced Spain to a darkness and backwardness from which it has never entirely recovered.

11. It was September 9, 1591.

12. Devon is a coastal county in southwestern England, that contributed far more than its share to the manning of the ships of the English fleet. Bideford was Devon's chief port on its northern coast along the Bristol Channel.

13. The poem is being narrated by a survivor of these events, apparently, but he is not identified anywhere in the poem.

14. The thumbscrew, a device by which the thumb could be squeezed beyond endurance by the turning of a screw, was an example of the tortures used by the Inquisition. The stake represented death by being burned alive. It was the common way of executing unrepentant heretics—to tie them to a wooden stake, around which combustible material was piled, and then set afire. And, of course, those who did these things were of the opinion that they were serving God's glory and delighting him with what they did—a belief that must surely anger a just God even more than the deeds themselves.

15. What really happened, we don't know. Tennyson's version

makes it appear that Grenville lagged behind to pick up the sick men whom the rest of the fleet was willing to abandon, and that by the time his ship put off to sea, the Spanish were between him and the rest of the English fleet. That may even have been the reason, or part of it, but whatever it was, he was trapped.

16. The Spanish warships tended to be large, with structures in the fore and rear resembling in appearance and purpose a kind of armored wooden castle. Indeed, the one in front was, and still is, called the "forecastle," usually abbreviated "fo'c'sle." The Spaniards saw their ships primarily as devices for carrying soldiers (and the Spanish infantry was unmatched at the time) who could board enemy ships and fight hand to hand. The English, however, had much smaller ships designed for maneuverability and for accurate gunnery. It was their intention to fight at long range. In the long run, it was the English tactics that prevailed. If the Spanish ships were prevented from coming close, their lack of maneuverability and their inferior gunnery put them at a fatal disadvantage. The very size that made them look so impressive helped defeat them.

17. The "weather bow" is on the side of the ship from which the wind is blowing. There must have been Spanish ships on the other side, too, or Grenville's ship need only have continued racing before the wind. He was very likely faster than the Spanish ships.

18. Seville is an important city in southwestern Spain. Aside from the fact that when pronounced English fashion it makes a handy rhyme for "devil," it was also the site of the Inquisition and therefore the very epitome of wickedness in the eyes of Spain's enemies.

19. "Don" is a Spanish term meaning Lord derived from the Latin *dominus*. Since almost any Spaniard with any pretensions to gentility, and some without such pretensions, affixed a Don before his name, it became a natural term for Spaniards in general.

20. This is the first occasion in the poem where Grenville's ship is named, if you disregard the poem's title. The English have a habit of naming their warships grandiloquently. The name was appropriate for many Englishmen looked upon the piracies against Spain as revenge for what they considered the mistreatment of their ships and sailors at the hands of arrogant Spaniards.

21. Tennyson was making it sound just a few lines before that Grenville was planning to attack the Spanish ships, rather than to fly, but of course that would have been an insane decision. The description here is of a ship trying to use its superior maneuverability to escape. The *Revenge* was racing between the lanes of Spanish ships in the hope that it would come out the other side and get away before the enemy could get itself into position for a cannonade (or at least for an accurate one).

22. The *San Philip* (St. Philip) was the largest of the Spanish ships and was named for the saint after whom the Spanish king, Philip II, was named. Philip II had become king of Spain in 1556 and was now in the last decade of his life. (He died in 1598, seven years after the events of this poem, having reigned for forty-two years.) Under him, Spain reached the peak of its power, but Philip's immoderate pursuit of the victory of Catholicism everywhere, without ever pausing to consider that his aims were beyond the capacity of his nation to sustain, ruined the land.

23. The advantage of high decks, fore and aft, was that guns could shoot down on the decks of lower vessels (a castlelike effect). At this moment, however, the advantage of height was that the *San Philip* could sail behind the *Revenge,* get between it and the wind thus forcing the *Revenge* to slow to a halt. Now Grenville had to fight—or surrender.

24. A galleon is a four-decked sailing vessel and was the typical ship used by Spain both for war and for commerce.

25. "Starboard" is to one's right as one faces forward on shipboard, and "larboard" to one's left. The "star—" was originally "steer" since the rudder, in early ships, was on the right. The "lar—" was originally "lade" since the ship was loaded from the left. The similarity in sound was confusing and larboard was replaced by "port." Obviously, if the ship is being loaded from the left, the port, or harbor, is located on the left, too.

26. This is unlikely, and Tennyson is just making a good story better. Had the Spaniards boarded the ship in any numbers that would have been the end. The only reason the *Revenge* lasted as long as she did was that she maneuvered successfully to keep from

being boarded while banging away with her superior gunnery at long distance.

27. The fight lasted fifteen hours.

28. "God of battles" is reminiscent of the biblical term "Lord of hosts" (see Psalms 80:7, for instance), a phrase that represents God in his role as a war deity.

29. He was not so terribly old; about fifty. Tennyson was sixty-nine when he wrote this poem.

30. The "lands they had ruined" were the Americas, so it was a west wind that arose.

The Landing
of the Pilgrim Fathers[1]

Felicia Dorothea Hemans[2]

(1620)

The breaking waves dashed high
  On a stern and rock-bound coast,[3]
And the woods, against a stormy sky,
  Their giant branches tossed;

And the heavy night hung dark
  The hills and waters o'er,
When a band of exiles[4] moored their bark
  On the wild New England shore.[5]

Not as the conqueror[6] comes,
  They, the true-hearted, came:
Not with the roll of the stirring drums,
  And the trumpet that sings of fame;

Not as the flying come,
  In silence and in fear,—

They shook the depths of the desert's gloom[7]
    With their hymns of lofty cheer.

Amidst the storm they sang,
    And the stars heard, and the sea;
And the sounding aisles of the dim woods rang
    To the anthem of the free![8]

The ocean-eagle soared
    From his nest by the white wave's foam,
And the rocking pines of the forest roared;
    This was their welcome home!

There were men with hoary hair
    Amidst that pilgrim-band;
Why had they come to wither there,[9]
    Away from their childhood's land?

There was woman's fearless eye,
    Lit by her deep love's truth;
There was manhood's brow, serenely high,
    And the fiery heart of youth.

What sought they thus afar?
    Bright jewels of the mine?[10]
The wealth of seas, the spoils of war?—
    They sought a faith's pure shrine!

Aye, call it holy ground,
    The soil where first they trod!
They have left unstained what there they found—
    Freedom to worship God![11]

1. The Protestant Reformation began in 1517, when the German monk, Martin Luther, began a controversy that ended with the Christian Church of Western Europe split into two warring camps. The fight of the *Revenge* had been an incident in the partly religious war between Protestant England and Catholic Spain.

There were struggles within the Protestant camp, too. The mild Protestantism of Elizabeth I, which was the official religion of England, was opposed by the more extreme Protestantism of the English Puritans. Elizabeth I was able to handle the opposition diplomatically, but not so her successor, James I (who as James VI had been ruling over Scotland for some decades previously).

Under James I, the Puritans found themselves increasingly harassed, and the monarch made no secret of his intention of driving them out of the country. Some did leave England, first for the more tolerant Netherlands and then, finally for the New World. Already, in 1607, a permanent English settlement had been established in Jamestown in the part of the North American coast called Virginia, and it was for Virginia that some of the Puritan dissenters headed.

They established a permanent colony well to the north of what we now call Virginia and for some time were referred to by their descendants and by settlers who came later as "Old Settlers" or as "Forefathers." About 1800, however, an old letter written by their leader was discovered which referred to the first band of settlers in the region as "pilgrims."

The word "pilgrim" comes from a Latin word for "traveler" and it came to be used, in particular, for one who traveled to a foreign land. In the Middle Ages the most common reason for distant travel, in a time when travel was both difficult and dangerous, was to visit the Holy Land, so a pilgrim came to be thought of as one who traveled for religious reasons.

The term didn't catch on till 1820, when Daniel Webster referred to those early settlers as "the Pilgrim Fathers" in one of his orations. This poem, written about ten years later, was very popular in its time and helped to establish the phrase in the consciousness of America by its use in the title.

2. Felicia Dorothea Hemans was born in Liverpool on September

25, 1793. At the age of twenty-five, she separated from her husband of five years. By that time she had five children, and she managed to support herself and them by the earnings derived from her prolific poetic output. Her reputation is not as great now as it was in her lifetime, but she is well known for several poems that have contributed often quoted lines to the English language.

One of her poems begins with "The stately homes of England!/How beautiful they stand." Another is *Casabianca*, which begins with "The boy stood on the burning deck/Whence all but he had fled." To American readers, however, her best-known poem is this one. She died in Dublin, Ireland, on May 16, 1835.

3. The Pilgrim Fathers left Plymouth, England, on September 16, 1620, and took nearly eight weeks to cross the Atlantic in their small sailing vessel. They landed at a point farther north than had been intended, well to the north of what had been marked out by English explorers as the limits of Virginia. On November 9, 1620, they found themselves at the tip of a curving peninsula, which had been named Cape Cod eighteen years earlier by an English explorer, Bartholomew Gosnold, after the codfish that abounded in the waters offshore. It was not the right time of year, really, to see that section of the coastline at its best. The Pilgrims did not remain but sought some better haven.

4. Some of the band were doubly "exiles." In 1607 a group of Protestant dissenters had made their way to the Netherlands. Although they could worship as they pleased in that tolerant land, they did not feel secure. The Protestant Netherlanders had been fighting a long war with Catholic Spain, and the English exiles were not sure that the war might not be renewed and might not end in disaster for them. Besides that, their children were learning Dutch and forgetting their English ways. It therefore occurred to some of them to find a new home in an empty land (at least, empty but for some savages with whom no well-bred European concerned himself) where they could worship freely and in security. They returned to England to arrange for ships and transport. One ship finally left, carrying 102 men and women, about one-third of whom were from the Netherlands group and who were now exiling themselves from England a second time.

5. The "bark" was the *Mayflower*, surely one of the most famous ships in American history, for this one voyage that it made. Having left Cape Cod, the Pilgrims explored the shore westward and northward and finally, on December 16, located a harbor that seemed more serviceable than any they had yet come across. As the winter was getting deeper, they settled for this site, which was some 40 kilometers (25 miles) west of the Cape Cod tip where they had made their first landfall.

John Smith, who had been with the earlier band of settlers who had settled in Jamestown, Virginia, thirteen years before, had explored the coast northward in 1614. It was he (not the Pilgrims) who named the region New England because it seemed to him to resemble England; and it was he who named the portion of the shore line Plymouth. The Pilgrims, having left England from Plymouth, found it fitting to accept the name.

We can't tell from the poem whether Hemans is referring to the first landfall at Cape Cod, or the final one at Plymouth. Perhaps she didn't know there were two and accepted the one at Plymouth as the significant one (as does almost everyone outside of Provincetown, Massachusetts, which is at the site of the first landing).

6. They may not have come as conquerors, but they were conquerors just the same. It is very sad that the general view of American history makes it seem as though the settlers landed in an empty region, when the fact is that the land was occupied by Indians who, on the whole, welcomed the newcomers in friendly fashion—in far more friendly fashion than the Europeans would have welcomed any intruders landing on *their* shores, but then the Indians were "savages," you see.

The Pilgrims were particularly fortunate, since a disease epidemic had struck the New England Indians in 1617 and the land was emptier than it had been.

In later years, however, the settlers in New England fought the Indians without ever feeling that they were wrong in doing so. The Indians were not Christians, and therefore not really human in the eyes of the settlers. The Indians were pagans to be converted, pushed aside, and, eventually, exterminated.

The American poet, Arthur Guiterman, writing on the same subject, a century later than Hemans, said:

> The Pilgrims landed, worthy men,
>   And saved from wreck on raging seas,
> They fell upon their knees, and then
>   Upon the Aborigines.

7. A desert is a region that contains no human beings. We think of it most often as a dry and sandy waste because those, plus the frozen waters of the polar regions, are the places on earth most dramatically empty of humanity. However, even a lush and verdant garden could be called a desert if no human beings are present. In that sense, the landing of the Pilgrim Fathers took place in a desert, as far as Hemans was concerned, since no human beings were present if one didn't count the Indians (and who did?).

8. As a matter of fact, the Pilgrim Fathers were freer than they had expected to be. Had they landed in Virginia they would have had to live under the rule of a governor appointed by the English company that controlled the Virginia settlements.

The "stern" and rockbound coast" on which they landed, however, was outside the jurisdiction of the company and they could, therefore, rule themselves. They had worked out a "Mayflower Compact" before they landed, one in which all those on the Mayflower agreed to obey the laws that were enacted by democratic procedure. When they landed, John Carver, one of those who had been in the Netherlands, was elected the first governor.

9. Unfortunately, many did "wither there." The Pilgrims had reached the Plymouth coast unprepared to deal with the hard winter that was beginning, and before spring came half of them were dead, including John Carver. The survivors hung on and elected William Bradford their new governor. He remained governor for thirty-five years, and it was in a letter of his that the band were referred to as pilgrims.

10. Columbus had reached America a century and a quarter before the Pilgrims' voyage. He had made *his* voyage in the hope of reaching the wealth of eastern and southeastern Asia. Even though

the land he discovered turned out to be not Asia but a "new world," colonists looked for gold when they arrived.

In some cases, as in Mexico and Peru, Europeans found the gold they sought, and that stimulated other searches of the sort. Even the English settlers in Jamestown were hoping for wealth and were not ready to settle down to the dull life of farmers, so that the settlement all but perished within its first two years of life.

The Pilgrim Fathers were the first band to come to the New World without any thought of finding wealth. They sought a new home where they could form a society to suit themselves, and having done that, they found, for their descendants, vast wealth as well, for the land, of which Viriginia and New England were the seeds, was to become the wealthiest the world had ever seen.

11. Not quite. It is common to say that the Pilgrims came seeking freedom of religion, but that is not so if what we mean is freedom of religion for *everybody*. They came seeking it for *themselves*, and for no one else. In New England a theocracy was set up that was far less tolerant of dissent than Old England had been. Dissenters were driven out, and a few were even executed.

One of those driven out was Roger Williams, who was the first man in America to take up the position that everyone must have the right to worship (or not worship) in his own way. His crime, you see, was in *really* believing in freedom of religion. In 1635 he founded Rhode Island where freedom of religion was established, and for years afterward it was treated as a leper colony by the rest of New England because of its radical beliefs.

In fact, at the time this poem was written, over two centuries after the landing of the Pilgrim Fathers, Massachusetts still maintained the Congregational Church as the official state church, and collected taxes for its support even from non-Congregationalists. It was not till 1833 that the Church was disestablished and Massachusetts accepted full religious freedom at last.

On the Late Massacre in Piedmont[1]

JOHN MILTON[2]

(1655)

Avenge, O Lord, thy slaughtered saints,[3] whose bones
   Lie scattered on the Alpine mountains cold[4];
   Even them who kept thy truth so pure of old,
   When all our fathers worshipped stocks and stones,[5]
Forget not: in thy book record their groans
   Who were thy sheep,[6] and in their ancient fold
   Slain by the bloody Piemontese, that rolled
   Mother with infant down the rocks. Their moans
The vales redoubled to the hills, and they
   To Heaven. Their martyred blood and ashes sow
   O'er all the Italian fields, where still doth sway
The triple Tyrant[7]; that from these may grow
   A hundred-fold,[8] who, having learnt thy way,
   Early may fly the Babylonian woe.[9]

---

1. Under the rule of Charles I, the son of James I, the Puritans in England grew stronger, and eventually led a rebellion against

Charles, who was attempting to rule without a Parliament that was increasingly Puritan-dominated. The Puritans won, under the military leadership of Oliver Cromwell, and King Charles was executed in 1649. The eleven-year period that followed saw England a republic, usually referred to as the Commonwealth.

England remained the ideological leader of European Protestantism during this period and reacted with vehement concern to an event in Piedmont in 1655. It was with this event that the poem concerns itself.

Piedmont (Piemonte, in Italian) is a district in northwestern Italy. It is bounded by mountain ranges on three sides so that its name ("foot of the mountain") makes sense. Piedmont came under the house of Savoy in the eleventh century and in 1655 was ruled by Charles Emmanuel II, Duke of Savoy.

2. John Milton was born in London on December 9, 1608, and stands second only to Shakespeare in the list of English poets, chiefly on the strength of his great epic, *Paradise Lost*. In his middle years, between 1641 and 1660, he was the great pamphleteer on the side of the Puritans, championing religious and civil liberty. During the time of the Commonwealth, Milton was a power in the state, being the editor of the most important newspaper of the time, and in 1655 he wrote his sonnet on the massacre in Piedmont.

In the winter of 1651–52 he went blind. After 1660, when the Commonwealth ended and the son of Charles I was restored to the English throne as Charles II, Milton was for a while a hunted man. It was then, in his blind retirement, that he composed his greatest works. He died in Chalfont St. Giles, Buckinghamshire, on November 8, 1674.

3. The "saints" (a term Milton used for those with whose religious principles he agreed) were the Waldensians. This sect was named from its founder, a French religious reformer named Peter Waldo.

About 1173 Waldo got the notion of founding a group of lay preachers, who would be celibate, live in poverty, and go about teaching the Scriptures. Because those who followed him, the Waldensians, based their teachings directly on the Bible and rejected the traditions that had accumulated in Catholicism, and because they tended to bypass the clergy and be hostile to them, they were considered in later centuries to have been precursors of Protestantism.

Although the Waldensians were poor, virtuous, and harmless, they were, in the view of the established Church, heretics and therefore dangerous. Attempts were made to stamp out them and their views, and for some three centuries they survived partly by the intensity of their beliefs and partly by their withdrawal into nooks and corners of mountainous areas where they were less noticeable. By the 1500s those that survived were concentrated mostly in the high valleys of the mountain range that separated France and Piedmont.

4. The massacre of 1655 took place when Charles Emmanuel II authorized an Easter attack on the Waldensians in those high valleys where they were still to be found. In the course of the attack, men, women, and children were slaughtered indiscriminately.

Cromwell protested vigorously. Since the religious wars had ended and since Europeans were no longer finding much pleasure in religious persecution, his voice rang loudly. The Waldensians had been notoriously harmless and inoffensive, and the killing of them had been clearly unprovoked, so general public opinion was unfavorable to the Piedmontese. Milton's sonnet helped, in particular, to make England favor the cause of the Waldensians, and it was with English help that the remnants of the sect took root again after 1689. There are colonies of Waldensians to this day in Italy and in the United States.

5. This is a reference to the fact that the Waldensians had what seemed like a Protestant theology for centuries before Martin Luther. During those centuries the English ("our fathers"), in common with the rest of western Europe, was firmly Catholic, and permitted statues of Jesus, Mary, the apostles, and saints to fill their churches. To the Puritans, such statues were idols that were being sinfully worshipped. They were "stocks and stones," where a "stock," in its oldest English meaning, is a block of wood.

6. In the Bible, God's care for the people is likened to that of a shepherd for his flock of sheep. Thus, with reference to the Exodus, God "made his own people to go forth like sheep, and guided them in the wilderness like a flock" (Psalms 78:52).

Again, at the time of the Day of Judgment before Jesus, "shall be gathered all nations: and he shall separate them one from another, as a shepherd divideth his sheep from the goats: And he shall set the sheep on his right hand, but the goats on the left" (Matthew 25:32–33). Since those represented by the sheep are then described as going to heaven while the others go to hell, it is customary to consider sheep as symbolizing saints, and goats as symbolizing sinners.

7. The "triple Tyrant" is the Pope, because he wore a triple crown. Italy was at the time of the poem (and since, too) firmly Catholic and was therefore under the Pope's "sway."

8. The early Christian Church father, Quintus Septimius Tertullian (155–255), in defending the Church against its Roman persecutors said, "We multiply whenever we are mown down by you; the blood of Christians is seed." This thought is sometimes expressed, "The blood of the martyrs is the seed of the Church." Milton is saying so when he hopes that God will "their martyred blood and ashes sow over all the Italian fields" and "that from these may grow a hundred-fold."

9. The "Babylonian woe" is Catholicism. In Revelation, Rome, which was then persecuting the Christians, was described as a wicked woman. Since it would have been dangerous to speak against Rome directly, however, the description was of "Babylon the Great, the Mother of Harlots and Abominations of the Earth" (Revelation 17:5). Since Babylon was an earlier persecutor of God's chosen, the substitution was a clear one.

It was easy for the more extreme Protestants to see in the woman described as "Babylon the Great, the Mother of Harlots" a representation of the Papacy, which now ruled in Rome and which directed the persecution of them as the Emperors had once directed persecution of the early Christians. Indeed, "the Whore of Babylon" was an almost routine way of referring to the Pope and to the Church he ruled over on the part of the more extreme Protestants.

The Deacon's Masterpiece,[1] or the Wonderful "One-Hoss Shay"[2]

A Logical Story[3]

OLIVER WENDELL HOLMES[4]

(1755)

> Have you heard of the wonderful one-hoss shay,
> That was built in such a logical way
> It ran a hundred years to a day,
> And then, of a sudden, it—ah, but stay,
> I'll tell you what happened without delay,
> Scaring the parson[5] into fits,
> Frightening people out of their wits,—
> Have you heard of that, I say?
>
> Seventeen hundred and fifty-five.[6]
> *Georgius Secundus*[7] was then alive,—
> Snuffy old drone from the German hive.[8]

That was the year when Lisbon-town
Saw the earth open and gulp her down,[9]
And Braddock's army was done so brown,
Left without a scalp to its crown.[10]
It was on the terrible Earthquake-day[11]
That the Deacon finished the one-hoss shay.

Now in building of chaises, I tell you what,
There is always *somewhere* a weakest spot,—
In hub, tire, felloe,[12] in spring or thill,[13]
In panel, or crossbar, or floor, or sill,
In screw, bolt, thoroughbrace,[14]—lurking still,
Find it somewhere you must and will,—
Above or below, or within or without,—
And that's the reason, beyond a doubt,
That a chaise *breaks down,* but doesn't *wear out.*

But the Deacon swore (as Deacons do,
With an "I dew vum," or an "I tell yeou,")[15]
He would build one shay to beat the taown
'N' the keounty 'n' all the kentry raoun';
It should be so built that it *couldn'* break daown:
"Fur," said the Deacon, "'t's mighty plain
Thut the weakes' place mus' stan' the strain;
'N' the way t' fix it, uz I maintain,
                    Is only jest
T' make that place uz strong uz the rest."

So the Deacon inquired of the village folk
Where he could find the strongest oak,
That couldn't be split nor bent nor broke,—
That was for spokes and floor and sills;
He sent for lancewood[16] to make the thills;
The crossbars were ash, from the straightest trees,
The panels of white-wood,[17] that cuts like cheese,

126

But lasts like iron for things like these;
The hubs of logs from the "Settler's ellum,"—[18]
Last of its timber,—they couldn't sell 'em,
Never an axe had seen their chips,
And the wedges flew between their lips,
Their blunt ends frizzled like celery-tips;
Step and prop-iron, bolt and screw,
Spring, tire, axle, and linchpin too,[19]
Steel of the finest, bright and blue;
Thoroughbrace bison-skin,[20] thick and wide;
Boot,[21] top, dasher,[22] from tough old hide
Found in the pit when the tanner died.
That was the way he "put her through."
"There!" said the Deacon, "naow she'll dew!"

Do! I tell you, I rather guess
She was a wonder, and nothing less!
Colts grew horses, beards turned gray,
Deacon and deaconess dropped away,
Children and grandchildren—where were they?
But there stood the stout old one-hoss shay
As fresh as on Lisbon-earthquake-day!

EIGHTEEN HUNDRED;[23]—it came and found
The Deacon's masterpiece strong and sound.
Eighteen hundred increased by ten[24];
"Hahnsum kerridge"[25] they called it then.
Eighteen hundred and twenty came—[26];
Running as usual; much the same.
Thirty and Forty at last arrive,[27]
And then come Fifty, and FIFTY-FIVE.[28]

Little of all we value here
Wakes on the morn of its hundredth year
Without both feeling and looking queer.

In fact, there's nothing that keeps its youth,
So far as I know, but a tree and truth.[29]
(This is a moral that runs at large;
Take it.—You're welcome.—No extra charge.)

FIRST OF NOVEMBER,—the Earthquake day,—[30]
There are traces of age in the one-hoss shay.
A general flavor of mild decay,
But nothing local, as one may say.
There couldn't be,—for the Deacon's art
Had made it so like in every part
That there wasn't a chance for one to start.
For the wheels were just as strong as the thills,
And the floor was just as strong as the sills,
And the panels just as strong as the floor,
And the whipple-tree[31] neither less nor more,
And the back-crossbar as strong as the fore,
And spring and axle and hub *encore*.[32]
And yet, *as a whole*, it is past a doubt
In another hour it will be *worn out!*

First of November, Fifty-five!
This morning the parson takes a drive.[33]
Now, small boys, get out of the way!
Here comes the wonderful one-hoss shay,
Drawn by a rat-tailed, ewe-necked bay.[34]
"Huddup!" said the parson.—Off went they.

The parson was working his Sunday's text,—[35]
Had got to *fifthly*,[36] and stopped perplexed
At what the—Moses—[37] was coming next.
All at once the horse stood still,
Close by the meet'n'-house on the hill.
First a shiver, and then a thrill,

Then something decidedly like a spill,—
And the parson was sitting upon a rock,
At half past nine by the meet'n'-house clock,—
Just the hour of the Earthquake shock![38]
What do you think the parson found,
When he got up and stared around?
The poor old chaise in a heap or mound,
As if it had been to the mill and ground!
You see, of course, if you're not a dunce,
How it went to pieces all at once,—
All at once, and nothing first,—
Just as bubbles do when they burst.[39]

End of the wonderful one-hoss shay.
Logic is logic.   That's all I say.[40]

---

1. A deacon is a member of the lowest rank of the ministry, below the priest or minister. In some church sects, they are laymen, elected by the congregation to assist the minister and to handle administrative and financial affairs which the minister himself is too unworldly to tend to.

2. "Chaise," pronounced "shayz," is the French word for "chair" and it can be used for a small, light carriage on two wheels—one that is so small and light that it is just about a sedan chair on wheels. It is generally small and is light enough to be pulled easily, even with a human load, by a single horse. It is, therefore, a "one-horse chaise."

When the vehicle was introduced into the colonies, the colonials, innocent of French, took "shayz" to be a plural, so that a single vehicle of that sort was referred to as a "shay." A one-horse chaise came, in New England dialect, to be a "one-hoss shay."

3. The point of the satire is its attack on blind logic, deriving results remorselessly from false assumptions. The poem is sometimes taken to be a satire on New England Puritanism.

4. Oliver Wendell Holmes was born in Cambridge, Massachusetts, on August 29, 1809. He studied law, but changed his mind and became a physician. He was a successful one—inventing the term "anesthesia," calling attention to the fact that childbed fever was contagious, rising to the post of professor of anatomy and physiology at Harvard, and, eventually, becoming dean of Harvard Medical School.

His fame in after years, however, has rested with his poetry. He first rose to national prominence in this respect with *Old Ironsides* which was published in 1830, when Holmes was only twenty-one years old. (It will appear later in the book.) *The Deacon's Masterpiece* was published in 1858. Holmes died in Cambridge, on October 7, 1894.

5. "Parson" is a term frequently used for a minister, and it has the same origin as "person." The parson is a "person of the church," with the last three words understood. This particular parson will show up later in the poem.

6. The story starts in the year 1755. As the third line of the poem implies, it will end a hundred years later in 1855, which is three years before the poem was written.

7. *Georgius Secundus* is the Latin form of the name of the monarch more commonly known as George II. He was King of Great Britain in 1755. (In 1707, the Act of Union combined England and Scotland into one nation under the name of Great Britain.) He was to continue to reign five additional years till his death in 1760.

8. In 1714 Queen Anne of Great Britain, a granddaughter of Charles I, died. She had no children of her own. Her father had been James II, and he had been driven from the throne in 1688 because he was both unpopular and Roman Catholic, and the British Parliament had determined that no Roman Catholic was to rule them thereafter.

The nearest relative of Queen Anne who was a Protestant was George Louis, Elector of Hanover (see page 66), and he succeeded as George I. He came to Great Britain reluctantly, for he spoke no English and his heart remained in Hanover. He brought with him his son, the future George II, who was twenty-nine at the time, and who was as German as his father.

Neither George I, nor George II who had devoted to
interested in British affairs, and the real business
ministers (the origin of the tradition that the crown reigns but
does not rule). They were therefore fighting in the
hive," since they did no work and were Ger

"Snuffy," means, literally, snuff-covered,
neat. In those days when one took snuff, one
away if one were neat. Snuffy came to mean
greeable, generally.

9. In 1755 a great earthquake, possibly the most
ern times, struck the city of Lisbon, demolishing eve
lower part of the city. Since the epicenter of the qua
the nearby ocean floor, a tsunami or "tidal wave" was se
funneled into Lisbon harbor and completed the devastai
thousand people were killed.

The shock was felt over an area of one and a half million
miles, doing substantial damage in Morocco as well as in Port
All over southern Europe, the chandeliers in churches (it was
All-Saints Day that the quake took place) danced and swayed.

The Lisbon disaster made a great impression on the scholars of
the day, since it was a time of optimism concerning advancing sci-
ence. The blow showed that man was still helpless before natural
forces and sobered much of the light-heartedness that prevailed.
Much was written about it, and in Holmes's day, a century later, it
had not been forgotten.

10. General Edward Braddock came to North America in 1755
with the largest army Great Britain had ever sent to North
America. He arrived for the purpose of chastising the French who
were expanding into the Ohio Valley from Canada and who had
established themselves at the site of what is now Pittsburgh, Penn-
sylvania.

Braddock marched from Virginia northwestward, along with a
contingent of Virginian troops under Colonel George Washington.
Refusing Washington's suggestion that the troops fight Indian style,
taking cover behind trees, Braddock tried to fight as though he were
on the plains of Europe. The result was that on July 9, his troops
were ambushed by the French and Indians, and in three hours of

g nearly two-thirds of the British soldiers were killed or
led. No doubt some of the killed were scalped by the Indians.

may seem heartless of Holmes to refer so lightly to the terrible
at, but it must be remembered that in the century between the
ted States had fought two wars with Great Britain, and that
n in 1858 Great Britain remained the traditional enemy. A Brit-
h defeat could be viewed with equanimity.

Besides, it was no defeat for Washington's American troops. They
ook to the trees, fought well, and saved the remnant of the British
regulars.

11. The Earthquake day was November 1, 1755. Naturally, the
Deacon didn't know it was the Earthquake day at the time. The
only way news was carried between the continents, in those days,
was by sailing vessel, and it was at least seven weeks before New
England could learn the news concerning Lisbon.

12. Hubs, tires, and felloes are all parts of the wheel. The hub is
the central portion to which the spokes are attached, and the felloe
is the outer wooden circle to which the other end of the spokes are
attached. The tire is the material placed around the rim of the
wheel (its "attire" of which "tire" is the shortened version). We are
used to thinking of tires as made of rubber, but in the days before
automobiles the tires were metal bands fitted tightly around the
wheel.

13. The thills are the two long wooden bars between which a
horse is harnessed.

14. The thoroughbrace is a band of leather, stretching from front
to back under the carriage and serving, by its limited elasticity, as a
kind of spring.

15. The Deacon, being a cut above an ordinary layman in holi-
ness, could not use the ordinary blasphemous ways of emphasizing
his statements. He had to use diluted version (sometimes non-
sense) that sounded the same but avoided the wicked syllables.
Thus, in place of "I do vow," he would say "I do vum," and in
place of I swear to you," he would say, "I tell you." (We do the
same. In place of using the name of Jesus Christ in vain, we will
say, "Gee" and "Geez" and "Gee whiz" and "Jiminy Christmas"
and a hundred other things.)

The Deacon's Masterpiece

The misspellings here and in later lines are intended to reproduce the New England regional pronunciations of the time.

16. Lancewood is hard and durable and has a particularly uniform grain so that any long thin object made of it (such as a lance; which gives it its name, or, as in this case, a thill) is tough and springy and very difficult to break. The Deacon had to send for the lancewood because the lancewood tree grows in the American tropics and cannot be handily obtained in the neighborhood.

17. White-wood is a soft, light-colored wood from any of a number of trees, such as the tulip tree or the cottonwood.

18. The Settler's elm was undoubtedly an old tree that had existed and played some part of note at the time that Europeans had first settled the region. Such trees were often regarded with sentiment and were protected and cared for as living memorials to past generations—but even trees do not live forever and the Settler's elm had come to its end.

19. A linchpin is a locking element of metal that holds two pieces together, as a wheel to an axle.

20. Bison skin was easily available in those days, for the bison (miscalled "buffalo") roamed the western plains in the tens of millions both in the Deacon's time and at the time the poem was written. Fifteen years after the poem was written, however, a deliberate policy of killing off the bison as a way of fighting the Sioux Indians was instituted, and by the time Holmes died, the bison herds were reduced to a few pitiful scattered remnants.

21. A boot is a leather container attached to the vehicle into which one can put packages—the equivalent of an automobile "trunk," which is called the "boot" by the British.

22. A dasher is a screen of leather or wood placed across the open front of the vehicle, against which water, snow, or mud can be "dashed," with the passengers themselves being protected. Another name is "dashboard," and modern automobiles still have a dashboard which has the position but not the function of the old dasher.

23. The shay was forty-five years old now and had undoubtedly suffered less change than the colonies. The colonies had rebelled against Great Britain and declared their independence when the shay was twenty-one years old, won their fight when it was twenty-

eight, established a Constitution when it was thirty-two, and now, with the shay forty-five, John Adams was completing his term as second President of the United States. There were sixteen states in the Union.

24. Thomas Jefferson had completed his eight years as third President when the shay was fifty-three, and now, with the shay fifty-five years old, James Madison was fourth President, and there were seventeen states in the Union.

25. A "hansom carriage" was something like a shay, except that it was used as the rough equivalent of what we now call a taxicab. There was a seat for the driver next to the passenger and, eventually, the driver sat in a place to the top and rear of the passenger compartment.

The reason for its name is that it was first designed by an English architect, Joseph Aloysius Hansom. Holmes is anachronistic here, by the way, since the hansom carriage wasn't patented till 1834. In 1810 Hansom was only seven years old.

26. James Monroe was the fifth President of the United States and had just been re-elected in 1820 when the shay was sixty-five years old. The second war with Great Britain had been fought, and the United States had survived. There were twenty-two states in the Union.

27. By 1840, when the shay was eighty-five years old, Martin Van Buren was the eighth President of the United States, and the nation had passed through eight hectic years of Andrew Jackson. There were twenty-six states in the Union.

28. In 1855 the shay was one hundred years old and Franklin Pierce was the fourteenth President of the United States. There were thirty-one states in the Union, and the United States had expanded to the Pacific and had, indeed, by 1853, gained the boundaries with Canada and with Mexico that still exist today.

29. At that, mankind does very well. The human being is the only mammal, as far as we know, that ever lives to wake on the morn of its hundredth year. In fact, the only other animal that definitely exceeds the human life span of up to 114 years (in the case of the oldest verified human age) are certain tortoises. Many trees, however, live to be over a hundred years old, and some trees,

such as the sequoia and the bristlecone pines, live to be several thousand years of age. As for truth, however, that seems to change from one generation to the next.

Holmes himself, by the way, lived to reach the morn of his eighty-fifth birthday, and had his son, the more famous Oliver Wendell Holmes, Jr., lived two days longer, he would have witnessed the morn of his ninety-fourth birthday. Not bad, really.

30. On that day, November 1, 1855, the civil war in Kansas between whose who favored the establishment of a slave state, and those who wanted a free state, was in high gear, and the new Republican Party was girding its loins to mount its first campaign for the Presidency the next year.

31. The whipple-tree is the swinging bar to which the traces of the harness are attached, and by which the horse pulls the shay.

32. *Encore* is French for again. Holmes needed a rhyme and *encore* is familiar enough to educated Americans, even those who don't speak French.

33. Apparently the one-hoss shay has remained in ecclesiastical jurisdiction. This is the parson, by the way, who is referred to in the sixth line of the poem.

34. A bay is a bay-colored horse, one that is of a reddish-brown chestnut color. It couldn't be a very good horse, for a rat-tail is one that has little or no hair, and a ewe-neck is one that is thin and without the arch that spirited steeds are supposed to have.

35. The parson got an early start, since November 5, 1855, was a Monday.

36. Sermons, especially New England sermons, are carefully organized with all the points numbered: firstly, secondly, and so on. The parson was well along in his work if he had reached fifthly.

37. The parson had obviously just stopped himself from using a stronger word than "Moses," one that was quite parsonically improper.

38. The life of the shay ended with a tiny earthquake as it had begun with a planetary one.

39. Undoubtedly bubbles break at some given point first. The rest of the hollow sphere contracts into droplets so quickly, however, that the structure *seems* to have gone all at once.

40. The fallacy is, of course, not Holmes, for he was making fun of New England theology. However, let's consider—

Taken more literally, the fallacy is that even if a complex device could be made equally strong throughout, it wouldn't stay equally strong. The unpredictable viscissitudes of use would weaken some points more than others, and in the end it would still break down and not wear out.

Nevertheless, there is an odd echo in modern structural chemistry of the old deacon and his one-hoss shay. Crystals (metallic and otherwise) are built up of atoms and groups of atoms in orderly array, and their strength depends on the tightness with which atoms hold on to their neighbors. Chemists can calculate what the theoretical strength of such crystals should be, of how much force they can withstand without breaking or deforming, and real crystals—real steel, for instance—never come near the theoretical. Apparently, in every crystal there are deformities, where the atoms are not perfectly orderly. There are missing atoms, intruding atoms, unaligned atoms, and these represent weak points where the crystals deform or break far below the theoretical force they should withstand.

Structural chemists are now trying to do exactly what the deacon tried to do: to form crystals without such weak points, crystals where every place is just as strong as every other. A steel bar without atomic deformities will still break eventually when subject to steadily increasing force (nothing is infinitely strong, short of a black hole) for a deformity will be finally introduced. Exactly where it is introduced will be decided by the random luck of the game if nothing else, but a steel bar without weak points will do so only under a far greater force than that which would suffice if a deformity already existed.

Paul Revere's Ride[1]

Henry Wadsworth Longfellow[2]

(1775)

Listen, my children, and you shall hear
Of the midnight ride of Paul Revere,
On the eighteenth of April, in seventy-five[3];
Hardly a man is now alive
Who remembers that famous day and year.[4]

He said to his friend, "If the British march[5]
By land or sea from the town to-night,[6]
Hang a lantern aloft in the belfry arch
Of the North Church tower[7] as a signal light,—
One, if by land, and two, if by sea[8];
And I on the opposite shore will be,[9]
Ready to ride and spread the alarm
Through every Middlesex village and farm,[10]
For the country folk to be up and to arm."[11]

Then he said, "Good night!" and with muffled oar
Silently rowed to the Charlestown shore,
Just as the moon rose over the bay,

Where swinging wide at her moorings lay
The Somerset, British man-of-war[12];
A phantom ship, with each mast and spar
Across the moon like a prison bar,
And a huge black hulk, that was magnified
By its own reflection in the tide.

Meanwhile, his friend, through alley and street,
Wanders and watches with eager ears,
Till in the silence around him he hears
The muster of men at the barrack door,
The sound of arms, and the tramp of feet,
And the measured tread of the grenadiers,
Marching down to their boats on the shore.[13]

Then he climbed the tower of the Old North Church
By the wooden stairs, with stealthy tread,
To the belfry-chamber overhead,
And startled the pigeons from their perch
On the sombre rafters, that round him made
Masses and moving shapes of shade,—
By the trembling ladder, steep and tall,
To the highest window in the wall,
Where he paused to listen and look down
A moment on the roofs of the town,
And the moonlight flowing over all.

Beneath in the churchyard, lay the dead,
In their night-encampment on the hill,
Wrapped in silence so deep and still
That he could hear, like a sentinel's tread,
The watchful night-wind, as it went
Creeping along from tent to tent,
And seeming to whisper, "All is well!"

A moment only he feels the spell
Of the place and the hour, and the secret dread
Of the lonely belfry and the dead;
For suddenly all his thoughts are bent
On a shadowy something far away,
Where the river widens to meet the bay,—
A line of black that bends and floats
On the rising tide, like a bridge of boats.[14]

Meanwhile, impatient to mount and ride,
Booted and spurred, with a heavy stride
On the opposite shore walked Paul Revere.
Now he patted his horse's side,
Now gazed at the landscape far and near,
Then, impetuous, stamped the earth,
And turned and tightened his saddle-girth;
But mostly he watched with eager search
The belfry-tower of the Old North Church,
As it rose above the graves on the hill,
Lonely and spectral and sombre and still.
And lo! as he looks, on the belfry's height
A glimmer, and then a gleam of light!
He springs to the saddle, the bridle he turns,
But lingers and gazes, till full on his sight
A second lamp in the belfry burns![15]

A hurry of hoofs in a village street,[16]
A shape in the moonlight, a bulk in the dark,
And beneath, from the pebbles, in passing, a spark
Struck out by a steed flying fearless and fleet:
That was all! And yet, through the gloom and the light,
The fate of a nation was riding that night;
And the spark struck out by that steed, in his flight
Kindled the land into flame with its heat.[17]

He has left the village and mounted the steep,
And beneath him, tranquil and broad and deep,
Is the Mystic,[18] meeting the ocean tides;
And under the alders that skirt its edge,
Now soft on the sand, now loud on the ledge,
Is heard the tramp of his steed as he rides.

It was twelve by the village clock,
When he crossed the bridge into Medford town.[19]
He heard the crowing of the cock,
And the barking of the farmer's dog,
And felt the damp of the river fog,
That rises after the sun goes down.

It was one by the village clock,
When he galloped into Lexington.[20]
He saw the gilded weathercock
Swim in the moonlight as he passed.
And the meeting-house windows, blank and bare,
Gaze at him with a spectral glare,
As if they already stood aghast
At the bloody work they would look upon.[21]

It was two by the village clock,
When he came to the bridge in Concord town.[22]
He heard the bleating of the flock,
And the twitter of birds among the trees,
And felt the breath of the morning breeze
Blowing over the meadows brown.
And one was safe and asleep in his bed
Who at the bridge would be first to fall,[23]
Who that day would be lying dead,
Pierced by a British musket-ball.

You know the rest. In the books you have read,
How the British Regulars fired and fled,—[24]
How the farmers gave them ball for ball,
From behind each fence and farmyard wall,[25]
Chasing the red-coats down the lane,
Then crossing the fields to emerge again
Under the trees at the turn of the road,
And only pausing to fire and load.

So through the night rode Paul Revere;
And so through the night went his cry of alarm
To every Middlesex village and farm,—
A cry of defiance and not of fear,
A voice in the darkness, a knock at the door,
And a word that shall echo forevermore!
For, borne on the night-wind of the Past,
Through all our history, to the last,
In the hour of darkness and peril and need,[26]
The people will waken and listen to hear
The hurrying hoof-beats of that steed,
And the midnight message of Paul Revere.

---

1. Though Braddock had been defeated in 1755, the British finally won the war against France and by 1763 had driven them off the continent. The British had North America to the Mississippi and as far north as they could penetrate.

The disadvantage of this was that the war had saddled the British with a huge debt which they tried to pay off, at least in part, by taxing the colonies for whose sake (they said) the war had been fought. The colonists, on the other hand, no longer in fear of the French, and certain they had done their fair share in fighting the war were not willing to be taxed at the will of a distant government.

From 1763 to 1775 the battle of wills grew sharper and a possible recourse to arms seemed increasingly likely. When the bloodshed began it came through events with which the name of Paul Revere has become indelibly linked.

Revere was born in Boston, Massachusetts, on January 1, 1735, the son of a Huguenot refugee named Apollos Rivoire. Paul anglicized the name. He was a successful silversmith and became a leader of the artisans of Boston.

His connection with the American opposition to British policies began in 1770 when he published a drawing of the "Boston Massacre." This was a set-to between Boston civilians and British soldiers which the civilians had provoked and in which several of them were killed. The drawing greatly exaggerated the bloodiness of the affair and made it look like an organized army assault on peaceful citizens (instead of the other way around). The cartoon was widely circulated and roused much indignation among the colonists.

Revere then became a mounted messenger for the Rebels. His most famous ride was the one described in this poem. Despite his real services in the Revolutionary era he was, however, quite forgotten, till this poem was published, and it was the poem, not his deeds, that made Paul Revere immortal.

2. Henry Wadsworth Longfellow was born in Portland, Maine, on February 27, 1807. In 1839 he published a volume of poetry that contained *The Psalm of Life*, which contained the verse:

> Lives of great men all remind us
> We can make our lives sublime,
> And, departing, leave behind us
> Footprints on the sands of time

The poem became immensely popular and made his reputation. His popularity continued to grow until he was the most successful poet of the nineteenth century and the first American to make a good living at poetry.

Beginning in 1863, Longfellow published *Tales of a Wayside Inn* modeled in form on *The Canterbury Tales*. The device was of a meeting of friends in the Wayside Inn (actually, the Red Horse Inn at Sudbury, Massachusetts), about 27 kilometers (17 miles) west of

Longfellow's home in Cambridge, with each person present telling several stories in verse, each in his turn.

The very first story is told by the landlord of the inn, and that was *Paul Revere's Ride,* a natural since it deals with events that took place between Cambridge and Sudbury—with Concord, the focus of the tale, lying but 10 kilometers (6 miles) north of Sudbury.

Longfellow died in Cambridge on March 24, 1882.

3. George III, who had succeeded his grandfather, George II, in 1760, was a stubborn man determined not to give in to the rebellious colonists. On December 16, 1773, a party of rebels (one of whom was Revere) dressed as Indians, boarded ships carrying tea (for which the colonials were supposed to pay a tax), and dumped 342 chests of it into the harbor. The furious George III decided to place Boston under martial law, an act which drove the Bostonians to greater extremes of opposition until, by the spring of 1775, the question was no longer whether there would be an uprising, but merely when and where it would take place.

4. Longfellow means, of course, an actual physical memory by someone old enough to have been alive on April 18, 1775 as more than a babe in arms. Since the poem was published in 1863, someone would have had to be well into his nineties to "remember that famous day and year."

5. The British army of occupation in Boston was under General Thomas Gage, who was also serving as royal governor of Massachusetts. The people of Massachusetts did not consider Gage their governor, however, but their oppressor. They had chosen a kind of "government in exile" which ruled from the city of Concord, 28 kilometers (17 miles) northwest of Boston. There the leaders of the rebellion met, and there arms and ammunition were gathered.

In April, Gage decided to send a troop of men to Concord to seize those arms and, if possible, to arrest the two ringleaders of the rebellion, Samuel Adams and John Hancock. Gage, however, could not conceal his intentions. He made no particular effort to be secret, and there were many rebel-sympathizers in Boston who reported the least action of Gage and his troops. Already on April 16,

Revere had ridden to Concord to warn them to convey their military stores to a safer place, and it was known that any day the British would move. By April 18, it was known that *that* was the day.

6. Since Concord was an inland town, the British could not actually go there by sea. Their choice was one of two alternatives. They might march southwestward by way of the narrow neck of land that, in those days, connected Boston to the mainland, and then westward to some point where the Charles River might be easily crossed. They would then head northwestward to Concord. This was "by land."

Or else they might take ships across the relatively wide estuary of the mouth of the Charles River and be on the north bank of the river at once—and then march from there. That would be "by sea."

7. The spires of the churches were the highest points in town, and the Old North Meeting House was the most northerly church in Boston. A signal could most easily be seen from its spire if Revere wanted to start on the other side of the Charles and get a good headstart in the race to Concord.

8. In the poem it would seem that Revere must know the route so that he can carry the warning to those who would be most affected by the march of the British.

In actual history there was no need for him to know the route at all, for despite Longfellow's account, which makes Revere the single hero of the occasion, there was more than one rider that night. Paul Revere spread the alarm north of the Charles, the route "by sea," while another man, William Dawes, slipped across the neck of land between Boston and the mainland and spread the alarm south of the Charles (the route "by land").

9. The opposite shore was occupied by the small town of Charlestown, then a separate entity, but eventually absorbed by Boston.

Revere's position on the opposite shore *before* knowing the route makes no sense if he were indeed the only rider of the night. If he cared which route the British took, it could only be because he wanted to rouse the rebels on the line of march, but he was already in position to do that only if they went by sea. What if they were going by land?

The fact was that he was taking the north shore as a matter of course, either way. Others would take the south shore.

10. Middlesex county lies to the northwest of Boston all the way to the New Hampshire line. Cambridge is its county seat and Concord is near its geographical center. The entire British march from Boston to Concord was within the bounds of Middlesex county. (Boston itself lies in Suffolk county, which is made up of that city plus three northeastern surburbs.)

11. The year before some of the farmers had banded together as "Minutemen," so-called because they pledged to be ready to grab their guns and dash to the scene of any fighting at a minute's notice. It was Revere's intention to supply rather more than a minute's notice.

12. British ships had arrived in Boston harbor in May 1774 bringing the troops of occupation. Eventually, they brought five regiments.

13. It was clear that the British were going to move across to the north shore of the Charles River. In other words, they were going "by sea."

14. The British are crossing the Charles.

15. Longfellow doesn't give the name of the "friend" who gave the signal, and we can suspect that there was no signal necessary under the real circumstances of the ride, no signal given, and therefore no friend to give it.

16. The village is Charlestown.

17. The events of that march, thanks in part to the warning rides by Revere and others, led to the first fighting of the American War of Independence. After that the fighting never ceased till independence was won.

18. The Mystic River flows southeastward on the north side of Charlestown, joining the Charles River to form a united mouth.

19. Longfellow doesn't say so, but Medford represents a detour. Revere rode out of the peninsula on which Charlestown was located, intending to take the road westward to Cambridge (6.5 kilo-

meters, or 4 miles, away) from which the most direct road to Con-
cord would be found.

When not yet halfway to Cambridge, however, he was inter-
cepted by mounted British soldiers. Revere's horse was fast, and he
saw them in time to turn about and gallop safely away, taking the
road to Medford, 7 kilometers (4.5 miles) north of Cambridge.
There he turned westward again and joined the Cambridge-Con-
cord road just northwest of the town of Arlington, which lay 6 kilo-
meters (4 miles) west of Medford.

20. Lexington is 10 kilometers (6 miles) west of Medford.

21. The British soldiers, in no particular hurry, and marching
much more slowly than Revere's horse was galloping, reached Lex-
ington at dawn. There were seven hundred of them. As a result of
Revere's warning, some forty minutemen gathered on the village
green to oppose them. Major John Pitcairn, who led the advance
British contingent, called out to the minutemen to disperse. This the
minutemen ought to have done and probably would have done, for
they were outnumbered nearly twenty to one, but from behind a
stone wall there came the first shot of the American Revolution.
Who it was who fired the shot no one knows to this day, but it was
enough. The British soldiers, without orders, fired point-blank at
the minutemen, killed eight and left ten more wounded. The min-
utemen returned the fire briefly, then ran. The British marched on
with a single wounded soldier as their only casualty.

This was the "bloody work." It wasn't much, as battles go, but it
was plenty and to spare for those who died. It was also the first
blood spilled in a war that was to last eight years and bring about
the recognition of the independence of the United States by Great
Britain and the rest of the world.

22. *No, he didn't.* Paul Revere never reached Concord that fate-
ful night. Never!

Here's what happened. While Revere had galloped to Lexington
via Medford and Arlington, William Dawes, south of the Charles,
had given the alarm in Roxbury and Brookline, then crossed the
Charles into Cambridge and pounded up the road toward Concord.
He reached Lexington just behind Revere.

Adams and Hancock happened to be spending the night in Lexington. They were roused by the two riders and got away. That was important, since they were the ringleaders of the rebellion, and had they been captured, that would have been a sharp blow at rebel morale.

In Lexington, also, Revere and Dawes were joined by a twenty-four-year-old physician named Samuel Prescott. He was still awake because he was with a girl. On becoming aware of what was going on (and having, perhaps, done with the girl) he mounted his horse.

The three headed for Concord but almost at once were stopped by a British patrol. Revere was arrested and was taken back to Lexington and his ride was over. He was released the next morning. Dawes managed to escape, but he had apparently been disheartened by the incident and returned home.

Only Samuel Prescott continued on, and it was he who reached Concord to give the alarm—but because Longfellow found it more dramatic to describe one man as doing the job, and because he chose Paul Revere to do it, Prescott rests in oblivion.

23. For this second skirmish of the day, see page 150.

24. The British Regulars were the trained fighting men of the British Army. Against them were untrained farmers. That the farmers stood up against the soldiers was remarkable in itself; that they fought effectively was even more remarkable. By noon, the British had had enough and prepared for the march back to Boston.

But now came the worst. The whole countryside swarmed with angry militia, four thousand of them according to some estimates.

25. The Massachusetts farmers didn't fight in army fashion. They sought cover and had time to take the careful aim of huntsmen. The British soldiers were not marksmen and didn't have the type of guns that could aim accurately anyway. The guns were designed for quick loading and then it was intended that a whole volley be fired from an even line of soldiers all shooting in the same direction in the hope that some of the balls, more or less by accident, would hit the targets.

The bewildered British soldiers—perfect targets in their bright red uniforms (hence "redcoats")—found themselves being shot down by an enemy they could not see and who offered no target to shoot back at. They could just stagger on, as one after another was hit. They might all have been mowed down before reaching Boston but for a strong relieving contingent sent to rescue them.

As it was, the trip to Concord had resulted in ninety-nine British soldiers dead and missing, and 174 wounded—some 40 per cent of the entire force. The total rebel casualties were ninety-three.

26. The poem was published in 1863 when the Civil War was at its very height. "The hour of darkness and peril and need" was never more on the nation, and the glimpse at a triumphant moment in the past, with its almost mystical indication that somehow the ghost of Paul Revere was still riding for the salvation of the country, contributed to the poem's instant popularity. At once, Revere became one of the nation's great heroes. And before 1863 was over, Union armies had taken Vicksburg and won the Battle of Gettysburg, so that the danger had passed its peak.

Concord Hymn[1]

RALPH WALDO EMERSON[2]

(1775)

By the rude bridge that arched the flood,[3]
  Their flag to April's breeze unfurled,[4]
Here once the embattled farmers stood,[5]
  And fired the shot heard round the world.[6]

The foe long since in silence slept;
  Alike the conqueror silent sleeps[7];
And Time the ruined bridge has swept
  Down the dark stream which seaward creeps.[8]

On this green bank, by this soft stream,
  We set today a votive stone;
That memory may their deed redeem,
  When, like our sires, our sons are gone.[9]

Spirit, that made these heroes dare
  To die, and leave their children free,
Bid Time and Nature gently spare
  The shaft we raise to them and thee.[10]

1. The same event is commemorated in this poem as in the previous one. Concord was founded in 1635, the first inland town in New England to be settled. It received its name because the settlement was arranged in peaceable agreement with the Indians.

2. Ralph Waldo Emerson was born in Boston, Massachusetts, on May 25, 1803. He was a Unitarian minister early in life, but abandoned that post and became one of America's great lecturers. His essays are more famous today than his poetry is, but of his poems, none is better known than this one, written to celebrate the memory of the battle of Concord, a town in which he had taken up his permanent residence in November 1834.

3. Concord lies at the place where the Sudbury River flows northward into the Concord River. It is the Concord River that is "the flood" and at a point just downstream from where the Sudbury River joins it, there was, in 1775, a "rude bridge" of wood—the North Bridge.

4. It is April 19, 1775. The British are marching to Concord and the farmers of the area have been warned of their coming by Samuel Prescott (see page 147).

5. Almost all New Englanders outside Boston itself and some of the other coastal towns were farmers, and it was the farmers who had grouped together in associations of "Minutemen" (see page 145).

6. The confrontation was at North Bridge. The British soldiers had killed eight men at Lexington (see page 146) en route to Concord and expected no more trouble here. They called on the rebels to disperse, and the rebels refused. Again, as at Lexington, a shot was fired, and again a melee followed, but this time it was not one-sided at all. There were fourteen British casualties—plus many more once the British decided to retreat to Boston (see page 148)—and the American Revolution had begun, and never ceased till it was successful.

By the time the commemoration was being held at which this hymn was sung, the United States had survived a second war with Great Britain. It had doubled the territory it had had at the time of independence and had quintupled its population. It was rising rapidly in wealth, strength, and prestige. There was no question but that the nation, which had had its beginnings at North Bridge, was to play an increasing role in the affairs of the world, and Emerson could fairly speak of someone having "fired the shot heard round the world."

7. The commemoration took place on April 19, 1836, on the sixty-first anniversary of the battle. Any survivor would have to be eighty years old at least.

8. The Concord River flows northward into the Merrimack River which, in turn, flows eastward into the Atlantic Ocean.

9. The lines possess a taken-for-granted male chauvinism. It is "our sires" who have already died, and "our sons" who are yet to die, and, undoubtedly, the "we" who set the stone are men as well. Mothers and daughters don't count.

10. Emerson's wish was amply fulfilled. In 1875, thirty-nine years after the commemoration and on the hundredth anniversary of the battle, the famous statue by Daniel Chester French, "The Minute Man of Concord," was dedicated on the site. Emerson lived to see that centennial celebration, dying on April 27, 1882, eight days after the 107th anniversary of the battle and a month short of his seventy-ninth birthday.

And, today, two centuries after the battle, there is still an annual pilgrimage to Concord on the anniversary days so that Americans may stand on the site of the shot heard round the world.

On the Extinction
of the Venetian Republic[1]

WILLIAM WORDSWORTH[2]

(1797)

Once did She hold the gorgeous East in fee,[3]
And was the safeguard of the West[4]; the worth
Of Venice did not fall below her birth,
Venice, the eldest child of liberty.[5]
She was a maiden city,[6] bright and free;
No guile seduced, no force could violate;
And, when she took unto herself a mate,
She must espouse the everlasting Sea.[7]
And what if she had seen those glories fade,
Those titles vanish, and that strength decay[8];
Yet shall some tribute of regret be paid
When her long life hath reached its final day[9]:
Men are we, and must grieve when even the shade
Of that which once was great, is passed away.[10]

---

1. What may have kept the British from viewing the new Ameri-
can Republic with unceasing and implacable hostility, and of

laboring incessantly to bring it down, was that a much more dangerous enemy arose against Great Britain in the years after the American success. In 1789 the French Revolution broke out threatening traditional values throughout Europe. Before long, Great Britain was rallying Europe against the new revolutionaries and embarking on a war that was to last more than twenty years.

Most of that war was fought against a French general who was to become Emperor—Napoleon Bonaparte. In 1716 and 1797, when Napoleon was yet merely a general, he defeated the Austrians in Italy in the first of his major campaigns and began what was to be a habit of his to the end of his military career—the carving and recarving of Europe into new boundaries. In 1802 this poem was written to commemorate one of the consequences of Napoleonic map-shuffling after this first campaign.

2. William Wordsworth was born at Cockermouth, Cumberland, on April 7, 1770. The French Revolution was greeted by him with enthusiasm at first. He visited France and, for a while, felt more French than English. He ran out of funds, however, had to return to England in December 1792, and there gradually grew disillusioned with the increasing violence of the French Revolutionaries. He spent the rest of his life shaking off his early liberalism and growing more and more conservative.

In 1798, in collaboration with his friend, Samuel Taylor Coleridge, he published *Lyrical Ballads* which established his reputation as a poet. The first edition was published anonymously, but a second, enlarged edition in 1800 bore his name. Though his poetic career declined in the last half of his life, he became Poet Laureate in 1843. He died in Grasmere, Westmoreland, on April 23, 1850.

3. For 2,500 years Europe had been awestruck at the wealth and resources in Asia. The barren city-states of Greece were struck by the wealth of the rulers of the larger states of Asia, by Midas of Phrygia, Croesus of Lydia, the various kings of Persia. The feudal barbarians of medieval Europe were similarly struck with the culture and wealth of the Moslem East at the time of the crusades, and in early modern times, the Europeans thought that the "Indies" of the Far East were a treasure-trove of gold, pearls, silk, and spices.

The phrase "gorgeous East" was first used by Milton in *Paradise*

Lost, written a century and a half earlier, and Wordsworth borrows it here.

Part of the gorgeous East in the Middle Ages was the Byzantine Empire, a yet-unfallen remnant of the Roman Empire. In A.D. 1000, its capital, Constantinople, was the greatest city in Europe, perhaps in the world. The Byzantine Empire was the most civilized land in Europe and was the strongest in the military sense, too, under a conquering Emperor, Basil II.

Commercially, however, it was weak, and was not to be compared with the Italian city of Venice in the northern Adriatic. It had a navy, a merchant marine, and a traditional connection with the Byzantines. The Byzantines found it profitable to allow the Venetians to establish a trading post in Constantinople. For two centuries, however, Venice grew stronger and the Byzantines weaker. In 1204 Constantinople was taken over outright by the Venetian navy carrying crusading knights. Half a century later Constantinople regained its independence, but thereafter the Byzantine Empire was but a minor power.

For two centuries, then, Venice, referred to as "She" in the poem, held the gorgeous East (the Byzantine Empire) in fee; that is, as a private estate run for the profit of the owners.

4. In A.D. 635, the Arabs, under their new religion of Islam, began their career of conquest. For over a thousand years, they pushed an offensive against Europe which, time and again, the Europeans repelled by a hair. For the first four centuries, it was the Byzantine Empire that met the brunt of the Moslem advance and turned it back. The weaker European powers west of the Byzantine Empire were thus protected, and the Empire was the safeguard of the west in that period.

Eventually, though, the Byzantine Empire began to fold under the strain, and Crusaders from the west came to join in the fight against the Moslems. But then the Crusaders, with Venice, took Constantinople, and after that the Byzantines were unable to counter the Moslems effectively.

In the fourteenth century, the Ottoman Turks became the strongest Moslem power, and in 1345 they crossed into Europe. In

On the Extinction of the Venetian Republic

1453 they took Constantinople, and the Byzantine Empire finally came to an end. By 1529 they were at the gates of Vienna and at the peak of their power, though they retained enough strength to try to take Vienna again in 1683. It was only thereafter that the Turkish power started its final decline.

During this three-century period of the Turkish danger—from 1345 to 1683—tiny Venice kept forever nipping at the flanks of the Turkish giant, and in this unequal battle, thanks to its fleet, Venice held its own.

Venice fought the Turks in 1416, again in 1425, and then in a major war between 1463 and 1479 was forced to give up some of its holdings in the Balkans which it had gained at the time of the taking of Constantinople. Even after another war—from 1499 to 1503—Venice retained outposts in the east, including, chiefly, the island of Cyprus. That survived another war from 1537 to 1540. In 1571 the Venetians were part of the coalition that inflicted the first major defeat on the Turks in the great naval battle of Lepanto (see pages 80ff). Despite that, Venice lost Cyprus. Finally, in another war—from 1645 to 1699—Venice lost Crete.

Although Venice never, in those centuries of on-and-off warfare, decisively defeated the Turks, she kept them constantly occupied and weakened—by just enough, perhaps, to allow the Turks never quite enough strength to extend their conquests into western Europe. In that sense, Venice "was the safeguard of the West."

5. Venice traced its history back to 452, when the dread Attila the Hun was invading Italy. The Huns laid seige to Aquileia, a city at the northern tip of the Adriatic Sea, and after three months took and destroyed it. Some of the inhabitants, fleeing from the devastation, took refuge among the swampy lagoons to the west where, helped by the undesirable nature of the surroundings and the lack of anything to tempt the looting hordes, they retained their independence. There were more refugees joining them in 568 when the Germanic tribe of the Lombards invaded Italy.

In this way, Venice alone of all the west-European portion of the Roman Empire remained untaken by the barbarians. It could therefore be considered "the eldest child of liberty."

6. After her foundation, Venice remained untaken by anyone, and for 1,400 years never felt the footsteps of a conquering army. In this sense she remained a "maiden city," never having been violated.

7. The Venetians always realized their strength lay upon the sea; that her defense was her navy, and her wealth was her merchant marine. A rather dramatic custom began in 1177 that symbolized this. In that year the Venetians had used their sea power to help Pope Alexander III defeat the German Emperor Frederick Barbarossa. The Pope therefore gave a gold ring to the elected Venetian ruling magistrate, the doge, and ordered him to use it to wed the sea, symbolically. Each year, on Ascension Day (the fortieth day after Easter), the Doge (a title which is the Italian equivalent of "Duke") threw a ring into the Adriatic Sea, saying, "We wed thee, O sea, in token of perpetual domination." Thus, the city did "espouse the everlasting Sea."

8. Venice was at the height of her power, military, commercial, and artistic, in the last decades of the fifteenth century, but events conspired against her. The wars against the Turks were costly and weakening; the discovery of the Americas and of the sea routes to the East meant that she was bypassed commercially. Furthermore, in 1508 France and Spain combined with the Pope in the "league of Cambrai" for the purpose of breaking the power of Venice. Venice survived, but was badly shaken. She declined in power steadily, and her final wars with the Turks, especially the one between 1645 and 1669, lost her all her posts beyond the Adriatic, and thereafter she stagnated and grew steadily weaker and more shadowy.

9. The "final day" was May 12, 1797. Napoleon had defeated Austria and intended to extract concessions from her. In order to pacify the defeated power and keep her from preparing for revenge, he planned to give her territory elsewhere—someone else's territory of course.

On that day, then, the Grand Council of Venice met for the last time. Ludovico Manin was then the 120th and last doge of an unbroken line since 687, when the first doge had been elected. (During all that time there had been only one civil disturbance or rebel-

lion against the Venetian government, and that had been in 1310).
Manin was forced to put an end to the Venetian Republic and turn
it over to Napoleon, who then turned it over to the Austrians.

10. Venice never regained its freedom. It remained Austrian for
seventy years until, in 1866, Austria was defeated by Prussia and
forced to cede the Venetian territory to the new kingdom of Italy.
Venice has remained part of Italy ever since.

Incident of the French Camp[1]

ROBERT BROWNING[2]

(1809)

You know, we French stormed Ratisbon[3]:
   A mile or so away,
On a little mound, Napoleon[4]
   Stood on our storming-day;
With neck out-thrust, you fancy how,
   Legs wide, arms locked behind,
As if to balance the prone brow
   Oppressive with its mind.[5]

Just as perhaps he mused, "My plans
   That soar, to earth may fall,
Let once my army-leader Lannes[6]
   Waver at yonder wall,"—
Out 'twixt the battery-smokes there flew
   A rider, bound on bound
Full-galloping; nor bridle drew
   Until he reached the mound.

Then off there flung in smiling joy,
　　And held himself erect
By just his horse's mane, a boy[7]:
　　You hardly could suspect—
(So tight he kept his lips compressed,
　　Scarce any blood came through),
You looked twice ere you saw his breast
　　Was all but shot on two.

"Well," cried he, "Emperor, by God's grace
　　We've got you Ratisbon![8]
The Marshal's in the market-place,[9]
　　And you'll be there anon
To see your flag-bird flap his vans[10]
　　Where I, to heart's desire,
Perched him!" The chief's eye flashed; his plans
　　Soared up again like fire.

The chief's eye flashed; but presently
　　Softened itself, as sheathes
A film the mother-eagle's eye
　　When her bruised eaglet breathes[11];
"You're wounded!" "Nay," the soldier's pride
　　Touched to the quick, he said:
"I'm killed, Sire!" And his chief beside,
　　Smiling the boy fell dead.[12]

---

1. This poem deals with an incident in the continuing Napoleonic Wars, one that took place a dozen years after the end of the Venetian Republic.

2. (See pages 65–66).

3. Ratisbon is the French version of the name of Regensburg, a Bavarian city on the upper Danube River, about 320 kilometers

(200 miles) upstream from Vienna and 10 kilometers (70 miles) north of the Bavarian capital at Munich. The day is April 23, 1809.

4. Napoleon Bonaparte had been leading French armies for thirteen years now. He had been a simple general when he was fighting against the Austrians in Italy in 1796. In 1799 he seized dictatorial control of France, and then beat the Austrians in Italy again in 1800.

In 1804 he made himself Emperor Napoleon I, and then beat the Austrians (with their Russian allies) a third time in 1805. This time, he beat them on their own territory and won the greatest of all his victories at Austerlitz. He then went on to destroy the Prussian armies, beat the Russians again, and by the end of 1807 was virtual master of Europe. Only Great Britain, which controlled the sea and which Napoleon couldn't reach with his armies, stood out against him.

But then Napoleon overreached himself in Spain. He threw out the worthless Spanish king and made his own brother, Joseph (also worthless), king instead. The Spaniards, in a choice of worthless monarchs, wanted their own and rose in rebellion with aid reaching them steadily from Great Britain.

It took all of 1808 for Napoleon to get some semblance of control over Spain, and he had to go there himself to do it. Austria, feeling that Napoleon's preoccupation in Spain was her opportunity, decided to prepare for a fourth trial of arms. On April 9, 1809, one Austrian army marched into Bavaria, which was an ally of France, and another moved into Italy. Both won initial victories, and the French, minus Napoleon, were in retreat everywhere.

Napoleon had left Spain when news of the Austrian preparations reached him, and he got to the scene of the battle on April 16, a week after the Austrian invasions had begun. Napoleon struck hard at the center of the overextended Austrian lines, and the northern half fell back on Regensburg, with Napoleon in pursuit. On April 23, the French stormed the town.

5. Napoleon has caught the fancy of mankind as no other military captain has since the day of Alexander the Great. Everyone has a picture of him in his mind—his shortness, his forelock, his habit of placing his hands behind his back or one hand inside his vest. There

is always the feeling that, like Alexander, he was superhuman; that with his driving energy, he could do more than any other seven men, whether it was in dictating letters, in planning a legal system, or in outlining a battle campaign. Hence, the picture here of a brain too heavy for his head.

6. Jean Lannes, born on April 11, 1769, just four months before Napoleon, was the son of a stable hand. As a result of the French Revolution, most of the French officer corps deserted or were killed, and the Republican Army had to make officers out of peasants and artisans. The result was that Napoleon, detecting native talent unerringly, collected about himself the most remarkable group of military leaders under a single dominating personality that the world had seen since the time of Alexander the Great.

Lannes had been the prime instrument in beating the Austrians in 1800, winning a great victory at Montebello. He had been created Duke of Montebello in consequence. Despite Browning's rhyme scheme, by the way, his name is pronounced "lan," without the final "s."

7. Napoleon's many victories had their price. He never hesitated to spend his men freely, and as the years went by, he was forced to call younger and younger men to the colors.

8. Yes, but Napoleon's enemies were learning, bitterly and painfully, how to fight from the hard lessons he was teaching them. In an earlier campaign, the Austrian Army would have disintegrated at this point. This time, though they lost Regensburg, they retreated in good order and would fight again.

9. Presumably this is Lannes, who was mentioned earlier. Actually, it was another marshal, Louis Nicolas Davout, who was most active on this particular occasion and who distinguished himself.

10. The "flag bird" is the eagle, of course, which seems to have represented more armies and nations than any other animal who existed (see page 38).

11. Napoleon had the instinctive feel for public relations. He knew how to remember soldiers' names; how to give awards and medals; how to make them feel he was personally concerned—as here. That this represented a *real* concern, we may doubt. He abandoned an army in Egypt in 1798 without a twinge, and when

he lost half a million men in Russia three years after the events described in this poem, he sent a message back to Paris assuring his people that his own health was excellent, as though that were all that mattered.

12. Napoleon, by the way, was himself slightly wounded in this battle.

The victory at Ratisbon did not settle the campaign. Napoleon went on to take the Austrian capital of Vienna, but the Austrian Army could still fight. On May 21–22, 1809, just four weeks after the fall of Ratisbon, the Austrians actually *defeated* Napoleon (the first defeat he suffered in his years of fighting) and mortally wounded Lannes in the process. Napoleon recovered and inflicted a final defeat on the Austrians on July 5—but that was the last time he could dictate a victorious settlement over a foe.

The Star-Spangled Banner[1]

Francis Scott Key[2]

(1814)

O say, can you see, by the dawn's early light,
  What so proudly we hailed at the twilight's last gleaming?[3]
Whose broad stripes and bright stars,[4] through the perilous fight,
  O'er the ramparts[5] we watched, were so gallantly streaming!
And the rockets' red glare,[6] the bombs bursting in air,
Gave proof through the night that our flag was still there[7]:
  O say, does that star-spangled banner[8] yet wave
  O'er the land of the free and the home of the brave?

On the shore, dimly seen through the mists of the deep,
  Where the foe's haughty host in dread silence reposes,[9]
What is that which the breeze, o'er the towering steep,
  As it fitfully blows, now conceals, now discloses?
Now it catches the gleam of the morning's first beam,
In full glory reflected now shines on the stream:
  'Tis the star-spangled banner![10] O long may it wave
  O'er the land of the free and the home of the brave!

And where is the band who so vauntingly swore
  That the havoc of war and the battle's confusion
A home and a country should leave us no more?
  Their blood was washed out their foul footsteps' pollution.[11]
No refuge could save the hireling[12] and slave
From the terror of flight,[13] or the gloom of the grave:[14]
  And the star-spangled banner in triumph[15] doth wave
  O'er the land of the free and the home of the brave!

Oh! thus be it ever, when freemen shall stand
  Between their loved homes and the war's desolation![16]
Blest with victory and peace, may the heaven-rescued land
  Praise the Power that hath made and preserved us a nation.
Then conquer we must, for our cause it is just,[17]
And this be our motto: "In God is our trust."[18]
  And the star-spangled banner in triumph shall wave
  O'er the land of the free and the home of the brave![19]

---

1. During the Napoleonic Wars, Great Britain tried to strangle Napoleon by controlling the sea commerce of the world. In doing so, she ran into trouble with the young United States, which was the most important sea-going neutral at the time. Neither the United States nor Great Britain wanted war, but the logic of events seemed to be making it inevitable.

In 1812 the United States, driven to distraction by high-handed British action at sea, was ready to declare war. Great Britain therefore decided to take up a conciliatory attitude since Napoleon was about to invade Russia, and if Russia fell, Great Britain would be left without a land ally and might be forced to make peace.

Before news of Great Britain's concessions could reach the United States, however, war had been proclaimed and it was then too late to back out.

The United States was unprepared and her armies on land did poorly, though her naval vessels did unexpectedly well. And then Napoleon met with utter disaster in Russia in 1812 and again in

Germany in 1813. On April 1, 1814, he abdicated and was exiled to the Italian island of Elba.

Great Britain then prepared to send substantial expeditionary forces across the Atlantic. On August 9, 1814, one British force landed in Maryland. Under General Robert Ross, the British took the American capital of Washington against almost no resistance on August 24. They set fire to the Capitol and to the Executive Mansion, as well as to most of the other public buildings, which had been left vacant when President Madison and the rest of the government had fled precipitously into Virginia at the approach of the British.

The next day, the British forces boarded their ships once more and were taken up the Chesapeake to the more important target of Baltimore. There they disembarked on September 13, and at Godly Woods, five miles east of Baltimore, they met a contingent of Americans and were badly battered. General Ross was killed.

The British then decided to let the Navy bear the brunt of the fight, and on the night of September 13–14 Fort McHenry, the chief American stronghold in the area, was placed under bombardment. This poem deals with that bombardment, and when written, therefore, it was given the title of *The Defense of Fort McHenry*.

Fort McHenry, by the way, was named for James McHenry, an Irish-born American who served in the Continental Army during the American Revolution as a surgeon, and who, for a couple of years, was George Washington's private secretary.

He settled in Maryland after the war, served in the state legislature, represented the state at the Constitutional Convention, was one of the three signers from Maryland, and was Secretary of War under President John Adams. McHenry was sixty years old and still alive and in Baltimore at the time of the bombardment. He died in 1816.

2. Francis Scott Key was a lawyer, born in Frederick County, Maryland, on August 1, 1770. He eventually practiced his profession in the new city of Washington. Key had come to the British fleet on September 13, to attempt to secure the release of an aged physician, William Beanes, who had been taken prisoner in an earlier action. After he had come aboard ship, the bombardment of

Fort McHenry began and nothing could be done before morning. Key remained on board throughout the night watching the bombardment. He and his friend were released in the morning and Key scribbled the poem down while being taken ashore. That night in a Baltimore hotel, he put it into final form and it was published anonymously in the *Baltimore Patriot,* on September 20.

The meter of the poem was chosen by Key to match a popular drinking ballad, "The Anacreontic Song," which had been written by John Stafford Smith about 1779 for the Anacreontic Society, a London club much given to the pleasures of wine. The song was better known by its first four words, "To Anacreon in Heaven." (Anacreon was a Greek poet who lived in the sixth century B.C. and who was best known as a writer of odes praising wine and women.)

The combination of patriotic words and a popular tune made the poem popular at once, and although its range is uncomfortably wide, it has remained popular ever since. It is the only thing of importance that Key wrote, but it is enough!

3. The American flag was flying over Fort McHenry as night fell, but if the fort surrendered during the night, that flag would be lowered and once the surrender took place, Baltimore would certainly be occupied, with dread consequences for the American cause. Throughout the night, Key and Beanes kept wondering, in heartsick fashion, if the fort had withstood the bombardment, and if the flag would still be flying in the morning. As the first streaks of dawn lit the eastern sky, Beanes, relying on the better eyes of the younger man, kept asking, "Is the flag still there? Is the flag still there?"

4. The red and white stripes of the American flag, and the white stars on a blue background ("union") in the upper right, were so characteristic of the flag when it was first designed, so completely different from other flags, that it was sufficient identification merely to call it "the stars and stripes." That phrase may have first been used in print by an American businessman, Elkanah Watson, in 1782. The composer John Philip Sousa immortalized the phrase by composing "The Stars and Stripes Forever" in 1897—the most famous of his marches and certainly one of the most successful ever written.

Nevertheless, the flag for which Key and Beanes were watching was by no means the one we are accustomed to. When the flag was first designed there were thirteen stripes, seven red and six white, and thirteen white stars in the blue union. Both stars and stripes were intended to indicate the thirteen states that had joined to form the United States. Not much thought was given at the time to the possibility of new states entering the Union, but in 1791 Vermont was admitted as the fourteenth state, and in 1792 Kentucky became the fifteenth.

As of May 1, 1795, then, Congress decreed that the American flag was to consist of fifteen stripes (eight red and seven white) and fifteen stars. Still more states were formed, however. Tennessee entered in 1796, Ohio in 1803, and Louisiana in 1812, so that at the time of the bombardment of Fort McHenry, there were eighteen states in the Union. Nevertheless, there had been no change in the flag, since it was obvious that putting in too many stripes would just wash out the color of the flag to a pink, if seen from any distance.

Indiana entered the Union in 1816 as the nineteenth state and Mississippi in 1817 as the twentieth, and then Congress decided, in 1818, on a sensible compromise. Let the stars in the Union increase to represent the number of states, but let the stripes be fixed at thirteen. That rule has been followed ever since so that at this time of writing the American flag has fifty stars and thirteen stripes.

The flag that flew over Fort McHenry, however, was one that bore fifteen stars and fifteen stripes. It was the only official flag of the United States that ever had more than thirteen stripes.

5. "Ramparts" are the broad embankments that a fortification like Fort McHenry would use as a foundation. The flag was being watched as it was waving over the fort on top of those ramparts.

6. Rockets seem a surprisingly modern reference in a poem written in 1814, but it is not anachronistic. The Chinese, as long ago as the thirteenth century, invented and used small rockets for psychological warfare—to frighten the enemy. They used gunpowder for the purpose, and knowledge of this eventually reached Europe, perhaps as a result of the Mongol invasions of that century. Rockets remained in use in the Far East.

In 1801 a British artillery expert, William Congreve, learned about rockets in India, where they had been used against the British in the 1780s. He adopted the notion and devised a number of rocket varieties that could be used as artillery. The British Army adopted these, and some were used at the bombardment of Fort McHenry.

Rocket weapons faded out rapidly after that as improvements in orthodox artillery outstripped them and made them useless. It was not till World War II that rockets were restored to prominence in warfare. In their brief earlier incarnation, however, they had lasted long enough to be immortalized in this phrase.

7. By the intermittent flashes of light produced by the rockets and bombs, Key and his friend could catch glimpses of the flag still flying. But then, when the bombardment ceased, nothing could be seen. Had the bombardment ceased because the fort had surrendered or because the British had given up?

8. *The Defense of Fort McHenry* proved a pallid title for a rather florid poem, and before the year was out, the phrase "the star-spangled banner" substituted as the title—and a good thing, too.

9. The British forces were waiting, as Key was, for the outcome of the bombardment.

10. The flag was still visible in the morning, still flying over the fort. The British bombardment had failed. The use of the expression "In full glory" may have helped fix another nickname to the flag in years to come. Captain William Driver of Salem was given a large American flag for his ship in 1831. In hoisting it, he said, "I name thee Old Glory."

11. Key was being rather vaunting himself, here. The British suffered three hundred casualties to two hundred for the Americans at the small battle of Godly Woods, and that is scarcely enough to count as vengeance for the burning of Washington. However, there is an odd prescience here. The poem was written on September 14, 1814. Not quite four months later, on January 8, 1815, the battle of New Orleans was fought, with Andrew Jackson in command of the American forces. The treaty of peace had been signed at Ghent, Belgium, twelve days earlier, but news of that had not yet reached the fighting front.

The battle was an unmitigated disaster for the British. The British were sent charging against entrenched American sharpshooters, and they were wiped out. The British endured two thousand casualties to twenty-one for the Americans. Although the war had been a draw, and the treaty of peace had simply restored things as they were before the war had started, without settling any of the issues over which the two nations had fought, the Battle of New Orleans turned it into an effective American victory. British blood had indeed "washed out their foul footsteps' pollution," and in the more than a century and a half that has passed there has never been another battle between the two countries.

12. During the War of 1812, George III was still on the throne of Great Britain. He was quite mad and there reigned in his place his eldest son as "Prince Regent." He remained a symbol of what had taken place in the past, however.

During the Revolutionary War, George III had found both the war and himself quite unpopular at home, and he had difficulty recruiting soldiers. He searched for foreign mercenaries and found them chiefly in the two small German states of Hesse-Darmstadt. The rulers of these vest-pocket lands had absolute powers. Since they were in financial difficulties, they simply detailed thousands of their subjects for service with the British in return for generous payments which went, of course, to the rulers and not to the soldiers.

The American Revolutionaries made much of these "Hessians" since it was easier to rouse a people who had long considered themselves "Englishmen" to fight against Germans than to fight other Englishmen. It was also a good club with which to beat George III, who could be accused of having hired foreigners to kill his own subjects.

It remained a good propaganda point after the war, too, so that it seemed only natural to accuse the foe of being "hirelings," though mercenaries weren't used in the War of 1812.

13. Actually, the Americans fled more often than the British did in the course of this war, but Key was hoping for the best here, and in a way, he proved right.

The British fleet, having failed in the bombardment, decided to give up the campaign. Three days after the poem was written, the

British soldiers on the shore reboarded their ships, and the fleet left Baltimore. A month later the fleet left Chesapeake Bay altogether and made for the West Indies.

They hadn't actually fled, and what they did wasn't in terror, but they had *left* and that was what counted.

14. Another vaunting remark that somehow harks forward to the grisly battle of New Orleans.

15. The war ended in a draw, but that, too, was triumph. The United States was a small country and Great Britain was, at the moment, the strongest in the world. To fight Great Britain for two and a half years, and end by not losing an acre of land, was a kind of triumph for the United States.

16. Amen! Such victories do not always come, alas, and freemen have been destroyed by the overwhelming force of tyranny. Still, freemen win often enough to give a lift to the soul. Great Britain itself, a century and a quarter after the bombardment of Fort McHenry, withstood a far more dreadful bombardment by a far more fearful and ruthless enemy, over a far longer period of time— but *did* withstand it, with the help of the very power that they did not destroy in 1814.

17. This ties victory to the justice of the cause for which the war is fought. The United States has, thus far, suffered only one major defeat in its military history, and that was in the Vietnam War, which many Americans felt to be an unjust war on our part.

18. The motto is from a biblical quotation: "In God have I put my trust: I will not be afraid what man can do unto me" (Psalms 56:11). In time to come a version of this motto, perhaps partly influenced by this last stanza of *The Star-Spangled Banner,* became official. In 1864, in the course of the heart-breaking Civil War, during some parts of which there seemed little ground for faith, a bronze 2-cent piece was issued with the words "In God We Trust" upon it, on the direction of Salmon P. Chase, Secretary of the Treasury. It appeared on other coins, on and off, and in 1955, a law was passed making its use mandatory on all American coins.

19. Key died in Baltimore on January 11, 1843, and during the remainder of his lifetime saw the United States enjoying peace and a reasonable prosperity and continuing to display remarkable

growth. At his death, the star-spangled banner boasted twenty-six stars.

As for the poem itself, it remained unfailingly popular, became the national anthem by popular acclaim, even though the fact was not made official till 1931.

On First Looking
into Chapman's Homer[1]

JOHN KEATS[2]

(1816)

Much have I travelled in the realms of gold,
 And many goodly states and kingdoms seen;
 Round many western islands have I been
Which bards in fealty to Apollo hold.[3]
Oft of one wide expanse had I been told
 That deep-browed Homer ruled as his demesne[4]:
 Yet did I never breathe its pure serene
Till I heard Chapman[5] speak out loud and bold:
Then felt I like some watcher of the skies
 When a new planet swims into his ken[6];
Or like stout Cortez,[7] when with eagle eyes
 He stared at the Pacific[8]—and all his men
Looked at each other with a wild surmise—[9]
 Silent, upon a peak in Darien.[10]

---

1. Napoleon's stay on Elba was brief. Within the year he had es-
caped and was back in France, back at the head of the government,

and back at war. The new war lasted only three months, however. On June 8, 1815, Napoleon fought and lost his last battle at Waterloo in what is now Belgium, and the Napoleonic Wars were over.

Great Britain emerged from these wars, and from her lesser war with the United States, as the wealthiest power in the world and as absolute controller of the world's ocean. For a century, she maintained that status and added continually to the extent and power of her Empire.

This poem was published soon after Waterloo. It was a time when the poets were celebrating the Romantic Era and hymned the beauties of nature and of an idealized past. Above all, there was the magnetic pull of the culture of ancient Greece, as this poem evidences.

2. John Keats was born in London, England, on October 31, 1795. His mother, who died in 1810 of tuberculosis (which finally killed Keats, too), had encouraged him to read, and though he headed toward a medical career, poetry won him. This sonnet is the first important poem he wrote—in October 1816, just as he was turning twenty-one. Although it remains one of the most familiar and popular of his poems, it was met with silence when it appeared. Keats died in Rome on February 23, 1821, at the age of twenty-five with a poetic career of only five years, which, nevertheless, sufficed to make him immortal.

3. The Greek god Apollo was the god of light, of medicine, of prophecy, of youth, and so on. One of the most important of his attributes, and the one made use of here, is that of being the god of music, poetry, and the fine arts, generally, and as the personified means by which these were produced by human beings. Artists of various kinds worked, so it was thought, under a kind of possession by the inspiring god, and what they produced was the god's work rather than their own. The "enthusiasm" that inspires the creative artist is from Greek words meaning "god within."

In these first four lines of the poem, then, Keats represents poetry ("the realms of gold") in feudal terms. Apollo is the overlord and the various poets owe their products to him "in fealty," as barons owe their land in that fashion to the king. ("Fealty" is from the Latin word for "loyal" and represents the pledge of loyalty to the overlord taken by the underling.) The "western islands" that Keats has explored are, of course, the products of west-European literature.

4. The works of Homer represent the oldest surviving great works in the Western tradition (though parts of the Bible—not truly Western in the narrow sense—may be older). Homer is the poet (of uncertain place of birth, uncertain century, even uncertain existence) who produced two epics, *The Iliad,* which dealt with the siege of Troy by Greek troops and with events taking place during the last year of the siege, and *The Odyssey,* dealing with the prolonged and adventurous homecoming of Odysseus (Ulysses) one of the Greek heroes of the Trojan War. These two epics are the "wide expanse" and the "demesne" (domain) ruled by Homer.

5. George Chapman was the first to translate Homer's epics into English, and it is this translation that is "Chapman's Homer" referred to in the poem's title. The first portion of the translation was published in 1598, the last in 1616. Until then Englishmen interested in the Homeric tales had to go back to the original Greek, or else to rely on the medieval versions of the tale, as Chaucer and Shakespeare did in their stories of the love of Troilus and Cressida.

Chapman's Homer was by no means an exact translation. In fact, Chapman not only translated Homer into English, but into the Elizabethan idea of English poetry complete with rhymed fourteen-syllable verse and with added moral homilies. Perhaps, for that reason, it proved extremely popular, remaining so even after Alexander Pope, between 1713 and 1726, translated Homer into urbane heroic couplets in equally artificial manner. It wasn't till modern times that more or less literal translations appeared.

6. On March 13, 1781, thirty-four years before this poem was written, the German-British astronomer William Herschel, while meticulously surveying the heavens, spied an object that turned out to be a new planet—later named Uranus. It proved to be about twice as far from the Sun as the farthest till-then-known planet, Saturn, was.

So ingrained into human thinking had been the notion of the naked-eye planets as being all there was that it seemed a virtual intellectual earthquake to add a new, dim one to the list. It was the most famous astronomical discovery of its time and made Herschel, at a bound, the most famous astronomer the world had yet seen.

The feat had not yet lost its luster in Keats's time, especially since between 1801 and 1804 four additional planets (very small ones—now called asteroids) were discovered in the space between the orbits of Mars and Jupiter. The glamour of such discoveries was such that it was a natural metaphor for Keats to use.

7. This may well be the most remarked-on mistake in great poetry. Hernando Cortez was a Spanish soldier-explorer who, in 1519, defeated the Aztec rulers of Mexico, and annexed that land to the Spanish crown. It was three centuries before Mexico was to regain its independence, and by that time there was a strong Spanish strain among its inhabitants.

Cortez had, however, nothing to do with the event described immediately afterward in the poem.

8. When Columbus, in 1492, first discovered what came to be called the New World, he thought it to be the eastern coast of Asia and maintained that belief to the day of his death. The first person to maintain something else—that the lands reached by Columbus were *not* parts of Asia but were newly found continents, separated from Asia by a second ocean at least as large as the Atlantic—was the Italian navigator Americus Vespucius in 1502. It was for this reason that the new continents were justly named for him rather than for Columbus.

To talk of a second ocean was one thing, to prove its existence was another. In 1513 the governor of what we now call Panama was Vasco Nuñe de Balboa. Exploring southward from its settled northern coast, he came upon what seemed to be a vast body of water, which he called the South Sea and which he suspected might be the second ocean. It was in 1519 that the Portuguese navigator, Ferdinand Magellan (in Spanish employ) first sailed across the South Sea and proved it to be an ocean larger than the Atlantic. Because he entered it in calm weather, after a very stormy trip through what is now called the Strait of Magellan, he named it the Pacific Ocean.

It was Balboa, then, and not Cortez who "stared at the Pacific."

9. The surmise was, of course, that they had located the much-speculated-upon second ocean.

10. The first European settlement in the isthmus that connects North and South America was one founded by the Spaniards in 1510 on the Atlantic shore of what is now Colombia. It was named Santa Maria de la Antigue del Darien and is invariably referred to as Darien. It didn't last long, and in 1519 Panama City was founded 270 kilometers (170 miles) to the west, on the Pacific shore of the isthmus. Panama City became the most important city of the region, something it has remained to this day, while Darien died.

Darien lived long enough to give its name to the "Isthmus of Darien," which, however, eventually became the "Isthmus of Panama," occupied by the nation of Panama. The southernmost part of the Caribbean Sea, occupying an inlet at the boundary of Panama and Colombia, is called the "Gulf of Darien" to this day.

At any rate, the isthmus was still the Isthmus of Darien in 1513 when Balboa reached the South Sea, so he and his men did stand, presumably speechless with astonishment, upon a peak in Darien. Keats wasn't wrong there.

A Visit from St. Nicholas [1]

CLEMENT CLARKE MOORE [2]

(1822)

'Twas the night before Christmas, when all through the house
Not a creature was stirring, not even a mouse;
The stockings were hung by the chimney with care,
In hopes that St. Nicholas[3] soon would be there;
The children were nestled all snug in their beds,
While visions of sugar-plums[4] danced in their heads;
And mamma in her 'kerchief, and I in my cap,[5]
Had just settled our brains for a long winter's nap,
When out on the lawn there arose such a clatter,
I sprang from the bed to see what was the matter.
Away to the window I flew like a flash,
Tore open the shutters and threw up the sash.
The moon on the breast of the new-fallen snow
Gave the lustre of mid-day to objects below,
When, what to my wondering eyes should appear,
But a miniature sleigh, and eight tiny reindeer,[6]
With a little old driver, so lively and quick,
I knew in a moment it must be St. Nick.
More rapid than eagles his coursers they came,

And he whistled, and shouted, and called them by name;
"Now, *Dasher!* now, *Dancer!* now, *Prancer* and *Vixen!*
On, *Comet!* on *Cupid!* on, *Donder* and *Blitzen!*[7]
To the top of the porch! to the top of the wall!
Now dash away! dash away! dash away all!"
As dry leaves that before the wild hurricane fly,
When they meet with an obstacle, mount to the sky,
So up to the house-top the coursers they flew,
With the sleigh full of toys, and St. Nicholas too.
And then in a twinkling, I heard on the roof
The prancing and pawing of each little hoof.
As I drew in my head, and was turning around,
Down the chimney St. Nicholas came with a bound.
He was dressed all in fur, from his head to his foot,
And his clothes were all tarnished with ashes and soot;
A bundle of toys he had flung on his back,
And he looked like a peddler just opening his pack.
His eyes—how they twinkled! his dimples how merry!
His cheeks were like roses, his nose like a cherry!
His droll little mouth was drawn up like a bow,
And the beard of his chin was as white as the snow;
The stump of a pipe he held tight in his teeth,
And the smoke it encircled his head like a wreath;
He had a broad face and a little round belly,
That shook, when he laughed, like a bowlful of jelly.
He was chubby and plump, a right jolly old elf,[8]
And I laughed when I saw him, in spite of myself;
A wink of his eye and a twist of his head,
Soon gave me to know I had nothing to dread;
He spoke not a word, but went straight to his work,
And filled all the stockings; then turned with a jerk,
And laying his finger aside of his nose,
And giving a nod, up the chimney he rose;
He sprang to his sleigh, to his team gave a whistle,

And away they all flew like the down of a thistle.
But I heard him exclaim, ere he drove out of sight,
"Happy Christmas to all, and to all a good night."[9]

---

1. The United States entered a generation-long period of peace after the War of 1812. In 1820 the first national row over slavery arose in Congress over the admission of Missouri, but the matter was settled with the "Missouri Compromise" to general American relief. Between 1817 and 1825 James Monroe was in the White House (so-called after it had been painted white to hide the scorching produced when the British had taken Washington in 1814) as the fifth President, and it was the "Era of Good Feeling" when partisan politics seemed at a low ebb. It seems appropriate that it was at this time that the most popular and influential non-religious Christmas poem ever written came to be.

The poem was written in 1822, supposedly just before Christmas, for the children of the poet. Apparently, it was not intended for publication, but a copy was made by a house guest and eventually it reached the press. It was published for the first time in the *Troy Sentinel* on December 23, 1823.

2. Clement Clarke Moore was born in New York City on July 15, 1779. He was the son of an Episcopalian bishop who also served as President of Columbia University. Moore was himself a Hebrew scholar, and served eminently in the field of ancient literature. His real claim to fame, however, is his casual construction of *A Visit from St. Nicholas*.

3. St. Nicholas, according to tradition, was Bishop Nicholas of Myra (a city on what is now the south Turkish coast) in the fourth century A.D. There is no firm knowledge of anything concerning his life, no contemporary references or any accounts in sober histories. There are only late legendary accounts of good deeds and miracles, some of which involve his rescue of children from tragedy, or his kind donation of money to those in need. Consequently, he became associated with gifts, especially to children.

He was popular enough in legend to be accepted as the patron saint of Russia. Two tsars bore his name, and it was Nicholas II who was overthrown by the Russian Revolution and then executed by the Revolutionaries. There were also popes bearing the name, and it is a fairly common given name in Great Britain and the United States. In origin, the name is Greek, by the way, from words meaning "victorious army."

The nature of the Christmas celebration is, in part, an outgrowth of the Roman Saturnalia which celebrated the Winter Solstice with a season of joy, feasting, and gift-giving. Since the Christians could not wipe out so happy a holiday, they adopted it and set the birth of Jesus at the solstice season even though there is absolutely no biblical justification for this. As Saint Nicholas was associated with gift-giving, he eventually became associated with the gift-giving aspect of Santurnalia/Christmas, all the more so since his feast day came on December 6, when the approaching Christmas season was in all minds.

The association on Saint Nicholas with Christmas gift-giving was strengthened in Germany at the time of the Protestant Reformation since the St. Nicholas aspect was one way of getting away from the complex religious ritual associated with Catholicism.

The habit spread to the Netherlands, and the Dutch settlers of New Amsterdam brought the association to the New World, using their own name for Saint Nicholas, which was "Sinter Claas" (*Claas* being their diminutive for "Nicolaas"). The Dutch legends persisted even after the English took over and converted New Amsterdam to New York in 1664. The Dutch name of the saint became Santa Claus (and who can now imagine, without tracing the legend, that Santa Claus is the patron saint of Russia).

4. A "sugar-plum" is what we would today call "a piece of candy." It was a sweet concoction in the shape of a ball. Originally, Christmas gifts were small things, such as extra dessert treats or simple toys that could be made to fit into a child's stocking. Under the stress of advertising, the ante has been raised steadily, till it has become doubtful if American department stores could exist without the artificially intensified tradition of Christmas expenditure.

5. In the days before central heating, keeping warm on a winter night was a problem. This was a special concern because, in the absence of knowledge of the cause of disease, night air was considered

dangerous. Hence, it was customary to cover the head with kerchiefs or caps. (A "kerchief" is from the French *couvrechef* meaning "to cover the head.")

6. Perhaps because Christmas is in the winter season and is associated with snow in the Protestant lands of northern Europe in which the modern legend of Santa Claus took shape, the legend arose that Santa Claus dwelt at the North Pole. The existence of the North Pole was known since ancient times, but at the time the Santa Claus legend arose nothing was known about the nature of its surroundings. It would seem from the steadily increasing cold and ice as one approached the polar regions that the North Pole must be bleak indeed, but there were many who held that beyond the snow and ice there was open sea and a pleasant environment.

Nevertheless, it was the polar cold that influenced the legend, and Santa Claus travels as one would expect an inhabitant of the polar regions to travel—by sleigh. That the sleigh is drawn by reindeer is not at all surprising. At the time the Santa Claus legend was taking over its modern form in Germany, the best-known people of the polar regions were the Lapps in northern Scandinavia. They had learned to make use of the reindeer (or caribou), using it for meat, milk, and even as a draft animal. Why shouldn't Santa Claus travel Lapp-fashion?

In this introduction of a reindeer-drawn sleigh and in other respects, the poem proved to be the most important Christmas event in modern history since, in the United States at least, it fixed the image and function of Santa Claus indelibly to this day. And, we must remember, Santa Claus and all he stands for in the way of institutionalized greed means far more to children and to American business than the more formal religious connotations of Christmas.

Notice that the poem speaks of "a miniature sleigh" and "tiny reindeer." The description is of a magic phenomenon, not a realistic one. The necessity of presenting Santa Clauses in department stores in the shape of full-grown men has weakened this aspect of the legend.

7. These names have become traditional for Santa's reindeer. One hangover from the Germanic past is "Donder and Blitzen," which means "thunder and lightning." All the names are suggestive

of liveliness and speed (even Cupid is a winged god) except for Vixen, which is the word for a female fox, or, by extension, that for a shrewish female human being. It seems the one inappropriate name, but Moore needed a rhyme or near-rhyme for Blitzen, we might suppose.

8. An elf, in legend, is usually viewed as a diminutive creature, which matches the poem's picture of Santa, his sleigh, and his reindeer, as all being in miniature. The description of Santa given here has become fixed in legend, too. The white hair and beard, the fur on his costume, the obesity, and, most of all, the rather wearisome continual ho-ho-ho.

9. The cliche is, of course, "*Merry* Christmas." So firm is the combination of syllables that goes "Merry Christmas and a Happy New Year" that to say the reverse, "Happy Christmas and a Merry New Year" would be laughed at as the mistake of a foreigner who didn't know English well, even though the meaning is essentially unchanged.

"Merry" is virtually archaic in present-day English and is not used except in this phrase and in other stock phrases dating back to an earlier time, as in "God rest you merry, gentlemen" and "Robin Hood and his merry men." Most children, in learning to parrot "Merry Christmas" probably don't know what "merry" means, and it is interesting that in this most famous of all non-religious Christmas poems, the phrase is "Happy Christmas" after all.

Old Ironsides[1]

OLIVER WENDELL HOLMES[2]

(1830)

Ay, tear her tattered ensign down![3]
    Long has it waved on high,
And many an eye has danced to see
    That banner in the sky[4];
Beneath it rung the battle shout,
    And burst the cannon's roar;—
The meteor of the ocean air
    Shall sweep the clouds no more.

Her deck, once red with heroes' blood,
    Where knelt the vanquished foe,[5]
When winds were hurrying o'er the flood,
    And waves were white below,
No more shall feel the victor's tread,
    Or know the conquered knee;—
The harpies of the shore shall pluck
    The eagle of the sea![6]

Oh, better that her shattered hulk
    Should sink beneath the wave;

Her thunders shook the mighty deep,
  And there should be her grave;
Nail to the mast her holy flag,
  Set every threadbare sail,
And give her to the god of storms,
  The lightning and the gale![7]

---

1. In peace there was long a tendency on the part of the American people to dismantle, in unsentimental fashion, the war machines it had used in strife. In 1832, for instance, the Navy was callously ready to do away with the most famous of all American warships. The ship was *Old Ironsides*.

That was the nickname of the American warship whose official name was *Constitution*. It was launched in Boston in 1797 at a time when a naval war with France threatened, but it saw its chief action in the War of 1812 against Great Britain.

In exactly which battle it obtained its nickname is disputed. One story is that during a fight against the British warship *Java*, off the coast of Brazil, on December 29, 1812, the American sailors, seeing the British cannon balls bouncing off the seasoned timbers of its hull, while their own shots were wreaking havoc with the foe, jubilantly termed their ship *Old Ironsides*. The nickname has stuck to the ship so tightly that the real name is little-known.

2. See page 130.

3. In 1830, the *Constitution* was thirty-three years old, which is aged for a warship, and it had grown obsolete. Her ensign, or flag, might be viewed as "tattered" from old age and hard service.

4. The *Constitution* had brought good news to the United States at a time when the national morale was low indeed, so that the mere sight of it brought a lift to the spirit ever afterward. In consequence, when the Navy decided, in 1830, that *Old Ironsides* was no longer seaworthy and should be broken up, the news shocked many, especially in the Boston area where it had been built and launched. Holmes therefore sat down to write his requiem.

5. As soon as the War of 1812 broke out, the *Constitution*, under

its commander, Isaac Hull, left Chesapeake Bay, where it was stationed, in order to join a naval squadron off New York. Four British ships, including the *Guerrière* ("Warrior") were waiting for it. The *Constitution,* designed to carry forty-four guns but carrying fifty-four, could outshoot any warship its size in the world, but it couldn't outshoot four. It had to be evasive, therefore, and it could outrun anything it couldn't outshoot. For three days and two nights it was pursued, but it got away.

Then on August 19, 1812, the *Constitution* encountered the Guerrière alone. At that time the United States was in deep distress. Three days before, the American Army stationed in Detroit had surrendered without a fight, and the news, when it came, was a shocking blow. The American general who had surrendered (and who was later court-martialed, convicted, and condemned to death —but reprieved) was William Hull, the brother of the captain of the *Constitution.*

Now the *Constitution* unlimbered its guns and, in the space of half an hour, shot the *Guerrière* into Swiss cheese that had to be sunk, inflicting seventy-nine casualties against fourteen of its own.

The news of this victory at sea against one of the ships of the proud British Navy sent a nation, starving for good news, hysterical with joy. When the *Constitution* got back to Boston, it received an unprecedented ovation, for it seemed to Americans that in half an hour they had wrested control of the seas from the British.

They almost had, for in a series of duels, American ships won victory after victory. A number of those victories were marked up to the score of the *Constitution,* which was never defeated.

Still, the weight of superior numbers of ships finally told, and one by one of the American ports were blockaded and the ships within it immobilized. The psychological effect remained, however. The United States did not do well on land against the British, but the American Navy, and the *Constitution,* in particular, made up for it all. The sea victories and the Battle of New Orleans (fought after the peace had been signed) converted the War of 1812 into a victory in American minds.

6. Harpies were mythical creatures in Greek legend, that were originally wind spirits, but eventually came to be viewed as beings

with heads of women and bodies of birds of prey. They were described as foul and stinking, snatching at food, and spoiling with their touch and excrement whatever they could not grab. They were the epitome of everything that was vile about a bird of prey, as the eagle invariably symbolizes all that is noble about one.

7. Who says nothing can be accomplished by a poem? *Old Ironsides* was published in the Boston *Advertiser* on September 14, 1830, and was quickly and widely reprinted. It promptly stirred up such a clamor among the American public that the Navy found it could not scrap the *Constitution* after all. The ship was repaired, refurbished, and put into action again. In 1855 she was converted into use as a training ship. In 1877 she was again repaired and in 1878 made her last trip across the Atlantic. But now, of course, it was the age of steam and of iron-hulled ships (the real "ironsides") and the *Constitution* was only nostalgia. She was restored again in 1931, and still exists in Boston harbor, the oldest commissioned ship in the United States Navy.

To Helen[1]

EDGAR ALLAN POE[2]

(1831)

Helen,[3] thy beauty is to me
    Like those Nicaean barks of yore,[4]
That gently, o'er a perfumed sea,
    The weary, wayworn wanderer bore
    To his own native shore.[5]

On desperate seas long wont to roam,[6]
    Thy hyacinth hair, thy classic face,
Thy Naiad airs,[7] have brought me home
    To the glory that was Greece
    And the grandeur that was Rome.[8]

Lo! in yon brilliant window-niche
    How statue-like I see thee stand,[9]
The agate lamp within thy hand![10]
    Ah, Psyche, from the regions which
    Are Holy Land![11]

1. The interest in ancient times was part of the Romantic Era in the United States as well as in Great Britain in the years after the Napoleonic Wars. This poem is an indication of this.

2. Edgar Allan Poe was born in Boston, Massachusetts, on January 19, 1809. He received his early education in Europe, went to the University of Virginia, and even got an appointment to the U. S. Military Academy at West Point (though he managed to get himself ejected from that establishment).

He was publishing poetry by the time he was eighteen, and though he did not really achieve nationwide fame till the 1840s, when he published many of his tales of Gothic horror, as well as his most famous single poem, *The Raven,* the poem *To Helen,* which some like best of all, appeared in 1831, when Poe was only twenty-two.

He died in Baltimore, Maryland, on October 7, 1849.

3. The poem might be referring to some actual woman, but, as a matter of fact, Helen happens to be a name that can be used to represent the ideal of beauty.

It was Helen who was queen of Sparta, and whom Paris carried off to Troy. It was she, commonly called "Helen of Troy," who was the occasion of the ten years war, parts of which were described in Homer's *Iliad.* She was, therefore, the center and cause, so to speak, of the greatest work of literature of the ancient world.

Helen might therefore represent a real woman, ideal beauty, the ancient world, or all three.

4. "Nicaean barks of yore" would be ships of ancient Nicaea. Nicaea (from a Greek word for "victory") was the name of several cities of the ancient Greek world. Of the two most important cities by that name, one was located in northwestern Asia Minor, and in the days of the Byzantine Empire was second only to Constantinople in importance. The other was on the Mediterranean coast near the boundary of what are now France and Italy. It is part of France now, and its present name is Nice.

Neither of these cities, nor any other Nicaea, was known in ancient times for its shipping or for any incident that bears any resemblance to the lines that immediately follow. One might conclude that Poe chose the adjective for its sound rather than its sense.

5. Here it is impossible not to think of Odysseus (Ulysses). For

ten years he wandered over the Mediterranean in his attempt to return from Troy to his home on the island of Ithaca off the western shores of Greece. (The tale is told in Homer's *Odyssey* so that both it and its companion piece, the *Iliad*, are evoked in the first stanza.

Finally, Odysseus landed on the island of Phaeacia, the only survivor of his original party. The raft he had used in the final stage of his journey was shattered, his clothes, even, were gone. He was cast ashore naked, alone, and worn out.

He was taken in by the kindly Phaeacians who clothed and fed him, listened to his sad tale, and then undertook to return him to his home. They put him on board one of their ships, where he fell asleep. While he slept, the ship completed the journey to Ithaca in a single night. The men of the ship then placed him, still sleeping, on his native shore.

Had the second line read, "Like that Phaeacian bark of yore" there would be no question about the first verse. Even so, it is perhaps clear enough that the beauty of Helen represents the means by which peace and security are finally to be achieved by the writer.

6. If Poe is speaking of himself, the line is clearly metaphor. He had crossed the sea to go to Europe in 1815, when he was six years old, and again when he returned to the United States in 1820 at the age of eleven, but he was no sea roamer.

7. None of these adjectives can be taken literally, anymore than "Nicaean" can. Each, however, gives an image of the ancient Graeco-Roman civilization. "Classic," meaning "of the first class" is commonly used to refer to the great achievements of the ancient world in art and literature.

"Hyacinth," which is a purplish color not generally found in women's hair (and not admired if artificially placed there), refers to the Greek myth of Hyacinthus, a Spartan prince with whom Apollo fell in love. Once, when they were competing amicably in the game of discus throwing, the West Wind, also in love with Hyacinthus and madly jealous, caught Apollo's discus in mid-air and sent it swerving into Hyacinthus's head, killing him. From the blood of Hyacinthus, there sprang up the purplish flower still called "hyacinth." Hyacinth was an ideal of manly beauty to the Greeks, corresponding to Helen as an ideal of womanly beauty.

A "naiad" (from a Greek word meaning "to flow") was the

name given by the Greeks to the nymphs, or nature goddesses, thought to inhabit springs, streams, rivers, and lakes. Like all nymphs they were pictured as beautiful and graceful.

All three adjectives then, regardless of their literal meaning, imply excellence—and an excellence associated with ancient learning and civilization.

8. If in the first stanza, it is possible to view Helen as an ordinary woman; in the second stanza, it is not. The impression one gets is that Helen represents the attraction of classical literature. Poe depicts himself as having drifted away into other pursuits ("desperate seas") and as having been brought back to what he truly valued ("home") by that attraction, very much as the "wayworn wanderer" of the first stanza had been.

9. Some of the most visible remnants of the ancient civilization Poe so admired (the "glory that was Greece/And the grandeur that was Rome"—perhaps the most quoted single lines that Poe wrote) are the statues that yet survive; particularly the serene faces and graceful proportions of the statuary of Greece's golden age. The word "statue-like" therefore fixes once again the view of Helen as the classical literature of the ancients.

10. An agate is a variegated stone, with different colors in stripes or bands or irregularly mixed. It was also considered, in ancient superstition, as bringing luck and warding off evil.

The general impression of the line would then be of classical literature spreading its beams outward, lamplike, in immensely variegated fashion. The good-luck charm of the agate might also reflect itself in the feeling that in the study of the ancient books, one could find happiness and protection from the vicissitudes of the modern world.

11. "Psyche" is the Greek word for soul, and Poe would seem to be apostrophizing his soul as it receives the radiation from the agate lamp, a radiation coming from the ancient civilizations that, to the mind, seem so wonderful as to be holy.

Anne Rutledge[1]

EDGAR LEE MASTERS[2]

(1835)

Out of me unworthy and unknown[3]
The vibrations of deathless music;
"With malice toward none, with charity for all."[4]
Out of me the forgiveness of millions toward millions,
And the beneficent face of a nation
Shining with justice and truth.[5]
I am Anne Rutledge who sleep beneath these weeds,
Beloved in life of Abraham Lincoln,[6]
Wedded to him, not through union,
But through separation.[7]
Bloom forever, O Republic,
From the dust of my bosom![8]

---

1. The quarrel over slavery in Missouri in 1820, though it seemed settled, broke forth again and again, as the issue of human slavery in "the land of the free" polarized the entire nation and finally brought on a massive Civil War that came within a hair of destroying the United States.

Everything about that war and, particularly, about its hero, President Abraham Lincoln, seemed larger than life in later years. Minor incidents in Lincoln's early life seemed fraught with a significance that cast their shadow before, as in the case of Anne Rutledge, who was born about 1816 in Illinois. She died, quite suddenly, in Sand Ridge, Illinois, on August 25, 1835.

2. Edgar Lee Masters was born in Garnett, Kansas, on August 23, 1869. A lawyer by profession, he published forgettable poetry until, in 1915, he produced his one masterpiece, *The Spoon River Anthology*. This consists of bitterly ironic epitaphs of the dead of the small town of Spoon River, supposedly delivered by each of them from the grave, and revealing the deficiencies of small-town life. The town in question seems to have been modeled on Lewistown, Illinois, which is near the Spoon River. *Anne Rutledge,* dealing with a historic person, is void of irony. Masters died in Philadelphia, Pennsylvania, on March 5, 1950.

3. Unknown, certainly. Anne Rutledge's nineteen years of life would never have remained in the nation's memory but for a tale told thirty years after her death—and an uncertain tale at that.

4. The reference is to the close of the inaugural address delivered by Abraham Lincoln on the occasion of his second inauguration on March 4, 1864. He said, "With malice toward none, with charity for all, with firmness in the right as God gives us to see the right, let us strive on to finish the work we are in—"

The Confederacy was, at the time, clearly *in extremis.* Lee's gaunt and famished army, pinned down by Grant's superior numbers, was no longer capable of striking. Sherman, having taken Georgia, was sweeping through the Carolinas, and Lincoln felt the work of winning the war and re-establishing the broken Union must now be completed in charity for the defeated and without the kind of malice that would burn into them generations-long hatred.

5. Lincoln's inaugural address finished with, "—to bind up the nation's wounds, to care for him who shall have borne the battle and for his widow and his orphan, to do all which may achieve and cherish a just and lasting peace among ourselves and with all nations."

There was no breath of anger or of revenge, but rather of healing and recovery. There is no question but that it was Lincoln's aim to forgive, to consider that at the moment peace came, the surrendered Confederates would cease being enemies and start being Americans again, and that only so could the nation's wounds be healed.

Lincoln was not able to oversee the carrying out of his aims for he was assassinated six weeks after the inaugural address (see pages 226–27) and, under a successor of far lesser stature, the forces of revenge and animosity gained far more ground than they would have (perhaps) if Lincoln had lived.

Even so, Lincoln set a tone that was not entirely forgotten, and the Union was not only victorious—but healed itself to a far greater extent than one might have supposed possible after so long, so bloody, and so desperate a civil war.

6. Actually, there is no real evidence of that. After Anne's death, Lincoln was engaged to Mary Todd, but was apparently reluctant to marry her and, in a fit of depression, broke the engagement—then reconsidered and on November 4, 1842, married her.

It can be supposed, romantically, that Lincoln did not want to marry Mary Todd because he was still haunted by his love for Anne Rutledge, who had died seven years before. But is that true? Lincoln did not need the memory of Anne Rutledge to send him into a depression; he was subject to depressions all his life. Nor was a possible lost love the only reason for Lincoln to dread marrying Mary Todd. Mary was of an aristocratic family with whom homespun Lincoln felt ill at ease. Mary had towering ambitions for her husband (any husband), and Lincoln's desires were far more limited in scope. Lincoln's practical sense might have told him it would be an unhappy marriage—and so, in fact, it was.

Lincoln was living in New Salem at the time of Anne Rutledge's death, and there is evidence that he was affected by her death, but so was just about everyone in the town, for Anne was a pretty and popular girl and her death was unexpected. She was engaged to a storekeeper who was, at the time, on a long trip to the East. There was no indication that she didn't entirely intend to marry him when he returned, nor any real reason to suppose that Lincoln was trying to make time with her in her fiancé's absence.

It was only in 1866, after Lincoln's death, that William Henry

Herndon, who had once been Lincoln's law partner, told the romantic story of the ill-fated love of Lincoln for Anne, and of its sudden blighting. The tale was accepted by the American public apparently because it was so touching that they felt it ought to be true, whether it was or not.

7. That was the essence of the romance of the story—that Lincoln always carried with him the shining vision of his lost love.

8. One can thread the romance further. The shining vision Lincoln was supposed never to have lost, deepened and strengthened him, giving him superhuman patience and tolerance, making it possible for him to endure the horror of the Civil War and his responsibility for seeing it through the dark days. Perhaps no one else might have had the firmness to persevere and see it through despite everything and, in the end, to be calm and tolerant and patient, and to direct the Union into the paths of forgiveness from which it did not entirely stray.

In that sense, one draws the connection between the dust of Anne Rutledge's body and the survival of the Union.

The Charge of the Light Brigade[1]

ALFRED TENNYSON[2]

(1854)

Half a league, half a league,
  Half a league onward,[3]
All in the valley of Death
  Rode the six hundred.[4]
"Forward, the Light Brigade!
  Charge for the guns!" he said[5]:
Into the valley of Death
  Rode the six hundred.

"Forward, the Light Brigade!"
Was there a man dismayed?[6]
Not though the soldier knew
  Some one had blundered[7]:
Theirs not to make reply,
Theirs not to reason why,
Theirs but to do and die[8]:
Into the valley of Death
  Rode the six hundred.

Cannon to right of them,
Cannon to left of them,
Cannon in front of them
   Volleyed and thundered[9];
Stormed at with shot and shell,
Boldly they rode and well,
Into the jaws of Death,
Into the mouth of Hell
   Rode the six hundred.

Flashed all their sabres bare,
Flashed as they turned in air
Sabring the gunners there,
Charging an army, while
   All the world wondered:
Plunged in the battery-smoke
Right through the line they broke;
Cossack and Russian
Reeled from the sabre-stroke,
   Shattered and sundered.[10]
Then they rode back, but not,
   Not the six hundred.

Cannon to right of them,
Cannon to left of them,
Cannon behind them
   Volleyed and thundered[11];
Stormed at with shot and shell,
While horse and hero fell,[12]
They that had fought so well
Came through the jaws of Death,
Back from the mouth of Hell,
All that was left of them,
   Left of six hundred.[13]

> When can their glory fade?
> O the wild charge they made!
> All the world wondered.
> Honor the charge they made!
> Honor the Light Brigade,
> Noble six hundred![14]

---

1. Although the end of the Napoleonic Wars saw Europe enter a century-long period of peace, there were occasional minor wars based on competing ambitions. Russia, for instance, had been expanding southward and eastward for three centuries, and Great Britain feared for the safety of her Indian dominions, the pride of her Empire.

In the 1850s Russia was concentrating on the Turkish lands, the Ottoman Empire. Since the days when the Turks had finally beaten Venice (see page 156), they had been declining steadily, and now it seemed as though their land might fall to Russia. Great Britain was determined to prevent that and joining her was France, now under Napoleon III, nephew of the great Napoleon.

In September 1854 British, French, and Turkish troops landed in the Crimea, a Russian peninsula jutting southward into the Black Sea, with Turkey on the opposite shore. The Crimean War had begun.

A month later, there came the incident involving the light brigade, with which this poem deals. A brigade is a fairly large body of troops, consisting of two regiments, generally, and under the command of a brigadier-general. In the nineteenth century, the cavalry brigades were divided into light, medium, and heavy, depending on the quantity of armaments carried by each horseman.

The light brigades, though carrying less weight and equipment, were for that very reason faster and more maneuverable and could be used for scouting. They were modeled on the Hungarian cavalry of the 1400s, and the Hungarian name, hussar, was used for them. The light cavalrymen were, by another tradition, colorfully uniformed, with a busby, or high cylindrical cloth cap, and with various sorts of gold braid.

2. See page 108.

3. The poem begins with the rhythmic imitation of horses galloping so the light brigade is already charging. (Half a league, by the way, is 2.4 kilometers or 1.5 miles.) What happened was this—

The British and their allies were hoping to take Sevastopol, the chief Russian port in the Crimea. In order to build the necessary offensive strength, their forces were being landed and supplied through the smaller port of Balaklava, about 12 kilometers (7 miles) south of Sevastopol. The Russians opened a drive intended to outflank the British forces probing toward Sevastopol and to strike at Balaklava. If the Russians could capture the port and destroy the shipping in the harbor, the British forces in the Crimea would be isolated and might then face the choice of surrender or destruction.

The Russians had initial successes, driving Turkish forces from two parallel ridges on either side of a valley near Balaklava and taking the guns on those ridges. The Russians could not, however, break through the wall of heavy cavalry at the British end of the valley, so that the main Russian forces fell back toward their own end.

Both sides now prepared for the next phase of the battle. The Russians might have regrouped and attacked once more, using, this time, the guns they had captured on both heights in addition to their own. The British might have planned a counterattack to retake the heights and then attempt to strike a presumably demoralized enemy and accelerate their retreat.

It was the British who struck first, but not in any rational way. The light brigade was ordered to charge on a totally useless and suicidal mission.

4. The charge was not aimed, in rational manner, at the relatively minor Russian forces on either (or both) of the two parallel ridges, where the sudden onslaught of 607 armed horsemen might have sent the Russians flying, without significant loss to the brigade. Instead, in complete madness, it went right down the valley between the heights, straight at the main Russian forces at the other end—an army that outnumbered the light brigade nearly twenty to one. That had to be a "valley of Death" for the charging horsemen.

5. The "he" who called the charge was Major-General James

Thomas Brudenell, 7th Earl of Cardigan. He was in that position not for any martial merit displayed on the battlefield. In those days, officers bought their commissions, and Lord Cardigan was rich— rich enough to buy promotion now and then and rich enough to equip his cavalrymen out of his own pocket till they gleamed by comparison even with other brigades. (The cardigan jacket is named for him, by the way.)

He was a quarrelsome and, indeed, half-mad individual protected from the consequences of his psychotic behavior by his social rank. He fought duels, and his generally vicious ways drove those subordinate to him mad with frustration. It was he, on October 25, 1854, just nine days after his fifty-seventh birthday, who lifted his sword, pointed at the Russian army and led the charge.

6. Was there a man dismayed? Why shouldn't every one of them be dismayed? Anyone could see the charge was a ridiculous mistake and would merely kill men to no purpose. But would dismay keep them from charging when refusal would mean court-martial and disgrace? Social pressure could overcome anything, even fear of death, and the men charged.

7. The fault lay initially with Fitzroy James Henry Somerset, 1st Baron Raglan. He was Commander-in-Chief of the British forces and was underequipped for the job. Distressingly indecisive, he made it possible for the Russians to fortify Sevastopol and set up a strong defense, when a quicker advance after landing in the Crimea might have taken the town.

Now, after having beaten off the Russian attack, he noticed that the Russians on one of the heights they had taken from the Turks were dragging away some of the guns they had captured. Raglan quickly ordered that the light brigade make an effort to prevent that and to retake those guns. Lord Raglan did not make it quite clear which guns he meant, and if he waved his hand in some direction, it was a characteristically indecisive wave that could have meant anything.

The aide who took the order somehow got the notion that the guns referred to by Lord Raglan were the guns of the main Russian forces, and by the time he brought the information to Lord Cardigan, he had made it a definite command to charge right at the main forces. Cardigan, dimly aware that this amounted to a sentence of death for his brigade, protested, but the aide repeated the order. Lord Raglan had spoken!

By the rules of command, Cardigan had no choice. Neither had the soldiers. Cardigan ordered the charge, and they charged.

8. These are the most famous lines of the poem, but when applied to anyone other than the light brigade of the poem, they are almost invariably used satirically or contemptuously. It is very difficult to decide whether people who don't make reply and don't reason why but just do and die are incredibly brave or incredibly stupid. Often the decision is based on whether the people involved are on your side or on your enemy's side.

Consider how dangerous it is to admire such unthinking "loyalty." Anyone convicted of war crimes insists he was merely following orders and that his was not to make reply and his was not to reason why. It is the Eichmann excuse. The Watergate crimes were committed by those who were just following orders. The real hero is the one who does *not* follow a stupid or a vicious order—but that way lies disgrace, ignominy, or worse, and the supply of heroes is always short.

9. There were the Russian cannon (recently captured) on the heights to the right and left of the valley and, of course, the Russian cannon of the main forces ahead of them. All began to fire, once the Russians got over their stupefaction at the sight of 607 cavalrymen voluntarily putting themselves up for target practice.

10. It did not take more than a few minutes for the charging horses to reach the Russian lines, and in that time there just wasn't opportunity enough for the gunners to kill all the cavalrymen. A substantial percentage reached the Russians, therefore, and attacked briefly and to no great purpose (and certainly not with the line breaking, shattering, and sundering that Tennyson's patriotism led him to insert into the lines). Having accomplished the letter of their order and attacked the Russians, they turned to ride back—those who had so far survived—without having captured any guns, of course.

11. The Russian guns from three directions had another chance at the target as they rode back.

12. It is sadly difficult, apparently, except for animal lovers, to remember that war takes its toll of forms of life other than human.

The soldiers voluntarily ran their risk and knew the nature of the risk, but by what right do human beings force their animal slaves to run those risks as well? Those 607 cavalrymen rode upon 607 horses, and 335 of those beautiful animals lay dead in the valley when it was over.

13. The whole thing, the charge, the sabre strokes, and the retirment, had lasted about twenty minutes, and in those twenty minutes, nearly half of the light brigade were killed or wounded. Lord Cardigan himself was slightly wounded and left the battlefield at once while the brigade was still fighting.

14. Twice Tennyson says that "All the world wondered." He did not say what it was that made them wonder. The loyalty of the men or the stupidity of the command. One remark was made on the spot that summed it up perfectly and has never been improved on. It was not made by an Englishman. The commander of the French forces was Pierre Jean François Bosquet. Watching the charge in disbelief, he said, "C'est magnifique, mais ce n'est pas la guerre." ("It's magnificent, but it isn't war!")

And what happened thereafter? The war dragged on until a crucial victory was won by the French over the Russians on September 11, 1855, just about a year after the charge of the light brigade. Austria-Hungary was threatening to join the allies, and the grim old Tsar, Nicholas I, had died. Russia saw no use in fighting any longer, and on February 1, 1856, she accepted the preliminary peace terms.

The war was a clear Russian loss since they were forced to give up their designs on Turkey for the moment. Great Britain didn't win much, however. Both sides had displayed a great capacity for running a war poorly, and both sides had showed themselves criminally indifferent to their soldiers, far more of whom died of disease and neglect than of battle action. It was in the course of this war that Florence Nightingale became famous—she founded trained nursing as a profession for women.

Lord Raglan died on June 18, 1855, while the war was going on and before it had taken a turn for the better for the allies. Lord Cardigan survived the war, had a hero's welcome in England, was promoted to lieutenant-general in 1861, and died on March 28, 1868, at the age of seventy.

Maryland, My Maryland[1]

James Ryder Randall[2]

(1861)

The despot's heel is on thy shore,[3]
　　Maryland!
His torch is at thy temple door,[4]
　　Maryland!
Avenge the patriotic gore
That flecked the streets of Baltimore,[5]
And be the battle-queen of yore,
　　Maryland, my Maryland!

Hark to an exiled son's appeal,
　　Maryland!
My Mother State, to thee I kneel,[6]
　　Maryland!
For life or death, for woe or weal,
Thy peerless chivalry reveal,
And gird thy beauteous limbs with steel,
　　Maryland, my Maryland!

Thou wilt not cower in the dust,
　　Maryland!

Thy beaming swords shall never rust,
   Maryland!
Remember Carroll's sacred trust,[7]
Remember Howard's warlike thrust,[8]
And all thy slumberers with the just,
   Maryland, my Maryland!

Come! 'tis the red dawn of the day,[9]
   Maryland!
Come with thy panoplied array,
   Maryland!
With Ringgold's spirit for the fray,[10]
With Watson's blood at Monterey,
With fearless Lowe and dashing May,[11]
   Maryland, my Maryland

Dear Mother, burst the tyrant's chain,
   Maryland!
Virginia should not call in vain,[12]
   Maryland!
She meets her sisters on the plain,—[13]
"Sic semper!" 'tis the proud refrain[14]
That baffles minions back amain,
   Maryland!
Arise in majesty again,
   Maryland, my Maryland!

Come! for thy shield is bright and strong,
   Maryland!
Come! for thy dalliance does thee wrong,
   Maryland!
Come to thine own heroic throng
Stalking with Liberty along,
And chant thy dauntless slogan-song,[15]
   Maryland, my Maryland!

I see the blush upon thy cheek,
   Maryland!
For thou wast ever bravely meek,
   Maryland!
But lo! there surges forth a shriek,
From hill to hill, from creek to creek,
Potomac calls to Chesapeake,[16]
   Maryland, my Maryland!

Thou wilt not yield the Vandal toll,[17]
   Maryland!
Thou wilt not crook to his control,
   Maryland!
Better the fire upon thee roll,
Better the shot, the blade, the bowl,[18]
Than crucifixion of the soul,
   Maryland, my Maryland!

I hear the distant thunder hum,
   Maryland!
The Old Line's bugle, fife, and drum,[19]
   Maryland!
She is not dead, nor deaf, nor dumb;
Huzza! she spurns the Northern scum!
She breathes! She burns! She'll come! She'll come![20]
   Maryland, my Maryland!

---

1. The slavery controversy within the United States, which had been gathering momentum and bitterness since 1820, reached a crisis in 1860, when Abraham Lincoln was elected sixteenth President of the United States. Before the end of the year, South Carolina, fearing that a Republican President would forcibly put an end to her way of life, seceded from the Union. Six other slave states quickly followed and formed the Confederate States of America.

Maryland, My Maryland

On April 12, 1861, South Carolina bombarded Fort Sumter in Charleston Harbor, to force the Union soldiers holding it to surrender. They did, and with that the Civil War began. On April 17 Virginia seceded and joined the Confederacy as its eighth state. This set off a new round of secessions, and for a while it seemed that Maryland, a slave state to the north of Virginia might secede, too. At least the Confederates hoped so, and this poem was written at just about this time as a call to Maryland's secession.

2. James Ryder Randall, a journalist and song writer, was born on January 1, 1839. An ardent Confederate sympathizer, he wrote the poem in April 1861, fitting its rhythm to the well-known German tune, "Tannenbaum." Randall survived the Civil War that followed by forty years, dying in Augusta, Georgia, on January 14, 1908. Next to "Dixie," this poem became the most popular and best-known of the Confederate songs.

3. The "despot" is the Union generally, or its army, or, most specifically, Abraham Lincoln himself. On the night of February 23–24, 1861, Lincoln, on his way to his new post in Washington, D.C., passed through Maryland secretly and by a devious route to prevent assassination attempts. Washington, D.C., was itself a part of Maryland originally, so that if Lincoln is viewed as the despot, his heel was literally on Maryland's shore.

Then, too, Lincoln was but too aware of Washington's vulnerability. It was just across the river from Virginia, the heart of the Confederacy (once it seceded) and was essentially part of the slave state of Maryland, which had some impulse to secede. The city needed military protection.

On April 19, 1861, then (the eighty-sixth anniversary of the Battle of Concord) a Union regiment marched through Baltimore toward Washington. The regiment was from Massachusetts (of all states, the most anti-slavery and the most hated by the Confederacy) and those soldiers could represent the "despot's heel," too.

4. In ancient times, when a city was taken by a conqueror and put to the torch, a special effort was made to burn the city's temples, since they represented the city's gods and were usually the emotional center of resistance. Thus, the Babylonians destroyed the Temple in Jerusalem in 586 B.C., and the Romans did the same in

A.D. 70. When the Persians took Athens in 480 B.C., they burned its temples. The picture of burning temples then is one that refers emotionally to a bitter and ruthless enemy.

5. Baltimore was a center of pro-Confederate sympathy in Maryland, and when the Massachusetts regiment marched through its streets it could not very well do so unnoticed. Crowds gathered to jeer, then to throw stones, then to attack. Before the crowds could be beaten off, four soldiers were killed and thirty-six wounded. Since the bombardment of Fort Sumter had been without casualties, these mobbed soldiers in Baltimore were the first military casualties of the Civil War.

It is, of course, not to these dead and wounded soldiers that Randall refers when he speaks of "patriotic gore." To him, the Union soldiers were invaders. In the course of the riot, there were casualties among the civilian attackers, too, and it was *their* blood he bemoaned.

6. Maryland was Randall's "Mother State" since he was born in Baltimore (so that the news of the deaths in Baltimore moved him, particularly, to write the poem). He was an "exiled son" out of personal choice. He did not live or work in Maryland, not because he had been driven out, but because he found congenial positions farther south. He taught for a while in Louisiana, for instance.

7. "Carroll" is Charles Carroll, born in Annapolis, Maryland, on September 9, 1737. He was one of the signers of the Declaration of Independence, the only Catholic among the signers and the last survivor among them, dying in Baltimore, on November 14, 1832, at the age of ninety-five. His "sacred trust" was the principle of rebelling against unjust authority.

8. "Howard" is John Eager Howard, born in Baltimore, Maryland, on June 4, 1752. He fought in the Revolutionary Army, reaching the rank of lieutenant colonel and receiving a medal for distinguished service at the battle of Cowpens. In 1781 he was severely wounded in action, but survived to be governor of Maryland from 1789 to 1791, and senator from Maryland from 1796 to 1803.

9. If the "red dawn" represents the beginning of a bloody war, Randall was more nearly correct than he probably knew. The Civil

War lasted four years, and was longer, bloodier, and crueler, than either side imagined it would be at the start.

10. Cadwalader Ringgold was born in Washington County, Maryland, on August 20, 1802. Ringgold was a naval officer whose greatest fame was as an explorer and surveyor. Between 1838 and 1842 he was on an exploring trip that, among other things, was the first to survey the coast of Antarctica.

11. Randall here rattles off a few more names of Marylanders who were eminent in his day for derring-do. The reference to "Monterey" is to the battle of Monterrey, fought in August 1846 in the course of the Mexican War, only fifteen years before the opening of the Civil War.

12. Virginia was the acknowledged leader among the slave states. She was the first to be colonized and she was the largest, most populous, and most influential state in the Union at the time of the Revolution. She was the home state of George Washington, Thomas Jefferson, James Madison, James Monroe, John Marshall, Patrick Henry, and Richard Henry Lee. When she seceded on April 17, she called on her neighbors to do likewise.

13. The "sisters" are those states that had already seceded. Virginia's importance to the Confederacy she was now joining is shown by the fact that on May 21 the capital of the new nation was moved from Montgomery, Alabama, to Richmond, Virginia.

14. "*Sic semper tyrannis*" (Thus always to tyrants) was Virginia's state motto, adopted in 1776 with George III in mind. Here, Randall turns it against the Union forces and, perhaps, against the new President, Abraham Lincoln. It is a sad thought that when John Wilkes Booth assassinated Lincoln, he shouted, "*Sic semper tyrannis.*"

15. What Maryland's "dauntless slogan-song" might have been in 1861 scarcely matters. In 1939, Maryland chose a new state song, and that was "Maryland, my Maryland."

16. The Potomac River marks off Maryland's southern border from east to west, while Chesapeake Bay bisects the state, running north and south. The verse seems to picture Maryland rising as one man, then, from border to border.

17. The "Vandals" were a Germanic tribe that occupied the midsection of northern Africa in the mid-fifth century, with Carthage as their capital. In A.D. 455, the Vandals, under their forceful leader, Gaiseric, sacked Rome. It was a very efficient sack with a minimum of bloodshed, cruelty, and needless destruction. The Vandals did, however, carry off everything portable that had any value. The indignant Romans spoke of any barbarous destroyers, thereafter, as Vandals, and the word gained its present meaning.

18. The bowl is the beggar's bowl, so that the verse is saying it is better to be killed or to be reduced to beggary than to give in.

19. The "Old Line" is the line of Maryland soldiers who demonstrated their bravery in various battles of the Revolution. Maryland is, to this day, known as the "Old Line State."

20. At the time Randall wrote this poem, it seemed as though Maryland might indeed come and join the Confederacy. The state legislature was pro-Confederate and so were many of its people. Had Maryland seceded, that would have isolated Washington, D.C., as an enclave within Confederate territory. Lincoln and the government might have had to flee to Philadelphia, and that would have been the kind of moral victory for the Confederates that might conceivably have broken enough of the Union will to force a permanent division of the nation.

But Lincoln quite understood this and he took decisive action. With the co-operation of Maryland's governor, who was pro-Union, Lincoln had many state officials arrested and imprisoned, and placed strong army units here and there in the state. By the end of 1861, despite Randall's call, Maryland was firmly in the Union camp, although individual Marylanders joined the Confederate Army (and many others joined the Union army).

Maryland never did "come." In fact, in 1862 and 1863, when Confederate General Lee twice moved north of the Potomac River, the Confederate soldiers marched through Maryland singing, "Maryland, my Maryland," but the state still did not rise.

Battle-Hymn of the Republic[1]

JULIA WARD HOWE[2]

(1861)

Mine eyes have seen the glory of the coming of the Lord[3];
He is trampling out the vintage where the grapes of wrath are
    stored[4];
He hath loosed the fateful lightning of His terrible swift
    sword[5];
      His truth is marching on.[6]

I have seen Him in the watch-fires of a hundred circling camps;
They have builded Him an altar in the evening dews and
    damps[7];
I can read his righteous sentence by the dim and flaring lamps;
      His day is marching on.[8]

I have read a fiery gospel, writ in burnished rows of steel:
"As ye deal with my contemners, so with you my grace shall
    deal[9];
Let the hero, born of woman, crush the serpent with his heel,[10]
      Since God is marching on."

He has sounded forth the trumpet that shall never call retreat[11];
He is sifting out the hearts of men before His judgment-seat[12]:
Oh, be swift, my soul, to answer Him! be jubilant, my feet!
    Our God is marching on.

In the beauty of the lilies Christ was born across the sea,[13]
With a glory in His bosom that transfigures you and me[14]:
As He died to make men holy,[15] let us die to make men free,[16]
    While God is marching on.

---

1. The first important clash between the two sides, North and South, after the southern states had seceded and formed the Confederacy, was at Bull Run in northern Virginia on July 21, 1861. The green Northern troops sustained a defeat, and the North, shocked and disappointed, began grimly to prepare for a long war. All winter long an army was trained by George B. McClellan, and the promise of blood and death hung ever more threateningly over the broken nation. This poem was written during the period of apprehension and uncertainty.

A hymn is a song of praise and adoration, and the word may have come from the Greek *hymen* referring to the shout of joy at a marriage. It is used almost entirely now to refer to a poem in praise of God. This poem, couched in biblical language and imagery, deals also with the waiting army and its mission, and it is therefore a "battle-hymn."

2. Julia Ward was born in New York City on May 27, 1819. She married a Boston philanthropist, Samuel Gridley Howe in 1843 and joined him in his dedication to the cause of the abolition of slavery. Between giving birth to six children, she helped edit an anti-slavery periodical to which she contributed poems and essays.

In the fall of 1861 she visited an army camp in Washington, D.C., and was moved to write this poem. It was published in the *Atlantic Monthly* in February 1862, and grew instantly popular. It has ever since been associated with the more solemn and tragic aspects of the Civil War and, particularly, with Abraham Lincoln.

Mrs. Howe long outlived the war and died in Newport, Rhode Island, on October 17, 1910, at the age of ninety-one.

3. God is seen as coming to visit destruction on the forces of evil, with the Union Army as his instrument. The language and images are biblical. Thus, when Isaiah has a vision of God, he fears that this is a sign of his imminent death: "Woe is me! for I am undone; because I am a man of unclean lips, and I dwell in the midst of a people of unclean lips: for mine eyes have seen the King, the Lord of hosts" (Isaiah 6:5). And in the description of that vision, Isaiah heard the seraphim chanting: "Holy, holy, holy, is the Lord of hosts: the whole earth is full of his glory" (Isaiah 6:3). The two lines combine to give the now familiar, "Mine eyes have seen the glory—"

"Glory," in one of its meanings, is the emanation of light emerging from objects of sanctity, and from God in particular, so that God, in Isaiah's vision, suffuses the world with light. (This notion is perhaps a remnant of primitive sun worship.)

4. This is an image of the day of judgment. The purple juice of the grapes symbolizes the blood of sinners being trampled to their destruction. The image is used twice in the Bible, and in both cases God is pictured as destroying his enemies in a paroxysm of rage:

"I have trodden the winepress alone; and of the people there was none with me: for I will tread them in mine anger, and trample them in my fury; and their blood shall be sprinkled upon my garments, and I will stain all my raiment" (Isaiah 63:3).

. . . and he shall rule them with a rod of iron: and he treadeth the winepress of the fierceness and wrath of Almighty God" (Revelation 19:15).

John Steinbeck, writing of another period in American history that seemed, in quite a different fashion, to have a judgment-day atmosphere—the Great Depression—published a novel in 1939 that he named *The Grapes of Wrath,* using the phrase from this line of the poem.

5. Another judgment-day image. In the passage in Revelation just before the reference to the winepress there come the words, "And out of his mouth goeth a sharp sword, that with it he should smite the nations" (Revelation 19:15).

The use of the word "lightning" is particularly apt, since it was quite customary in ancient times to picture the lightning bolt as a divine weapon. Zeus hurled the lightning bolt, and so did the Norse god, Thor.

In the Bible it is, of course, God who uses the lightning. In the colorful imagery of the psalms, God is, on one occasion, pictured as using the storm blast to war against His enemies: "The Lord also thundered in the heavens, and the Highest gave his voice; hail stones and coals of fire. Yea, he sent out his arrows, and scattered them; and he shot out lightnings and discomfited them." (Psalms 18:13–14).

6. Still another judgment-day image. A verse in the Bible describes God as follows: ". . . for he cometh to judge the earth: he shall judge the world with righteousness, and the people with his truth" (Psalms 96:13).

Mrs. Howe had deliberately adopted a meter for the poem which would enable it to be sung to the tune of "John Brown's Body," a popular marching song of those days, and one that commemorated the death of John Brown. Brown was a madman who centered his madness about the hatred of slavery. In October 1859 he attempted to raise a slave rebellion in Virginia, but was taken, tried, and condemned. He was hanged on December 2, 1859. The nature of his cause and the absolute courage with which he met his end made him into a hero of the anti-slavery cause, and they sang:

> John Brown's body lies a-mouldering in the grave;
> John Brown's body lies a-mouldering in the grave;
> John Brown's body lies a-mouldering in the grave;
> But his soul goes marching on.

The tune was stirring but the words, to say the least, were uninspired, and Mrs. Howe undoubtedly felt that she was performing a noble act in supplying much better words for so effective a tune, and who can fail to agree with her?

The tune was older than "John Brown's Body." It was borrowed from a hymn, which had as its refrain: "Glory, glory, hallelujah," three times repeated. That refrain was kept in "John Brown's

Body" and also in "Battle-Hymn of the Republic" when it is sung, although it does not appear in the poem proper. It goes:

> Glory, glory, hallelujah,
> Glory, glory, hallelujah,
> Glory, glory, hallelujah,
> His truth is marching on.

"Glory, glory, hallelujah" is not a set of nonsense syllables, but is a fitting line for a hymn. "Hallelujah" is a Hebrew word meaning "Praise God" and a meaning of "glory" other than that used in the first line of the poem, is "praise" as when one says, "Glory to God." The refrain, "Glory, glory, hallelujah," means, then, "Praise, praise, praise God."

7. This is Mrs. Howe's personal experience at the army camps and her vision of the army as the weapon of God.

8. The judgment-day motif is back with "righteous sentence." "His day" is, of course, the day of judgment, which term is used in the New Testament: "Verily I say unto you, It shall be more tolerable for the land of Sodom and Gomorrah in the day of judgment, than for that city" (Matthew 10:15). In the Old Testament, however, it is usually referred to as "the day of the Lord." Thus: "The great day of the Lord is near, it is near, and hasteth greatly, even the voice of the day of the Lord" (Zephaniah 1:14).

9. In the gospels, it says: "For if ye forgive men their trespasses, your heavenly Father will also forgive you: But if ye forgive not men their trespasses, neither will your Father forgive your trespasses" (Matthew 6:14–15).

Here, though, we have a "fiery" gospel of anger to be delivered by those "rows of steel" that represent the weapons of destruction. It is a gospel that seems to reverse the just quoted injunction from the Sermon on the Mount. The grace and forgiveness of God will go to those who deal with His contemners (those who despise Him) *un*forgivingly. Lest there be any question of this, it is made specific in the next line.

10. This harks back to the curse placed by God on the serpent after the incident with the fruit of the tree of knowledge in the Gar-

den of Eden. God tells the serpent, "And I will put enmity between thee and the woman, and between thy seed and her seed; it shall bruise thy head, and thou shalt bruise his heel" (Genesis 3:15).

In later times, the primitive tale of the garden of Eden, was idealized and given cosmic significance. The serpent was transmuted into Satan, the principle of evil, and the descendant of Eve who was to apply the final crushing destruction to Satan and win mankind to goodness forever, was Jesus. It is because of this Messianic significance given the biblical verse quoted above that the word "Hero" is capitalized in the poem.

The Confederate armies are thus linked to Satan, and the Union armies fight for Jesus. In such a battle, the forgiveness enjoined on man for man would seem to be outlawed.

11. The primitive trumpet had its use in war. It was not a musical instrument; rather, a device to sound a few simple notes much more loudly than the unaided human voice could. It was therefore a method for gathering and controlling large bodies of men whom the voice could not reach, particularly in the hurly-burly of battle.

It was natural, therefore, to imagine a trumpet used to gather people together at the time of judgment. Jesus, in describing the day of judgment says, "And he shall send his angels with a great sound of a trumpet, and they shall gather together his elect from the four winds, from one end of heaven to the other" (Matthew 24:31). There is a common legend that it is the Archangel Gabriel who will blow that last trump, but there is no mention of this in the Bible.

12. A judge always sits on an elevated dais, while the accused must stand and look up at him. Certainly God will sit on high at the time of the final judgment too, so that the reference to standing before "His judgment-seat" is one more image of the final day.

13. The reference to lilies harks back to Jesus' praise of the flower as the very epitome of beauty: "And why take ye thought for raiment. Consider the lilies of the field, how they grow; they toil not, neither do they spin: And yet I say unto you, That even Solomon in all his glory was not arrayed like one of these" (Matthew 6:28–29).

The Hebrew term *shoshannah,* translated as "lilies" (and giving rise to the feminine names, Susan and Susannah, by the way) does not refer to the white lilies with which we are familiar but to a more colorful flower, probably an iris. In Christian art, the lily, with its pure whiteness, has come to be an emblem for chastity, innocence, and purity, and it, too, is therefore a fit image to associate with the birth of Jesus.

14. To "transfigure," in its theological meaning, is to "glorify," to imbue someone or something with the brightness associated with God. Thus, at one point in the Gospels Jesus himself is reported to have appeared to three of his apostles in gleaming glory. Jesus "was transfigured before them and his face did shine as the sun . . ." (Matthew 17:2). This is referred to as the Transfiguration.

15. It is the general Christian belief that whereas Adam's original sin tainted all mankind afterward, the sacrifice of Jesus produced grace enough to neutralize all that sin and make it possible for mankind to be redeemed at the time of judgment. Thus, referring to Jesus, "And he is the propitiation for our sins; and not for ours only, but also for the sins of the whole world" (1 John 2:2). Since Jesus made it possible for mankind, generally, to share in God's glory, His coming "transfigured you and me."

16. In the Civil War, more people died in order that slavery might be abolished than Mrs. Howe perhaps expected at the time she wrote the poem. There were almost a million casualties—Union and Confederate—and misery and unhappiness beyond counting. Nor was the legacy of slavery so easily wiped out. Though the blacks were legally freed, it was long before they were socially freed —and not entirely even yet.

Barbara Frietchie[1]

JOHN GREENLEAF WHITTIER[2]

(1862)

Up from the meadows rich with corn,
Clear in the cool September morn,[3]

The clustered spires of Frederick[4] stand
Green-walled by the hills of Maryland.

Round about them orchards sweep,
Apple and peach tree fruited deep,

Fair as the garden of the Lord[5]
To the eyes of the famished rebel horde,[6]

On that pleasant morn of the early fall
When Lee marched over the mountain-wall[7];

Over the mountains winding down,
Horse and foot, into Frederick town.[8]

Forty flags with their silver stars,
Forty flags with their crimson bars,[9]

Flapped in the morning wind: the sun
Of noon looked down, and saw not one.[10]

Up rose old Barbara Frietchie then,
Bowed with her fourscore years and ten[11];

Bravest of all in Frederick town,
She took up the flag the men hauled down[12];

In her attic window the staff she set,
To show that one heart was loyal yet.

Up the street came the rebel tread,
Stonewall Jackson riding ahead.[13]

Under his slouched hat left and right
He glanced; the old flag met his sight.

"Halt!"—the dust-brown ranks stood fast.
"Fire!"—out blazed the rifle-blast.

It shivered the window, pane and sash;
It rent the banner with seam and gash;

Quick as it fell, from the broken staff
Dame Barbara snatched the silken scarf.

She leaned far out on the window-sill,
And shook it forth with a royal will.

"Shoot, if you must, this old gray head,
But spare your country's flag," she said.[14]

A shade of sadness, a blush of shame,
Over the face of the leader came;

The nobler nature within him stirred
To life at that woman's deed and word[15];

"Who touches a hair of yon gray head
Dies like a dog! March on!" he said.

All day long through Frederick street
Sounded the tread of marching feet;

All day long that free flag tossed
Over the heads of the rebel host.

Ever its torn folds rose and fell
On the loyal winds that loved it well;

And through the hill-gaps sunset light
Shone over it with a warm good-night.[16]

Barbara Frietchie's work is o'er,[17]
And the Rebel[18] rides on his raids no more.

Honor to her! and let a tear
Fall, for her sake, on Stonewall's bier.[19]

Over Barbara Frietchie's grave,
Flag of Freedom and Union, wave!

Peace and order and beauty draw
Round thy symbol of light and law;

And ever the stars above look down
On thy stars below in Frederick town![20]

---

1. The Civil War, which was largely in a state of preparation in 1861, reached its full fury in 1862, and this poem deals with an in-

cident that is supposed to have taken place during the campaigns of that year.

2. John Greenleaf Whittier was born near Haverhill, Massachusetts, on December 17, 1807. In the years preceding the Civil War, he was an Abolitionist and idealist, and many of his poems were written to express his political and social views. He was too gentle to go along with the extreme Abolitionists, however, and his pacifism and detestation of violence led him to disapprove of John Brown's attempt to end slavery by black rebellion. Once the southern states seceded, he would have preferred to have them go in peace rather than to attempt to force them back into the Union by war. This poem celebrates the victory of peaceful resistance over warlike passion.

He died in Hampton Falls, Massachusetts, on September 7, 1892.

3. The September is the September of 1862, and it was a bitter time for the Union. In March of that year General George B. McClellan, of whom much had been expected, was finally persuaded by President Lincoln to move the army that he had kept uselessly at home. Through May and June, McClellan fought battles in Virginia against a numerically inferior Confederate force. The Confederates were under the leadership of Joseph E. Johnston, and when he was wounded, the command of the army was taken over by Robert E. Lee, who fought with Thomas J. ("Stonewall") Jackson as his right-hand man.

The Union forces fought well, but McClellan was temperamentally incapable of fighting on the offensive, and the Confederates drove him off. Another Union army under General John Pope was beaten even more dismally by a small Confederate army under Lee and Jackson at the Second Battle of Bull Run on August 29 and 30.

With these victories under his belt, it seemed to Lee a good idea to march northward and invade the North. Maryland, which was a slave state and, to an extent, sympathetic to the Confederate cause (see page 208), might rise. Washington might then be isolated and the Union government might be forced to flee from it as it had had to do in the War of 1812 (see page 164). That would be a stunning propaganda victory that would bring in foreign aid and force a humiliated North to end the war.

So, on September 4, 1862, Lee's army began to move across the Potomac and into Maryland.

4. The town of Frederick, Maryland, received its name in 1745 in honor of Frederick, Prince of Wales, son of George II and father of George III. It is about 20 kilometers (12 miles) northeast of the Potomac River and 65 kilometers (40 miles) northeast of Washington.

5. The "garden of the Lord" is the garden of Eden and is referred to by that name in some verses in the Bible. Thus, when Abraham and his nephew, Lot, parted ways, Abraham gave Lot first choice of the place to settle in, "And Lot lifted up his eyes, and beheld all the plain of Jordan, that it was well watered everywhere . . . even as the garden of the Lord . . ." (Genesis 13:10).

6. One great advantage of the Union over the Confederacy was that the Union was industrialized and had an excellent transportation system it could keep in good repair. The Confederacy was undeveloped, rural in its economy, with a sparse railroad system and no facilities with which to maintain it. This meant that the Union, however often it might be defeated, could always rush reinforcements and supplies to its armies, something the Confederacy could not necessarily do. The Union soldiers were always well fed, the Confederate soldiers were always on short rations. They were a "famished rebel horde" indeed.

7. The Catoctin mountain range runs north and south just to the west of Frederick (the Maryland hills that are the green walls of Frederick as referred to in the fourth line of the poem). But Lee didn't send his army clamboring unnecessarily over mountain passes. He crossed the Potomac just south of the southern end of the ridge, then skirted it to the east and marched northward toward Frederick.

8. The Confederate army entered Frederick on September 7, 1862, actually still late summer rather than early fall.

9. The use of "bars" is unfortunate. The Confederate flag was like the American flag in some ways, but for one thing, differed in the fact that the red and white stripes were only three in number; red, white, red. The greater thickness of those stripes led to the Confederate flag being called the "stars and bars" as opposed to the "stars and stripes" of the American flag.

These lines made it look as though Confederate flags were flying in Frederick and were lowered as the Confederate troops marched in—but that was just because Whittier needed a rhyme for "stars." It was, of course, the Union flags—the stars and stripes—that were flying, and that came down.

10. It is understandable that this should happen. Prudence would dictate it, and few people would choose not to be prudent in the face of the actual presence of an enemy army. Prudence, however, was not enough for the Confederates. They didn't want the Marylanders just to take down their Union flags. They wanted them to rise, to join the Confederate cause, to flock to the Confederate army. This did not happen and the Confederate invasion hopes were, in a way, lost before any battle had been fought.

11. Born in 1772 (if the tale, as Whittier tells it is correct), Barbara Frietchie was four years older than the United States.

12. One might suspect, by the way, that at the age of ninety, one has little to lose and can afford to be brave. Perhaps, though, it is better to wait until one is ninety oneself and can determine through personal experience how much bravery has been increased by age before one indulges in easy cynicism.

13. Actually, this can't be right. At the time the Confederate army reached Frederick on September 7, Stonewall Jackson was at Harpers Ferry on the Potomac River, 32 kilometers (20 miles) southwest of Frederick.

However, Stonewall Jackson was the most skilled tactician ever born in the United States, and one of the most colorful generals. The feats he performed with his underequipped, underfed men were little short of miraculous. There hardly needed to be any communication between himself and Lee. Each knew the other's mind and they worked together perfectly.

There was no Confederate general so feared and so (grudgingly) admired as Stonewall Jackson, and his presence at the scene is a dramatic necessity.

14. These lines are the most famous in the poem, and are known even to people who don't know the poem.

15. This is extremely unlikely. Stonewall Jackson was a highly neurotic person, a thoroughgoing hypochondriac, and a religious fanatic who was quite convinced of the justice of the cause for which

he fought. There is no likelihood that "a shade of sadness, a blush of shame" would cross his face at the thought of shooting at the enemy flag. Once, when Union soldiers were dying under the rifles of Jackson's men, one Confederate officer admiring the gallantry of the foe expressed regret that so many brave Union men must die, Jackson said gruffly, "Shoot them all! I do not wish them to be brave!"

16. Frederick remained in the grip of the Confederacy only a few days. With McClellan advancing, Lee moved westward in order to outflank him and strike for the Susquehanna River. Unfortunately for Lee, his plan of campaign fell into the hands of McClellan. With any commander but McClellan this would have meant Lee's destruction as the Union army moved quickly to anticipate the known strategy of the foe. All that the slow-moving McClellan could do, however, was to fight a drawn battle with Lee at Antietam Creek, some 30 kilometers (19 miles) west of Frederick.

Even a drawn battle was enough to force Lee to abandon his plan of invasion, for his army had been too far weakened. He returned to Virginia, but McClellan dared follow him only at a distance—and that was too much for Lincoln. McClellan was relieved of his command and never fought again.

17. But, thanks to the poem, she is not forgotten. Her home in Frederick is restored and is now the site of a Civil War museum.

18. Since the poem was written in 1863, the "Rebel" cannot be a symbolic singular referring to the Confederate army as a whole. The Confederate armies were at work for more than a year after the poem was written. The "Rebel" is Stonewall Jackson himself, for at the time the poem was written, he would ride on his raids no more—he had been killed in action.

19. After the Maryland campaign, Union armies plunged into Virginia again and were twice more very badly defeated by the team of Lee and Jackson; once at the battle of Fredericksburg on December 13, 1862, and once at the battle of Chancellorsville from May 1 to May 4, 1863.

In the course of that second battle, however, Stonewall Jackson rode forward on the night of May 2 to reconnoiter and was shot, by mistake, by some Confederate troops who thought he was an enemy.

His left arm was shattered and had to be amputated. He might have survived that, but he caught pneumonia, and on May 10, 1863, eight months after the incident at Frederick, he died, at the age of thirty-nine.

20. Whittier's calm assurance of victory was justified. The Civil War was won by the Union in 1865, the Nation was reunited, and has remained united ever since. The "flag of Freedom and Union" waves over all the states today.

O! Captain My Captain!¹

WALT WHITMAN²

(1865)

O Captain! my Captain!³ our fearful trip is done,⁴
The ship has weathered every rack,⁵ the prize we sought is won,
The port is near, the bells I hear, the people all exulting,⁶
While follow eyes the steady keel, the vessel grim and daring;
   But O heart! heart! heart!
     O the bleeding drops of red,
   Where on the deck my Captain lies,
     Fallen cold and dead.⁷

O Captain! my Captain! rise up and hear the bells;
Rise up—for you the flag is flung—for you the bugle trills,
For you bouquets and ribboned wreaths—for you the shores
    a-crowding
For you they call, the swaying mass, their eager faces turning⁸;
   Here Captain! dear father!
     This arm beneath your head!⁹
   It is some dream that on the deck
     You've fallen cold and dead.

O Captain! My Captain!

My Captain does not answer, his lips are pale and still,
My father does not feel my arm, he has no pulse nor will,[10]
The ship is anchored safe and sound, its voyage closed and done,
From fearful trip the victor ship comes in with subject won;
    Exult O shores, and ring O bells!
      But I with mournful tread,
    Walk the deck my Captain lies,
      Fallen cold and dead.[11]

---

1. The turning point of the Civil War came at the beginning of July 1863. Lee invaded the North a second time and was defeated at the battle of Gettysburg. Meanwhile, the Union general Ulysses Simpson Grant took Vicksburg on July 4 so that the entire course of the Mississippi was in Union hands. Though the Confederacy fought on valiantly for nearly two years thereafter, its final defeat was assured. But then, with victory came a final tragedy, and it is with that event that this poem concerns itself.

2. Walt Whitman was born in West Hills, Long Island, on May 13, 1819. He grew up in Brooklyn and was editor of the Brooklyn *Eagle* from 1846 to 1848 (a newspaper that still existed when I was a teen-ager in Brooklyn). His book *Leaves of Grass* was published in 1855 and was controversial, indeed. It was "free verse" not bound by the rigid requirements of rhyme and scansion that was normal for nineteenth-century poetry, and it was not a popular success in its time. This poem, however, written more conventionally, was popular from the start, and has remained so. Whitman died in Camden, New Jersey, on March 26, 1892.

3. It is Abraham Lincoln, sixteenth President of the United States, who is here being addressed as the captain of the "ship of state."
The metaphor that likens a nation to a ship, and its history to a sail over smooth seas or through stormy waters, is a natural one to a sea-faring nation and is as old as the ancient Greek playwrights. Aeschylus and Sophocles both used it, and by 1714 Jonathan Swift, the English satirist, was complaining that the metaphor was stale.

What revitalized it, at least for American ears, was a poem by Henry Wadsworth Longfellow, in which the United States is addressed in that fashion at a time when there were growing doubts that the Union would long survive:

> Thou, too, sail on, O Ship of State!
> Sail on, O Union, strong and great!
> Humanity with all its fears,
> With all the hopes of future years,
> Is hanging breathless on thy fate!

The time was to come when Winston Churchill would quote that poem to Americans during the dark days of World War II.

4. The "fearful trip" is that of the Civil War, and the trip "is done" because the poem was written shortly after April 9, 1865, when Lee surrendered his army to Grant at Appomattox Courthouse and organized Confederate resistance came to an end.

5. During the first half of the war, the main theater in Virginia was the scene of an almost unrelieved series of disasters for the Union at the hands of gifted Confederate generals (see pages 219–20). In surviving those, the Union had "weathered every rack."

6. "The port is near," no more than that, for there were still some scattered Confederate forces in the field. They would surely have to surrender soon, but there would still be casualties. Galveston, Texas, did not surrender to the Union till June 2, eighty days after the event described in this poem, and that was the actual end of the war. Still, the celebration over Lee's surrender as the essential end was justified and the people, on the winning side at least, were "all exulting."

7. With Washington in a state of high hilarity, Lincoln, an enormous weight lifted from his shoulders, decided to see a play at Ford's Theater on the night of April 14, five days after Lee's surrender. The Secret Service guards, who were supposed to be watching Lincoln's box, were watching the play instead.

John Wilkes Booth, an actor, and a Confederate sympathizer, entered the box, shot the President at point-blank range, then leaped from the box to the stage, shouting the Virginia state motto of "Sic semper tyrannis" (Thus always to tyrants). He broke his ankle in the jump but managed to get away in the confusion. He was pursued and finally located and shot on October 26 in a barn near Bowling Green, Virginia, but what good was that? It didn't bring back Lincoln, who died at 7:22 A.M. on the morning of April 15.

8. Lincoln was not a popular President at the start. He was ungainly and, in some ways, uncouth. He had a high-pitched voice and an unfortunate sense of humor that broke forth at times when pomposity would have seemed to be the thing to small minds. The early misfortunes of the war were heaped on his shoulders. He was blamed for not prosecuting the war vigorously enough, for prosecuting it too vigorously, for not freeing the slaves early on, for being too concerned about the slaves. He was hounded from beginning to end by office seekers and by politicians who were sure they could do the job better than Lincoln, and by other politicians whose only interest was in lining their own pockets.

As 1864 approached, Lincoln might have decided that the unprecedented situation of an election coming up in the middle of a life-and-death struggle (the first presidential election to come in wartime) had to be treated unprecedentedly. He might have argued that the Union could not afford a divisive election at this stage and might therefore have canceled it. He did not. Even though he felt he would not be re-elected, he realized that the precedent of canceling an election—however good the reason—would be used later for no reason, or for bad reasons. To win the war at the cost of canceling the election was to lose the essence of America.

The election took place, and the tide turned clearly and irresistibly toward victory just in time for Lincoln to win re-election. It came to be realized in those last few months of the war that it had been Lincoln's patience and resolution that had held the Union steady through all the misfortunes; that his hand had been firm on the helm at all times, and that perhaps no one else could have seen it through. The realization came late but it came, and when victory washed over the Union, it was Lincoln who was the hero.

9. The picture of Whitman cradling the fallen figure is, in a way, out of real life. During the Civil War, Whitman worked in Washington, and spent his spare time visiting army hospitals and trying to cheer the wounded and dying—of both sides.

10. Twice Lincoln is addressed as "father." He has always given an impression of age. He was frequently called "Old Abe" and yet he was only fifty-one years old when he became President and only fifty-six years old when he died. The accident being named Abraham may have helped. Abraham, as the patriarch of the Israelite race, is pictured in the most dramatic stories about him in the Bible, as being an old, old man. He had his son, Isaac, at ninety-nine, and he died at the age of 175, and this symbolism of age carried over.

In 1862, when three hundred thousand men were needed for the badly mauled Union army, James Sloan Gibbons wrote a recruiting song which turned out to be very popular. It opened with the line: "We are coming, Father Abraham, three hundred thousand more."

11. Whitman was right to feel one should rather mourn the death than celebrate the victory, for without Lincoln the victory was hollow. Andrew Jackson of Tennessee succeeded to the presidency, an honest man but a poor politician. With *his* hand at the helm, the Ship of State veered off-course and was not prevented from entering a period of reconstruction that humiliated the defeated states needlessly, when conciliation was needed, and that used the newly liberated blacks merely as pawns to enrich political hacks and thieves rather than as human beings to be brought into American life with decency and self-respect. The evil results of that period are still with us.

Invictus[1]

William Ernest Henley[2]

(1875)

Out of the night that covers me,
  Black as the pit from pole to pole,[3]
I thank whatever gods may be[4]
  For my unconquerable soul.

In the fell clutch of circumstance
  I have not winced nor cried aloud.
Under the bludgeonings of chance[5]
  My head is bloody, but unbowed.[6]

Beyond this place of wrath and tears[7]
  Looms but the Horror of the shade,[8]
And yet the menace of the years
  Finds and shall find me unafraid.

It matters not how strait the gate,[9]
  How charged with punishments the scroll,[10]
I am the master of my fate:
  I am the captain of my soul.[11]

1. After the Crimean War, Great Britain entered a four-decade period of essential peace (excluding distant and unimportant colonial engagements) during which its empire and its prosperity grew steadily under the long-enduring reign of Queen Victoria.

To be sure, a new power was rising in Europe. The separate states of Germany, after having defeated France under Prussian leadership, had united into a strong German Empire in 1871. The German army was the strongest in the world, but the island nation of Great Britain, secure behind its fleet, felt unconquerable, and it is not surprising that individual Britishers might feel unconquerable as well.

The title of this poem, *Invictus* is the Latin word for "unconquerable," and it refers to the poet himself, whose half-century of life was spent in the golden summer of Victoria's reign.

2. William Ernest Henley was born on August 23, 1849, in Gloucester, England. During childhood, he contracted tuberculosis of the bones, and eventually one foot had to be amputated. The other might have had to go, too, but Henley made his way to Edinburgh to get the help of Joseph Lister, the greatest surgeon of the day, and the one who had introduced the technique of antiseptic surgery in 1865.

The leg was saved, but at a considerable price, for Henley had to remain in an Edinburgh infirmary for a nightmarish twenty months from 1873 to 1875. During this stay, afflicted by boredom, uncertainty, frustration, discomfort, and pain, he began to write verse that eventually earned him a modest reputation as a poet.

Among his, for the most part, quite forgettable poems, there appeared in 1875, toward the end of his hospital stay, this one, which instantly became enormously popular and has remained so ever since. Henley died on July 11, 1903, in Woking, near London.

3. Night covers one half of Earth at all times, of course, from North Pole to South Pole. It stretches exactly from pole to pole at the time of the equinoxes, only approximately so at other times.

The pit referred to is *the* pit, which, in the Bible, is one of the words used to represent Hell. Thus, the prophet Isaiah, when inveighing against the king of Babylon (whom he refers to, sarcastically, as Lucifer, the morning star) says, ". . . thou shalt be brought down to hell, to the sides of the pit" (Isaiah 14:15).

4. The phrase "whatever gods may be" is an expression of agnosticism (from a Greek word meaning "unknown"). When used in connection with religion, agnosticism refers to a view that neither affirms nor denies God, but places the question in the limbo of the unknown and, perhaps, unknowable. In the wake of Darwin's theory of evolution, which had been presented to the world in 1859, agnosticism became popular in British intellectual circles. Darwin was himself agnostic, and the word was coined in 1869 by the English biologist Thomas Henry Huxley, one of Darwin's most vocal supporters.

5. It is, of course, the standard belief among Christians that God is the author of misfortune. The proper attitude, preached in the Book of Job, is to bow to the Divine will and to accept it even if you don't understand it. It might even be argued that the spiritual discipline required for the purpose does the soul far more good than the misfortune can do harm.

The doctrine of Darwinian evolution, however, made it appear that chance ruled life, and that it was chance that led to the development of man. It was chance then that brought misfortune.

6. A line, if it is sufficiently powerful as an evoker of an image, becomes an instant cliché. "My head is bloody, but unbowed" said it so well that it has been said over and over and over uncounted times in the past century by everyone, from school children all the way down to politicians. No serious writer can now use it, except humorously.

7. "This place" could be the hospital, of course, but in a larger sense it is the earth, which faces, according to the traditional view, an eventual wrathful day of judgment. John the Baptist says, in admonishing those who came to him, "O generation of vipers, who hath warned you to flee from the wrath to come?" (Matthew 3:7). Along with the wrath, of course, will be the ineffectual tears of those who suffer condemnation. Angels shall seize the sinners and "cast them into a furnace of fire: there shall be wailing and gnashing of teeth" (Matthew 13:42).

8. After judgment, comes hell. The reference to "shade" recalls the nothingness of the Greek Hades, where the dead are but insubstantial shades without sense, memory, or feeling. Even without the active torture that fills all the descriptions of the Christian Hell, the negativity of Hades is nevertheless "Horror." Homer has the shade of the great warrior Achilles tell the still-living Odysseus in Book XI of the *Odyssey:* "I should rather labor as another's serf, in the home of a man without fortune, one whose livelihood was meager, than rule over all the departed dead."

9. "Strait" and "straight" are often confused, but the two are entirely different words. "Strait" is related to "strict" and implies an interference with free flow. Both "constrict" and "restrict" describe a choking of free flow, while a "strait" is a body of water whose flow is restricted by the encroachment of land on either side. We also see the word in "straitened circumstances," in "strait-laced," and "strait jacket," all words that, because of the obsolescence of "strait," run in continual danger of having "straight" substituted so that it is not at all unusual to see "straight jacket" or "straight-laced," which are meaningless words, actually.

In the Sermon on the Mount, Jesus says, "Enter ye in at the strait gate: for wide is the gate, and broad is the way, that leadeth to destruction, and many there be which go in thereat: Because strait is the gate and narrow is the way, which leadeth into life, and few there be that find it" (Matthew 7:13–14).

It is because of this passage that "strait and narrow" (the same meaning repeated in two synonymous words) is used to signify the path of virtue, so much more difficult to find than the "wide and broad" road to hell. Most people, of course, say "straight and narrow" thus vitiating the meaning of difficulty, since a straight road is easier to follow than a crooked one.

Henley, of course, uses the word correctly, making a direct reference to the passage in the Sermon on the Mount.

10. In the books of Daniel and Revelation, God is described as keeping records of the deeds of men for consultation at the time of judgment. Thus, we have: "And I saw the dead, small and great, stand before God; and the books were opened: and another book was opened, which is the book of life: and the dead were judged

out of those things which were written in the books, according to their works" (Revelation 20:12). In biblical times, books were in the form of scrolls of papyrus, so the reference in the poem is accurate.

11. To those who deny the existence of a guiding God, there is no choice but to be one's own guide. This was a relatively common attitude among pre-Christian pagans. Thus, in *Julius Caesar,* William Shakespeare has Cassius say to Brutus:

> Men at some time are masters of their fates:
> The fault, dear Brutus, is not in our stars,
> But in ourselves, that we are underlings.

It is not every poet that can snatch a phrase from Shakespeare and make it his own, but Henley does that here.

Henley proved master of his fate to the extent of eventually emerging from the hospital and resuming a busy and successful life as writer and editor. He had made friends with Robert Louis Stevenson while in the hospital, and the friendship continued afterward. They collaborated on four plays, and Stevenson is supposed to have used the one-legged Henley as a model for the one-legged Long John Silver in *Treasure Island.*

The Modern Major-General[1]

WILLIAM SCHWENK GILBERT[2]

(1880)

I am the very model of a modern Major-General,[3]
I've information vegetable, animal, and mineral,
I know the kings of England, and I quote the fights historical,
From Marathon to Waterloo[4] in order categorical;
I'm very well acquainted too with matters mathematical,
I understand equations, both the simple and quadratical,[5]
About binomial theorem[6] I'm teeming with a lot o' news—
With many cheerful facts about the square of the hypotenuse.[7]

I'm very good at integral and differential calculus,[8]
I know the scientific names of beings animalculous[9];
In short, in matters vegetable, animal, and mineral,
I am the very model of a modern Major-General.

I know our mythic history, King Arthur's[10] and Sir Caradoc's,[11]
I answer hard acrostics,[12] I've a pretty taste for paradox,[13]
I quote in elegiacs[14] all the crimes of Heliogabalus,[15]
In conics I can floor peculiarities parabolous.[16]

I can tell undoubted Raphaels[17] from Gerard Dows[18] and
    Zoffanies,[19]
I know the croaking chorus from the *Frogs* of Aristophanes,[20]
Then I can hum a fugue[21] of which I've heard the music's din
    afore,
And whistle all the airs from that infernal nonsense *Pinafore.*[22]

Then I can write a washing bill in Babylonic cuneiform,[23]
And tell you every detail of Caractacus's uniform[24];
In short, in matters vegetable, animal, and mineral,
I am the very model of a modern Major-General.

In fact, when I know what is meant by "mamelon" and
    "ravelin,"[25]
When I can tell at sight a chassepôt rifle[26] from a javelin,
When such affairs as sorties and surprises[27] I'm more wary at,
And when I know precisely what is meant by "commissariat,"[28]
When I have learnt what progress has been made in modern
    gunnery,
When I know more of tactics than a novice in a nunnery:
In short, when I've a smattering of elemental strategy,
You'll say a better Major-General has never sat a gee—[29]

For my military knowledge, though I'm plucky and adventury,
Has only been brought down to the beginning of the century[30];
But still in matters vegetable, animal, and mineral,
I am the very model of a modern Major-General.

---

1. Great Britain's military security during the Victorian era plus
a long tradition of freedom of speech and press made it possible for
writers to satirize British institutions and traditions with impunity.
This strengthened rather than weakened the nation since the great
danger is that stupid and/or corrupt institutions be maintained
unchanged because no one dares criticize them.

One obvious target of satire was the army officers corps which had shown itself, in the Crimean War, to have been incompetent— as was to be expected when promotion depended on birth and wealth, rather than ability. Since the British Army remained without serious challenge for the rest of the century, incompetence could reign undisturbed (except for satirists), and that fact has been forever enshrined in this poem.

2. William Schwenk Gilbert was born in Harrow Weald, Middlesex, England, on November 18, 1836. His early ambition was to be a lawyer, and he was actually called to the bar in 1863 (something that is reflected in a few of his works), but by then he was beginning to write comic ballads. His real fame began when he teamed up with Sir Arthur Sullivan to turn out fourteen comic operas, of which eleven are without doubt and beyond question the most deservedly successful productions of this type that ever existed. They are a century old now and show no signs of age or of ever losing the devotion of their hosts of fans.

One of the characteristics inevitable in a Gilbert and Sullivan production is the "patter song," a song with advanced vocabulary and complicated rhymes designed to be sung as fast as is humanly possible. Perhaps the most famous of the patter songs is to be found in *The Pirates of Penzance,* first produced in 1880. It is sung by Major-General Stanley, a "modern" Major-General, one who knows everything but his business.

Gilbert died in Harrow Weald, Middlesex, on May 29, 1911. Though he was a misanthrope and boasted of it, he died of a heart attack brought on by his efforts (at the age of seventy-four) to rescue a woman from drowning.

3. There are several ranks of general officers in the army. A brigadier-general, who commands a brigade, is the lowest rank. Above him is the major-general who commands a division (made up of several brigades.) There are additional ranks above that, too.

4. The phrase "from Marathon to Waterloo" was a natural at the time. The English historian Edward Shepherd Creasy had, in 1851, published a book, *Fifteen Decisive Battles of the World* which had proved enormously popular. Of the fifteen battles (dealt with

chronologically in the book) the battle of Marathon, fought in 490 B.C., was first. At that battle, the Athenians defeated the Persians so that the Greek cities of the mainland remained free for the two centuries during which they produced the civilization, arts, and literature that were ancestral to our own. The fifteenth was the battle of Waterloo, fought in 1815, in which the British and the Prussians defeated the French under Napoleon and won the twenty-year war against the French domination of Europe. Creasy died only two years before *The Pirates of Penzance* was produced.

5. In equations, one solves for unknown quantities whose mathematical relations are known. If we know, for instance, that $x+y=8$, and that $x-y=2$, then we can solve the equations by well-established procedures and show that $x=5$ and $y=3$. Equations in which the unknowns can be represented as simple letters are "simple equations."

Where the relationship involves an unknown multiplied by itself, then the equation must contain x multiplied by x, usually written as x^2 and read "x square." The reason for this is that in a square, in which all four sides are equal and can therefore be represented as x units of length, the area of the square is obtained by multiplying the length of one side by another. The area of the square is therefore x square, or x^2.

An equation that contains an x^2 or a y^2 or, for that matter, an xy, is therefore called a "quadratic equation" from the Latin word for "squared."

6. A binomial is any mathematical expression that is the sum or difference of two unknowns, such as, in simplest form, $x+y$ or $x-y$. If this sum or difference is multiplied by itself a number of times (raised to a power), then the binomial theorem advances a method for expressing the product of that multiplication in terms of x and y. The binomial theorem was first worked out by the English mathematician Isaac Newton in about 1665, though he didn't publish it till considerably later.

7. In a right triangle, two sides meet at a right angle (if one is exactly horizontal, the other is exactly vertical). The third side of the triangle is the "hypotenuse" from Greek words meaning

"stretched beneath." (If the triangle is drawn with the vertex of the right angle on top, the hypotenuse can be drawn as a horizontal line at the bottom, so that it is "stretched beneath.")

About 525 B.C., the Greek philosopher Pythagoras was able to show that if each side of a right triangle was made the side of a square, the sum of the areas of those squares was equal to the square of which the hypotenuse was one side. The usual way of expressing this "Pythagorean theorem" is: "The sum of the squares of the sides is equal to the square of the hypotenuse." It is the most famous of all geometric theorems.

8. Calculus is that branch of mathematics which deals with quantities that are changing in some regular manner. It was first worked out independently, and nearly simultaneously, by Isaac Newton and by the German mathematician Gottfried Wilhelm Leibniz, about 1680 or so.

There are two chief branches of calculus. In one, an equation that describes the manner in which a particular quantity is changing is converted into another equation according to fixed rules. The second equation is the "differential," and it tells something useful about the changing quantity. "Differential calculus" describes the methods for working out the differentials and putting them to use. The reverse technique, that of beginning with a differential and working out the original equation, is called "integration," and the branch of calculus dealing with integration is "integral calculus."

9. "Animalcule" is from a Latin diminutive meaning "small animals." The name was given by the Dutch lens maker Anton van Leeuwenhoek to the one-celled creatures he discovered in 1677. As better microscopes were produced, the one-celled creatures Leeuwenhoek saw (now called "protozoa") and still smaller living things now called "bacteria" could be seen in such detail that they could be classified into species.

In 1872, the German botanist Ferdinand Julius Cohn published a three-volume treatise on bacteria. This founded the science of bacteriology and introduced a complicated classification of the tiny creatures. It was these "scientific names" that were known by Major-General Stanley.

10. The tale of King Arthur had, as its kernel of truth, a battle of the post-Roman Britons against the invading Saxons about the year 500. It was a great Britonic victory, and it won a respite for the hard-pressed Britons for a generation.

Leading the Britons in the battle was one Ambrosius Aurelianus, and out of that battle and that leader, through centuries of distortion, a complex legend arose in which Arthur ruled the Britons in the sixth century, established a glorious united kingdom, defeated even the Romans, and became Emperor of Rome.

Knights serving under King Arthur and banqueting at a great "Round Table" were invented and endless romantic tales were spun about them. It was a "mythic history" indeed.

11. Sir Caradoc was one of the knights of the Round Table. He appears in an old ballad in which the wives and sweethearts of the various knights were asked to wear a mantle that had the property of remaining on only those ladies who had been absolutely faithful to their lords. Not one woman could wear it but the wife of Sir Caradoc.

12. An "acrostic" (from a Greek expression meaning "ends in order") is a literary composition, usually a poem, in which the initial letters of the lines, read downward, form a word or expression. Sometimes the final letters and middle letters do so also. It is possible to make a game out of this by having to guess words that will convert a poem into a given acrostic.

13. A paradox is something that seems true but is false, or seems false but is true, or seems straightforward but is self-contradictory. It can even be a play on words, taking advantage of the fact that one word (or two very similar words) may have opposite meanings. It is sometimes thought clever to invent such paradoxes.

14. An "elegiac" is a poem in which the lines have six feet and five feet in alternation. It is not a metrical scheme found in English verse, except as a kind of *tour de force,* but it was used by the Greeks and Romans for elegies (hence the name) that is, for sad songs of (usually) unrequited love.

15. Heliogabalus was a Syrian priest who, in A.D. 218, was made Roman Emperor. He was fourteen at the time and remained Em-

peror for four years before being assassinated. But in that interval he is reported to have made a career of effeminacy, debauchery, and decadence.

16. The intersection of a cone and a plane forms any of a family of curves that, altogether, are called "conic sections" or, more briefly, "conics." Depending on the angle the plane makes with the axis of the cone, the section can be a circle, an ellipse, a parabola, or a hyperbola.

17. Raphael was an Italian painter of the late Renaissance who produced his great works in the first two decades of the 1500s.

18. Gerard Dow, more properly Gerard Dou, was a Dutch painter (1613–75) who was a student of Rembrandt.

19. John Zoffany is the Anglicized name of a German-born painter who came to England in 1758 and who grew to be a very popular portraitist.

20. Aristophanes (448–340 B.C.) was an Athenian comedy-dramatist, the most successful and highly regarded of ancient times. He wrote forty comedies, of which eleven still survive. One of the surviving plays is *The Frogs,* so-called because there is a chorus of frogs that croak (the "croaking chorus") "Brekekekex ko-ax ko-ax."

21. A "fugue" is a complex musical composition in which a number of voices sing in parts. Bach and Handel were particularly noted for their fugues.

22. Here Gilbert makes fun of himself for, of course, H.M.S. *Pinafore,* was the Gilbert and Sullivan musical comedy that had just finished its run before *The Pirates of Penzance* had opened. Gilbert was perfectly safe in making this joke, since *Pinafore* had been an enormous success and is, to this day, second in popularity only to *The Mikado,* which was to be produced in 1885, five years after *The Pirates of Penzance.*

Gilbert was never above twisting a word to make a rhyme, and he introduced the phrase "din afore" (a vulgarized variation of "din before") in order to have a rhyme for Pinafore.

23. The ancient peoples who lived in the area that is now occupied by Iraq, used clay as a substance on which to write. They jabbed a sharp stylus into the soft clay, leaving wedge-shaped marks, which are "cuneiform" from Latin words meaning "wedge-shaped."

They would then bake the clay and have a permanent record in wedge symbols.

Cuneiform writing lasted for some three thousand years, dying out only in the first century, A.D., and many of the tablets can still be found in the ruins of ancient cities of the area. It was not until 1846, however, that cuneiform was deciphered. This was accomplished by an English archeologist, Henry Creswicke Rawlinson. Naturally, most of the cuneiform inscriptions found turned out, when deciphered, to be entirely prosaic bookkeeping lists—laundry bills or the equivalent.

24. Caractacus was one of the tribal rulers in Britain at the time the Romans launched their serious invasion of the island in A.D. 43. He fought valiantly and held the legions off for years but was finally defeated and captured in A.D. 50, and was carried off to Rome, where he died. Needless to say, uniforms are a relatively recent invention in the history of warfare, and Caractacus did not wear one.

25. Major-General Stanley now begins to reveal his trifling shortcomings. "Mamelon" and "ravelin" are both technical terms used in connection with fortifications. Both are from the French, as is most of the vocabulary of fortification.

26. The "chassepôt rifle" was a new type of musket that the French Army had adopted in 1866. It was designed by the French inventor Antoine Alphonse Chassepôt. In 1871 the German inventor-brothers, Peter Paul and Wilhelm Mauser, invented an even better model called the "Mauser rifle." Since this is easier to pronounce, those who sing this song always say "Mauser rifle," though the written version always has "chassepôt rifle."

27. A "surprise," militarily speaking, is any unexpected attack, while a "sortie is an attack by those under siege."

28. A "commissariat" is the military organization that oversees the food supply of the soldiers.

29. "Gee" and "haw" are exclamations used to guide animals pulling a plow, and "gee-up" is a common exclamation designed to cause a horse to move forward. Children use "gee-up" relentlessly in urging on their hobbyhorses, so it is only natural that "gee-gee" becomes a child's word for a horse. Hence "sat a gee" means to be-

stride a horse, although the distant implication of a hobbyhorse rather fits the Major-General's military competence.

30. Considering the time in which the song was first sung; that means only till 1800.

The New Colossus[1]

EMMA LAZARUS[2]

(1883)

Not like the brazen giant of Greek fame,[3]
With conquering limbs astride from land to land[4];
Here at our sea-washed, sunset gates[5] shall stand
A mighty woman with a torch,[6] whose flame
Is the imprisoned lightning,[7] and her name
Mother of Exiles.[8] From her beacon-hand
Glows world-wide welcome; her mild eyes command
The air-bridged harbor that twin cities frame.[9]
"Keep, ancient lands, your storied pomp!" cries she
With silent lips. "Give me your tired, your poor,
Your huddled masses yearning to breathe free,
The wretched refuse of your teeming shore.
Send these, the homeless, tempest-tost to me,
I lift my lamp beside the golden door!"[10]

---

1. In the years after the Civil War, the United States enjoyed a generation of peace and of growing prosperity and power. The development of a giant nation needed hands, and immigrants were welcome. Millions came from European lands where a hardened

caste system meant oppression for the lower classes, and to them the United States was the golden land of promised liberty. It is this role, played by the United States, that the poem commemorates, and it does so by referring to a gigantic statue designed to commemorate the same.

The Greeks used a word of unknown origin—*kolossos* (*colossus* in Latin)—for any statue that was larger-than-life size. The word has been used ever since and has been broadened to mean anything huge, especially in the adjectival form, "colossal." The large amphitheater of the early Roman Empire, the Colosseum, is not so-called because of its colossal size, but because it was built near the site at which a colossus (106 feet high) of Nero had been constructed by the Greek sculptor, Zenodorus.

The American statue that was to be, was a "new colossus."

2. Emma Lazarus was born in New York City on July 22, 1849. She was of a Sephardic family; that is, of a Jewish family that traced its ancestry back to Spain where, under the Moslems, the Jews had experienced a kind of golden age that withered as Christians reconquered the land, and ended when Jews were expelled in 1492. Lazarus was conscious of the fact that Jews had frequently been forced into exile and that in the United States they had freedom they had not known for many centuries. The poem is a reflection of this.

3. The most famous colossus of all time; the only one that was to rival, in the minds of humanity, the new colossus that was being erected, was the bronze statue of the Sun-god, Helios, built on the Greek island of Rhodes by the Rhodian sculptor Chares. That statue celebrated the successful defense of the island against a siege (305–4 B.C.) by a Macedonian general, Demetrius Poliorketes. It stood over a hundred feet tall and was supposed to have taken twelve years to build (292–80 B.C.). It stood in the harbor of the city of Rhodes for only a little over half a century, and then an earthquake in 225 B.C. tumbled it. Its fragments remained where they fell till carted away by Arabs in A.D. 653.

It is known as the Colossus of Rhodes and undoubtedly made an imposing spectacle for the ships sailing into the harbor, when it was standing, and, scarcely less so, after it had fallen. The ancients included it in their list of the Seven Wonders of the World, along with a smaller colossus, the thirty-foot statue of Zeus at Olympia.

4. In the Middle Ages, after the Colossus of Rhodes had fallen and been carted away so that no trace remained, the tales of its one-time existence exaggerated the fact. It came to be believed that the statue was so large that it straddled the harbor, with one leg on each shore and that ships, sailing into the harbor, passed between its legs. The statue wasn't that large and couldn't have been. The Greeks didn't have the techniques for supporting the weight of so large a statue on two legs of proportionate thinness at such a straddling angle.

The picture remains, however, not only in this poem, but even more memorably in William Shakespeare's ironic description of Julius Caesar's prestige in his last days. In *Julius Caesar* he has Cassius say to Brutus: "Why, man, he doth bestride the narrow world/Like a Colossus, and we petty men/Walk under his huge legs and peep about/To find ourselves dishonourable graves."

Nevertheless, Lazarus does the colossus an injustice. It did not represent triumphant tyranny; rather it symbolized the successful resistance of a small nation *against* tyranny. It was a statue of pacific calm, as much a tribute to freedom as the new colossus was to be.

5. The "sea-washed, sunset gates" are the opposing shores of New York Harbor, which are sea-washed, of course. Since, from the standpoint of a Europe from which most of the immigrants came, New York was far to the west, the narrow shores of the harbor were "sunset gates."

6. At the time this poem was written, the statue, in the form of a woman holding a torch aloft, was being constructed in France under the supervision of the sculptor, Frédéric-Auguste Bartholdi. It was intended as a gift to the United States and represented the friendship of the French people.

7. The imprisoned lightning is, of course, electricity. In 1879, four years before the poem was written, the American inventor Thomas Alva Edison had perfected the electric light bulb, and in 1881 he had built a generating station in New York that supplied

eighty-five subscribers with electricity on demand. Electric lighting was the wave of the future, and it was to light the torch of the new colossus.

8. Though that is the name given it by Lazarus, the name given it by the French was "Liberté Éclairant le Monde" which, in English, is "Liberty Enlightening the World." The torch in her raised right hand symbolizes, then, the soft and welcome light of liberty. In her left hand, she holds a tablet on which is inscribed the date July 4, 1776, so that no doubt is left as to the source of the liberty. Popularly, the structure is known as "The Statue of Liberty."

9. In the year the poem was written, Brooklyn Bridge, crossing the East River at the upper end of New York Harbor, was completed after fourteen years of construction. It was the first great suspension bridge, swinging from cables attached to large structures driven into the riverbed. Its design was such that it was higher than an ordinary bridge would be, and did not require supports all across the width of the water it spanned. There was, thus, an unprecedented amount of free space beneath it, both in the air and in the water—hence "air-bridged."

The "twin cities" were New York and Brooklyn, which lay at opposite ends of the Brooklyn Bridge. At that time Brooklyn was a city in its own right with a population of a million. New York (which occupied only the island of Manhattan) was the largest city in the United States and Brooklyn was the third largest. It was not until 1898 that Brooklyn and several other outlying districts joined the island of Manhattan to form what is sometimes called "Greater New York."

10. It is the last four and a half lines of the sonnet that are best remembered as representing the United States' traditional welcome to the immigrants. In the year the poem was written 603,322 immigrants entered the United States. The peak came in 1907 when 1,285,349 immigrants entered.

(In 1923, 522,914 immigrants entered, and among them were my parents and myself.)

The Statue of Liberty was brought to the United States and erected on what was then called Bedloe Island (and is now called Liberty Island). The Statue was dedicated in 1886, and Lazarus' poem was inscribed on a bronze plaque placed inside the base of the statue. Lazarus lived to see the Statue dedicated, but died in New York City on November 19, 1887.

In 1924, a year after my family and I arrived, the United States established a quota system for immigrants and cut off the free flow from which I, and millions like myself, had benefited. The golden door was never closed so tightly, however, that the land ceased to be the "Mother of Exiles."

Recessional[1]

RUDYARD KIPLING[2]

(1897)

God of our fathers, known of old—[3]
    Lord of our far-flung battle line—[4]
Beneath whose awful hand we hold
    Dominion over palm and pine—[5]
Lord God of Hosts,[6] be with us yet,
Lest we forget—lest we forget![7]

The tumult and the shouting dies—
    The Captains and the Kings depart—[8]
Still stands Thine ancient sacrifice,
    An humble and a contrite heart.[9]
Lord God of Hosts, be with us yet,
Lest we forget—lest we forget!

Far-called, our navies melt away—[10]
    On dune and headland sinks the fire—[11]
Lo, all our pomp of yesterday
    Is one with Nineveh[12] and Tyre![13]

Judge of the Nations,[14] spare us yet,
Lest we forget—lest we forget!

If, drunk with sight of power, we loose
   Wild tongues that have not Thee in awe—
Such boastings as the Gentiles[15] use,
   Or lesser breeds without the Law—[16]
Lord God of Hosts, be with us yet,
Lest we forget—lest we forget!

For heathen heart[17] that puts her trust
   In reeking tube and iron shard—[18]
All valiant dust[19] that builds on dust,[20]
   And guarding calls not Thee to guard,—
For frantic boast and foolish word,
Thy Mercy on Thy People, Lord![21] Amen.

---

1. By 1897 Great Britain was at the peak of its power. Victoria had been Queen for sixty years—sixty years that had seen the nation advancing steadily in population, prosperity, prestige, and power. Now the nation was celebrating the Diamond Jubilee, the sixtieth anniversary of Victoria's accession to the throne.

Great Britain ruled over an empire that had been expanding throughout the nineteenth century and was still expanding. To symbolize British glory and success, Victoria had been promoted to a higher title and had been made Empress of India in 1876. Small though Great Britain might be in area, she ruled nearly a quarter of the world directly, and dominated virtually all the rest financially.

And yet the most famous literary work to emerge from this ecstatic celebration turned out to be this somber poem. Its very name indicates the manner in which its mood went precisely contrary to that of the happy nation.

A recession is an act of retiring or withdrawing, and a recessional is a piece of music played at the end of some performance or ceremony, as the audience is leaving. The poem, therefore, deals with the possible decline of the Empire; its departure, so to speak, from the stage of history.

2. Joseph Rudyard Kipling was born in Bombay, India, on December 30, 1865, and India was the very epitome of Imperial success. It was India that was the most populous, the most historic, the most exotic, and the most impressive of all British possessions. It was of India that the British monarch became Empress. In the years Kipling spent in India, he grew interested in Indian life and culture but always from the viewpoint of a member of a master race.

Kipling came to be viewed as the outstanding literary spokesman for imperialism; for the view that men of European descent (and of British descent in particular) had a kind of natural right to rule over non-Europeans, and that it was even their duty to do so. Yet in the midst of the frantic Jubilee celebration, a chill foretaste of the nemesis of imperialism seemed to come over him.

He died in London on January 18, 1936.

3. The poem is biblical in tone and flavor. The British, in Kipling's view, were God's chosen people, destined for world rule, and it was impossible for him not to hark back to that other chosen people, the Israelites. Throughout the poem, the British are made into the contemporary equivalent of biblical Israel.

Thus, when Moses came to the Israelite slaves in Egypt with the news that God would rescue them, he had to assure them that it was no invention of his own that he was bringing, no unknown deity, but an ancestral God of proven work, one that was known of old. God's instructions to Moses were: "Thus shalt thou say unto the Children of Israel, the Lord God of your fathers, the God of Abraham, the God of Isaac, and the God of Jacob, hath sent me unto you" (Exodus 3:15).

And so Kipling, in addressing God, stresses the same historic continuity, the same ancestral respectability, to lend a more somber note to the prayer.

4. "Far-flung" indeed!

The empires of the past had been limited in size. The largest had been that of the Mongols, who from 1240 to 1340 had ruled over most of Asia and half of Europe. Even that empire had been contiguous, however, with all parts land-connected; it was not truly intercontinental; not truly a world empire.

It was only after the opening of the age of exploration that world empires became possible. In the course of the sixteenth century, Portugal and Spain each established trading posts on every continent and took over large land areas in the Americas. Indeed, from 1580 to 1640 Spain took over Portugal and combined both empires. These Iberian empires could only be held together feebly, however, in the days of sailing ships; especially since the home nations were in the grip of a depressed and declining economy.

It was with the coming of industrialization that a real gap opened between those nations that could impose colonialization and those that must suffer it. Great Britain, which was the first to industrialize, forged on to outstrip the earlier world empires in extent, far outstrip them in population, and far, far outstrip them in power.

Of the previous world empires, it had been said that the sun never set upon them. At every moment during earth's rotation some region forming part of the empire was on the day-lit portion of the globe. The earlier examples were forgotten, however, in the greater example of the newer empire. Throughout the nineteenth century, it was common to say that "the sun never set upon the British Empire." And it was easy to begin to believe that in the figurative sense, too; that the sun of history and power would never set and that the British Empire would remain basking in an eternal noon.

5. Again a reference to the wide extent of the British Empire. The palm is a characteristic tree of the tropics, and the pine the characteristic tree of the northernmost forests. The palm trees of India and the pine forests of Canada were both under the rule of the government in London. (Canada had dominion status and considerable self-rule to be sure.)

6. The ancient peoples all had war gods, lords of the hosts (armies), and why not? When did a people need their god more than when they were meeting their enemies in battle (and when, presumably, the enemy were busily calling upon *their* gods for help). Kipling specifically recognizes the role of God as generalissimo when he refers to him earlier as "Lord of our far-flung battle line."

In the Bible, the Creator is sometimes spoken of as "God of Hosts" or "Lord of Hosts," when the Divine role on the battlefield, or as an agent of destruction, is to be emphasized. Thus, when the

Bible describes the manner in which God will inflict military defeat upon the Egyptians, it says, "And the Egyptians will I give over into the hand of a cruel lord; and a fierce king shall rule over them, saith the Lord, the Lord of hosts." (Isaiah 19:4).

Again, in a plea to reverse the civil war that is giving the enemy an opportunity to destroy Israel, we have, "Turn us again, O Lord God of hosts, cause thy face to shine; and we shall be saved" (Psalms 80:19).

7. To the biblical writers, the military defeat and physical destruction of a land is the direct result of forgetting what is due to God, since God's people cannot suffer defeat except as punishment by an angry and forgotten God. Thus, the Bible quotes God as saying: "For Israel hath forgotten his Maker, and buildeth temples; and Judah hath multiplied fenced cities, but I will send a fire upon his cities, and it shall devour the palaces thereof" (Hosea 8:14).

8. Tumult and shouting evoke a picture of the clamor of battle, and "Captains" and "Kings" are the leaders of armies. There is a biblical passage describing the war horse that is reminiscent of these lines: "He saith among the trumpets, Ha, ha; and he smelleth the battle afar off, the thunder of the captains and the shouting" (Job 39:25).

But the noise dies and the warriors depart. Military glory *alone* is insufficient, for the wars end and there must be something to maintain the nation afterward.

These two lines also evoke the "tumult and the shouting" of the Jubilee, the gathering of royalty and of military notables from every European nation. The noise of the Jubilee has to die, too, and the celebrants must depart, and what then?

9. It is a common biblical notion that it is not the proud, the powerful, and the arrogant who are cared for by God, but the humble, the repentant, and the unassuming. The former are too apt to be tempted into feeling they have no need of God and are therefore likely to forget Him. The latter cannot forget Him because they have nowhere else to turn.

Thus: "The Lord is nigh unto them that are of a broken heart; and saveth such as be of contrite spirit" (Psalms 34:18). Again: "The sacrifices of God are a broken spirit: a broken and a contrite heart, O God, thou wilt not despise" (Psalms 51:17).

10. Great Britain's prime defense was its navy. It was through its navy's defeat of the Spanish Armada in 1588 that England became an important power on the stage of the modern world. It was because its navy patrolled and controlled the waters about itself that Great Britain was held inviolate from the armies of Philip II of Spain and of Louis XIV and Napoleon of France—armies that would have destroyed the nation, could they have but set foot on it.

What's more, it was British control of the sea beyond its own waters that controlled the trade of the world, poured wealth into the unblockaded island and, in the end, wore out and frustrated all the Continental conquerors and left their land victories useless.

But what if Great Britain, foolishly vainglorious, attempted tasks too great for her, or entered into tasks without careful forethought and planning? The navy, "far-called" (that is, spread thin over the waters of a world-wide Empire, too thin) would melt away. The links binding the Empire would be broken, and the homeland itself would be left defenseless before the attack of armies that could not be prevented from landing.

11. Dunes are sandy ridges common along seashores. Headlands are spits and capes, bits of land jutting out into the sea. Lighthouses on such places guide incoming ships at night or in fogs. They are necessary for a maritime nation, whose ships are its life line. They are unnecessary once a navy no longer exists, since trade can no longer be protected once the life line is cut. And with the life line cut, the sinking of the fire in the lighthouses becomes a symbolic way of representing the dying of the nation.

12. Nineveh was the capital of the Assyrian Empire in the seventh century B.C. during the days of its greatest glory. Under Ashurbanipal, it became not only the military center of western Asia, but the cultural center as well. It might have seemed to the proud warrior caste of Assyria that their power and rule was eternal, yet Ashurbanipal died in 627 B.C. with his empire essentially intact, and within twenty-five years it was all gone, forever.

Nineveh fell to Chaldean rebels from within the empire and to Median horsemen from without in 612 B.C. It was never rebuilt, and two centuries later, when a Greek army passed that way, they had to ask what the mounds were.

13. Tyre is a particularly close approximation to Great Britain.

It, too, was a naval power, with a citadel on an island that could not be forced while its ships controlled the seas about it. Tyre, too, built up a vast network of trading posts and flung its merchantmen and warships far out, from end to end of the Mediterranean and even into the Atlantic.

Tyre's prosperity declined slowly as it adjusted to the realities of the mighty Asian empires of Assyria and its successors. Finally, in 323 B.C., Tyre was besieged by Alexander the Great, who filled in the sea between the island and the coast. He took the city after nine months and destroyed it. It exists to this day as a small coastal city in Lebanon, but no shadow of its former glory remains.

14. This title, given to God, harks back to the biblical passage in which Abraham attempts to dissuade God from destroying Sodom with indiscriminate anger against its inhabitants. After all, there may be some people of Sodom who are righteous. Abraham said, "That be far from thee to do after this manner, to slay the righteous with the wicked; and that the righteous should be as the wicked, that be far from thee: Shall not the Judge of all the earth do right?" (Genesis 18:25).

15. It is the wild overweening pride, the *hubris,* of the Jubilee, that makes Kipling uneasy. The behavior is not British in his opinion, but is more suited to other and inferior people (a viewpoint which is itself an example of *hubris,* of course).

"Gentiles" are, strictly speaking, related members of a tribe or clan (from the Latin word *gens* meaning tribe or clan.) Any group that considers itself in a special relationship to God, or as having a special significance in history, is likely to lump all other people as Gentiles, as members of the (other) tribes. Thus, to Jews, all non-Jews are Gentiles; and to Mormon, all non-Mormons are Gentiles.

To Kipling, with his attitude that the British are the modern Israelites and the new-chosen of God, all non-British are Gentiles, and therefore inferior beings who know no better than to indulge in vainglorious boasting. That the British should do that as well would be shameful.

16. The agreement, or covenant, by which the Israelites became the chosen of God, required that, in exchange, they obey the Law as delivered to Moses on Mount Sinai. Thus, God says, "Now, there-

fore, if ye will obey my voice indeed, and keep my covenant, then ye shall be a peculiar treasure unto me above all people" (Exodus 19:5).

To be "without the Law," then, is not to be of the elect. Again, there is the flavor of inferiority about those not chosen. They are not British (Israelite), and therefore they are "lesser breeds."

17. The word "heathen" is used in the English translation of the Bible for those who did not worship the God of Israel: "Why do the heathen rage—" Psalms 2:1. The word means those of the heath, or backwoods, who are unsophisticated and cling to primitive traditions and worship.

18. The "reeking tube" is the gun barrel generally, of all sizes, and the "iron shard" is the bullet or other object fired from it. The trust in force exclusively, without regard to moral justification, is exemplified in a jingle that became current in Great Britain after the invention of a new and improved machine gun by the American inventor, Hiram Stevens Maxim in 1884—

> Whatever happens, we have got
> The Maxim-gun, and they have not.

Ironically enough, even as Kipling wrote, the word "reeking" became obsolete.

For six hundred years the chemical explosive used on the battlefield to propel bullets and balls had been gunpowder. That had produced smoke, soot, and reeking odors that fouled the guns, choked the gunners, and obscured the battlefield. In the last decades of the nineteenth century, however, smokeless powders were developed. In the wars of the twentieth century, various smokeless powders were used, and though the "tube" grew steadily more deadly, it was no longer "reeking."

19. From the biblical view, man was a creature compounded of dust: "And the Lord God formed man of the dust of the ground, and breathed into his nostrils the breath of life" (Genesis 2:7). In battle, man might display valor, but that did not dignify his origins; he was merely "valiant dust," a phrase William Shakespeare uses in *Much Ado About Nothing*.

20. This is a reference to the biblical parable of the "foolish man,

which built his house upon the sand: And the rain descended, and the floods came, and the winds blew, and beat upon that house; and it fell" (Matthew 7:26–27).

21. The last plea is, of course, biblical: "Be merciful, O Lord, unto thy people Israel—" (Deuteronomy 21:8), and Kipling here directly equates the British with Israel.

Yet God chose *not* to have mercy, for immediately after 1897, the year of the Diamond Jubilee, the British Empire began its decline.

Even while the Jubilee was being celebrated, British imperialism was pressing hard on the independent Boer Republics north of British dominions in South Africa. In 1899 this turned into open war which, to British surprise and humiliation, lasted nearly three years. The British won in the end after they had sufficiently reinforced their armies, but world sympathy was with the Boers.

The British, surprised at being cast in the role of villains, and cast down at finding they had not a friend in the world, lost the euphoria of 1897, and it was never, quite, to return.

Cargoes[1]

JOHN MASEFIELD[2]

(1902)

Quinquireme[3] of Nineveh[4] from distant Ophir[5]
Rowing home to haven in sunny Palestine,[6]
With a cargo of ivory,
And apes and peacocks,[7]
Sandalwood, cedarwood, and sweet white wine.

Stately Spanish galleon coming from the Isthmus[8]
Dipping through the Tropics by the palm-green shores,
With a cargo of diamonds,
Emeralds, amethysts,
Topazes, and cinnamon, and gold moidores.[9]

Dirty British coaster[10] with a salt-caked smokestack
Butting through the Channel in the mad March days,[11]
With a cargo of Tyne coal,[12]
Road-rails, pig-lead,
Firewood, iron-ware, and cheap tin trays.[13]

---

1. The British decline that began with the Boer War was only
very gradual at first, and it was not for a decade or so that the

change in the world balance of power was to become apparent. In 1902, when this poem was written, Great Britain was still the commercial leader of the world.

Of course, the bustle and change of "modern times" (at all times in history, probably) was not always to the taste of those who dreamed of the mythical romance of earlier times. This poem might be interpreted as such nostalgia for the unreal.

2. John Masefield was born on June 1, 1878 in Ledbury, Herefordshire. He spent time at sea and then in the United States, where he was employed in a carpet factory. He returned to Great Britain, where he worked on the Manchester *Guardian*. He was well-enough known for his poetry to be appointed Poet Laureate in 1930, the fifteenth of the line. He died on May 12, 1967 near Abingdon, Berkshire.

3. The word "quinquireme" is from a Latin phrase meaning "five oars." It was a galley which was propelled by oars arranged in five banks, but no one today is sure of the detailed construction. The workhorse of the ancient navies was the "trireme" with three banks of oars, and the quinquireme was the most complicated warship of the ancients. It came into use about 200 B.C.

4. Nineveh was the capital of Assyria which had no navy to speak of and was not a sea-trading nation. Besides, Nineveh was utterly destroyed in 612 B.C. (see page 253), centuries before quinquiremes existed. Of course, Masefield is interested in the dreamy sound of the line rather than in the accuracy of the content, and from a poetic standpoint, he is right.

5. No one actually knows what land is meant by Ophir. It is mentioned in the Bible always in connection with gold so that all sorts of romantic places were supposed to be its site: India, the far East, even Peru. Actually, it is most likely that Ophir was located somewhere along the Red Sea, possibly on the site of what is now known as Yemen. It would then be about 2,200 kilometers (1,400 miles) from Jerusalem and, by the standards of that time, it would be quite distant.

6. Solomon, who ruled over Israel at the height of its prosperity, about 950 B.C. (some two and a half centuries before Nineveh was founded), established a port at Eloth (the modern Elat) on the

Red Sea. He made use of ships and seamen supplied by his ally, Hiram of Tyre, and this navy "came to Ophir, and fetched from thence gold, four hundred and twenty talents, and brought it to King Solomon" (1 Kings 9:28).

7. The poem does not go on to describe the gold in this stanza, but switches to Solomon's other trading venture—in the Mediterranean, rather than the Red Sea. In the Mediterranean, another Phoenician fleet sailed westward to Tharshish (Tartessus) in Spain: "once in three years came the navy of Tharshish, bringing gold, and silver, ivory, and apes, and peacocks" (1 Kings 10:22).

8. The second stanza takes us to the sixteenth century, when the central meeting place of the Spanish cargo fleet, gathering from various parts of the Americas to leave for Spain, was at Nombre de Dios on the Isthmus of Panama.

9. Spain obtained the accumulated gold of the native cultures in Mexico and Peru, so that the New World became in the minds of the Europeans the counterpart of early Ophir. A "moidore" is a gold coin used in Portugal and Brazil. It is from a Portuguese phrase that means "gold coin."

10. A coaster is a vessel that sails from one point on a given shore line to another—a very dull task compared to the long-distance rowing and sailing of quinquiremes and galleons.

11. The "Channel" is the English Channel which is noted for its stormy weather, particularly during the winds of March.

12. The Tyne River is in northern England, and it is on that river that Newcastle is situated. Newcastle was the center of England's chief coal-mining district in the nineteenth century, and it was by the energy of coal that Great Britain's industrialization—and domination of the world—was made possible.

13. The items in the coaster cargo are typical of the new industrial society, even down to the "cheap tin trays" which are mass-produced for the masses. They might be viewed as dull and ugly in comparison to ivory, peacocks, and precious gems, but who got those luxury items in early days? Is the average man's share of useful tin trays not worth more than the knowledge that somewhere an aristocrat is using gold plates while you content yourself with a wooden bowl?

Miniver Cheevy[1]

Edwin Arlington Robinson[2]

(1910)

Miniver Cheevy,[3] child of scorn,
  Grew lean while he assailed the seasons[4];
He wept that he was ever born,
  And he had reasons.

Miniver loved the days of old
  When swords were bright and steeds were prancing;
The vision of a warrior bold
  Would set him dancing.

Miniver sighed for what was not,
  And dreamed, and rested from his labors;
He dreamed of Thebes[5] and Camelot,[6]
  And Priam's neighbors.[7]

Miniver mourned the ripe renown
  That made so many a name so fragrant;
He mourned Romance,[8] now on the town,
  And Art, a vagrant.[9]

Miniver loved the Medici,[10]
  Albeit he had never seen one;
He would have sinned incessantly[11]
  Could he have been one.

Miniver cursed the commonplace,
  And eyed a khaki suit with loathing[12];
He missed the medieval grace
  Of iron clothing.[13]

Miniver scorned the gold he sought,
  But sore annoyed was he without it;
Miniver thought, and thought, and thought,
  And thought about it.

Miniver Cheevy, born too late,
  Scratched his head and kept on thinking;
Miniver coughed, and called it fate,
  And kept on drinking.[14]

---

1. In 1898 the United States had a brief war with Spain. The land battles in Cuba were comic-opera affairs, but separate fleets of the American Navy, modern and efficient, utterly destroyed the Spanish ships near Cuba and near the Philippine Islands, without as much as an American scratch. With this victory, the United States was seen to be sufficiently formidable in war to make it a member of the ranks of the "great powers."

Great Britain, becoming aware of its isolation in the simultaneously fought Boer War, and seeing two foreign navies, the American and the German, rising to prominence, knew it would have to join with one of them if it were to oppose the other. Great Britain chose to cultivate the United States as ally, and the two nations, which had been "traditional enemies" all through the nineteenth century, became close allies through all the struggles of the twentieth century.

The American entrance onto the world stage was not as popular with everyone, of course, and there was nostalgia for an older, simpler time here, too—a nostalgia which is brutally satirized in this poem, written in 1910.

2. Edwin Arlington Robinson was born in Head Tide, Maine, on December 22, 1869. He was the first American poet to make popular the new trick of writing in a plain style rather than in the florid fashion of the English poets of the Victorian Era.

The first forty years of his life were spent in poverty and failure, but then, in 1905, President Theodore Roosevelt found hmself attracted by Robinson's poetry, and found a spot for him at the U. S. Customs House in New York. This didn't take up much of his time, and it enabled him to eat while continuing to write poetry. He died in New York City on April 6, 1935.

3. The name "Miniver Cheevy" was undoubtedly chosen primarily for its sound, but "miniver" is the name given to a kind of fur frequently used in medieval costumes. It is uncertain which animal yielded the fur, or whether it might not have come from any of a number of different animals. In any case, it is a good name for someone sunk in nostalgia.

4. We usually think of "season" as a fixed part of a year, but, less frequently, it is used as a synonym for "time." It is in this sense that we say something happens "in season." In this verse, Miniver Cheevy is assailing the times; that is, the century in which he lives.

5. Thebes was a Greek city that was the site of some of the famous Greek legends; for instance, that of Oedipus. It was also the capital city of Egypt at the time of Egypt's greatest power.

6. Camelot was the capital city and residence of King Arthur (see page 239).

7. Priam was the king of Troy at the time of the famous siege concerning which Homer wrote in *The Iliad*. Miniver longed for the romance of the legends of ancient and medieval times—which existed, of course, only in the minds of those who made them up and who converted the rough and grim reality into fragrant posies of charm and splendor.

Robinson himself, in the years after he had written *Miniver Cheevy*, went on to write long poems in blank verse on themes drawn from the Arthurian legend. There may thus be an element of rueful self-satire in the poem.

8. Romance is often taken to mean a love story. Actually, it is broader than that. It applies to all fiction dealing with picturesque and adventurous themes in which everything is larger than life, as opposed to Realism which attempts to depict life as it actually is. Romantic literature (both prose and poetry) reached its heights in the early nineteenth century and was losing out in favor of Realism in the twentieth.

9. Both "on the town" and "vagrant" can be used as euphemisms for turning to prostitution.

10. The Medici were an Italian merchant family that, at the height of the Renaissance, ruled over Florence, the most cultured city in the peninsula. Lorenzo the Magnificent was the most notable member of the line, ruling from 1469 to 1492. He was a wealthy patron of the arts, and his reign was a golden age for the city. The Medici family also supplied three Popes, and two of its members married into the royal House of France (one of these was the famous Catherine de Medici, whose three sons ruled France in succession from 1544 to 1589, and who was the power behind the throne for much of this period).

11. The ruling families of Renaissance Italy, since they had wealth and loved luxury, and since they lived in a time of lax sexual standards, were widely regarded, especially by later more sexually rigid people, as having been great sinners. They were certainly no saints, but it is doubtful that they sinned more than anyone else would have under similar circumstances. Lack of opportunity is, I suspect, a far greater barrier against sin than ever virtue was.

12. "Khaki" is a Hindu word meaning "dust-colored" and this brownish color was first used for uniforms by British troops in India. It had always been customary, prior to the twentieth century, to use bright colors for uniforms both to raise morale and for easy recognition. As weapons grew more accurate and longer-range, however, it came to be realized that bright colors made an easy mark. Khaki came into general use in the Boer War, in place of the traditional red of the British soldier. Of course, one can't grow enthusiastic about khaki, since the color is (and is designed to be)

dull. In fact, the winter uniform of the United States Army is designated "olive drab."

13. Anyone who tries to wear a suit of medieval armor, instead of merely dream about one, is sure to find that in the not-very-long run, khaki is better.

14. There are always Miniver Cheevys who mourn for a departed state of pastoral bliss that never existed, and think that they can abandon our modern industrial world by returning to the simple life. A few can, perhaps, provided the rest of us keep our noses to the grindstone. It is only our industrial technology that keeps four billion people alive on earth now. When that falters, most of those billions will die, and the rest will find themselves in a nonindustrial world they very probably won't like. We have only a slim chance of getting through the problems that face us now, but if too many Miniver Cheevys sit back to drink and long for a non-existent past, that slim chance will decrease to zero.

In Flanders Fields[1]

JOHN MCCRAE[2]

(1915)

In Flanders fields[3] the poppies blow[4]
Between the crosses, row on row,
   That mark our place[5]; and in the sky
   The larks, still bravely singing, fly
Scarce heard amid the guns below.[6]

We are the Dead. Short days ago
We lived, felt dawn, saw sunset glow,
   Loved and were loved, and now we lie
   In Flanders fields.

Take up our quarrel with the foe[7]:
To you from failing hands we throw
   The torch[8]; be yours to hold it high.
   If ye break faith with us who die
We shall not sleep, though poppies grow
     In Flanders fields.[9]

---

1. Great Britain, seeking allies after the ordeal of the Boer War
and recognizing Germany and its naval ambitions to be her greatest

danger, made friends with France and Russia as well as with the United States.

Growing rivalry between competing alliances finally led, more or less inevitably, to a general war. What we now call World War I, began on July 28, 1914, and Great Britain entered the war on August 4. There followed a four-year orgy of blood-letting that changed the world permanently. This poem was written in 1915, in the second year of the war, but was published only in 1919, after the war and after the death of the poet.

2. John McCrae was a Canadian physician, born in Guelph, Ontario, on November 30, 1872. When World War I began, he volunteered to serve as a medical officer with the first Canadian soldiers to go overseas and was stationed in Boulogne, France.

3. Flanders is a region that includes the seacoast of Belgium and northeasternmost France—the continental coast just across the English Channel from Dover and therefore that part of Europe of which England was always most conscious. Many medieval battles were fought in Flanders by English troops, including the great English victories at Crécy in 1346 and at Agincourt in 1415. In modern times it was the site of the great English victories at Malplaquet in 1709 and at Waterloo in 1815.

Now, in World War I, British troops were fighting in Flanders again, and McCrae, stationed at Boulogne, was himself in Flanders.

4. The word "blow" as used here means "bloom." Once World War I was over, the date of the Armistice (November 11, 1918) was celebrated annually in Great Britain as Remembrance Day, a time to remember the war veterans. It was also called "Poppy Day" since artificial poppies were sold, the proceeds to go to ex-servicemen. The use of poppies was inspired by this poem.

5. It is the dead who are speaking, and there were plenty of them. The number of incompetent generals in World War I was higher than was usual for that undemanding profession, and along the trenches on the Western Front, waves of soldiers were sent in suicide attacks against entrenched machine guns over and over again. Millions died to gain yards—worthless yards, at that. In 1914 and 1915 the British lost heavily in battles about the Belgian town

of Ypres (in Flanders), and the crosses were row on row on endless row.

6. McCrae is supposed to have been inspired to write the poem when he heard the song of larks during momentary halts in the sound of gunfire. It seemed to him a symbol of life carrying on resolutely amid an unbelievable carnage.

7. In all the previous great battles that England (and then Great Britain) had fought in Flanders, it had been France that was the foe. After all, France had been the nation that had dominated Flanders through the Middle Ages and right down to Napoleon's time. Now, however, the powerful German Army had burst into Flanders and they were the foe that Great Britain and France, in alliance, were both fighting.

8. The image is that of a relay race in which each runner carries a baton a specified distance, running himself to exhaustion in that distance in the knowledge that a fresh runner will take the baton from him and carry it over the next course. It was necessary to view the war thus, for in 1915, despite horrible casualties, the war was in a stalemate and it was to continue in an almost motionless struggle, in Flanders at least, for over two more years.

9. In 1917 the stalemate began to look as though it might break —and on the German side. Russia, the ally of Great Britain and France, had been ruined by incredible mismanagement and corruption. It collapsed into revolution, and left the war in defeat. Germany was now bringing all her armies to bear on the west.

The United States had joined the Anglo-French armies in April 1917, but it was questionable if American soldiers could be trained and brought over fast enough to save the situation. On January 28, 1918, while the issue still hung in the balance, McCrae died of pneumonia and himself became one of "the Dead."

Within a few months of McCrae's death, the German general Erich Ludendorff launched a last powerful offensive that seemed for a time to carry all before it. But Germany was worn out. At the last moment, she could not carry through, and with American men and supplies pouring into France, she collapsed.

And so Great Britain was one of the victorious powers and, indeed, expanded her Empire further, to its maximum extent, by absorbing German and Turkish colonial territories. This was at a fearful cost, however, for she became a debtor nation, giving up financial leadership and naval equality to the United States.

What's more, the changes begun with the Boer War were accelerated, and she suffered a permanent blow to her self-confidence. The British Empire began changing its structure. Several portions, largely British in culture, became virtually independent in 1931, and were held to London only by a sentimental attachment to British tradition and the British monarch. The Empire became the British Commonwealth of Nations, and eventually even the adjective "British" was removed as giving the homeland too great a preeminence by implication. Within a half century of the great Diamond Jubilee the great British Empire of Victorian times no longer existed.

Fire and Ice[1]

ROBERT FROST[2]

(1923)

> Some say the world will end in fire,
> Some say in ice.[3]
> From what I've tasted of desire
> I hold with those who favor fire.[4]
> But if it had to perish twice,
> I think I know enough of hate
> To say that for destruction ice
> Is also great
> And would suffice.[5]

---

1. Science and technology had advanced rapidly in the nineteenth century, and the Industrial Revolution spread from its beginnings in Great Britain to other nations, including the United States and Germany. After World War I the pace quickened, and the whole world began to undergo a remarkable—and in some respects, dangerous—industrialization. Amazing advances were made in science as well.

This short poem, written in 1923, almost seems to mirror the new science.

2. Robert Lee Frost was born in San Francisco, California, on March 26, 1874, and was perhaps the most successful of all twentieth-century American poets. His poetry seems to please the critics, and because it is plain-spoken, rhymes and scans, it pleases human beings as well. This one happens to be my own favorite. Frost had a moment of unusual fame when he read one of his poems at the inauguration of John F. Kennedy as President of the United States on January 20, 1960. He died in Boston, Massachusetts, on January 29, 1963.

3. This might signify the alternative suggested for a biblical Day of Judgment, but it might also be interpreted as pointing up an astronomical difference of opinion, as to the manner of evolution of stars and of the fate of the sun.

In 1914 the American astronomer Henry Norris Russell had noted the relationship of a star's brightness and temperature, as Dutch astronomer Eijnar Hertzsprung had done, in less detail, in 1905. As a result, the "Hertzsprung-Russell diagram" was produced, and in it most stars fell on a diagonal line called the "main sequence."

It seemed, if one followed what looked like the obvious line of argument, that a star slowly collapsed out of a cloud of dust and gas, growing hotter as it did so—red, then yellow, then blue-white in its glow. Once it had fully collapsed, it began to cool off to yellow and then red again. Thus, you began with a red giant and changed to, in order, a yellow giant, a blue-white star, a yellow dwarf, a red dwarf, and finally a cold, black object. By that line of argument our own sun had already reached the yellow dwarf stage and would eventually cool to the point where the world would die in ice.

There would scarcely seem room for argument here, but Frost, in allowing fire as an alternative, was prescient. In 1938, fifteen years after the poem was written, the German-American physicist Hans Albrecht Bethe worked out the nuclear reactions at the sun's core that kept the sun shining. By studying these reactions and their consequences, it became apparent to astronomers that the older interpretation of the Hertzsprung-Russell diagram was faulty. The red giant stage was late in a star's evolution, not early. The sun, as it grew older, would grow warmer and would expand so that the earth would end in fire.

4. Frost chooses between the alternatives by equating them with human emotions, and he ends up favoring what proved eventually (barring further advances in knowledge) to be the winning side.

5. The full power of hate, as magnified by science, was not, however, apparent in 1923. In 1933, ten years later, Adolf Hitler, at the head of the Nazi Party came to power in Germany. Steadily and brutally, he made his plans to reverse the decision of World War I and arrange for Germany to dominate the world. For the purpose, he enlisted the help of the ambitious rulers of other nations, notably Italy and Japan.

After a period of pusillanimity made inevitable by the loss of self-confidence, Great Britain girded to resist a Germany grown more powerful and more vicious than ever before. World War II broke out on September 1, 1939, and as in the earlier war, Germany won the initial battles. In 1940 Great Britain, at her nadir, faced Germany alone, and for a few months, Kipling's *Recessional* seemed decidedly prophetic (see page 248). (Kipling himself had died four years before.)

Far-called, the British Navy did indeed melt away, and it was only by obtaining American destroyers that the British life line was maintained. On dune and headland the fire sank and, indeed, went out altogether in a blackout, as German planes pounded the nation from the air. For a while, that autumn, it seemed almost certain that Great Britain's pomp of yesterday would indeed be one with Nineveh and Tyre—and only forty-three years after the great Diamond Jubilee.

With a last, supreme effort, Great Britain beat back the attack and was more the admiration of the world than ever before in its history. With the entrance of the Soviet Union in June of 1941 and of the United States in December of 1941 into the military coalition against Germany, the defeat of Hitler and his allies was assured.

Great Britain emerged from World War II again the victor, but now no longer a great power. There were only two great superpowers after World War II, the United States and the Soviet

Union. And a new threat hung over the world. Appearing at the very end of World War II was the atom bomb, and by 1949 both superpowers had them. It was plain that the hate spoken of by Frost, if allowed its full play, could indeed destroy the world, but not by ice after all—

Again by fire.